Pattern in the Teaching and Learning of Mathematics

Edited by
Anthony Orton

CASSELL

London and New York

Cassell
Wellington House
125 Strand
London WC2R 0BB

370 Lexington Avenue
New York
NY 10017–6550

www.cassell.co.uk

First published 1999

British Library Cataloguing-in-Publication Data
A catalogue record for this book is available from the British Library.

ISBN   0–304–70051–7 (hardback)
       0–304–70052–5 (paperback)

Typeset by York House Typographic Ltd.
Printed and bound in Great Britain by Redwood Books Ltd, Trowbridge, Wiltshire

Contents

iv   *Contents*

About the Contributors

Christopher S. Burke is a secondary school Head of Mathematics and a freelance artist. His research interests include graphics in mathematical education, and in particular the use of diagrams in mathematics teaching and learning. His doctoral study was entitled 'Referential thinking: the structures and processes of graphic representation'.

Len Frobisher is a former Mathematics Coordinator with the Mathematics at Key Stage 2 Assessment Project, having previously been a Lecturer in Mathematics Education at the University of Leeds, with particular responsibilities for primary mathematics. He is now working freelance as a mathematics education consultant. His particular interests include investigative approaches to learning mathematics and innovative ways of assessing achievement and attainment. He is the joint author of *Insights into Teaching Mathematics*.

Rosalind Garrick is a teacher of nursery and early years children. Her research interests are concerned with the development of mathematical thinking in young children. Her doctoral study is entitled 'The development of pattern-related abilities through play activities in young children'.

William Gibbs is a former Lecturer in Mathematics Education at the University of Leeds, now working freelance. He has previously worked as a mathematics educator in many parts of the world, including Bangladesh, Bhutan, India, Kenya, Sierra Leone, Solomon Islands and Zambia. His main interests now centre on the relationship of mathematics to the community it serves and the use of simple resources in the teaching of mathematics. He is the joint author of *Health into Mathematics*.

Melanie Hargreaves is a research assistant in the School of Education at the University of Leeds. Her research interests are based in psychological aspects of mathematical education and assessment. Her doctoral study is entitled 'Factors influencing the interpretation and generalisation of number patterns in children aged 7 to 12'.

Anthony Orton is a former Senior Lecturer in Mathematics Education at the University of Leeds. He is now retired, but working part-time as a Senior Fellow, with some teaching and research responsibilities. He has been actively engaged in research into learning mathematics for over twenty-five years, and has been involved in developmental work overseas for fifteen, particularly in South Africa. He is the author of *Learning Mathematics: Issues, Theory and Classroom Practice*, and joint author of *Insights into Teaching Mathematics*.

Jean Orton is a part-time Lecturer in Mathematics and Computer Education at the University of Leeds, with particular responsibilities for international students. She has previously worked for many years in secondary, primary and pre-school education, and has acted as a mathematics consultant overseas, particularly in Sierra Leone. Apart from pattern, her research interests include the development of algebraic understanding.

Tom Roper is a Senior Lecturer in Mathematics Education at the University of Leeds, with particular responsibilities for PGCE and undergraduate courses. He previously worked for seventeen years as a secondary school mathematics teacher and department head. His research interests include the applications of mathematics to other subjects in the school curriculum, mechanics teaching, and the assessment of Ma1. He has contributed to a number of texts on mechanics, and is the joint author of *Particle Mechanics*.

Diane Shorrocks-Taylor is Professor of Assessment and Evaluation in Education at the University of Leeds. She has directed the Mathematics at Key Stage 2 Assessment Project throughout and was formerly a Senior Lecturer in Educational Psychology. Her research interests include primary education, language development and assessment. She is the author of *Implementing National Curriculum Assessment in the Primary School*, and editor of *Directions in Educational Psychology*.

John Threlfall is a Lecturer in Mathematics Education at the University of Leeds, with particular responsibilities for primary mathematics. He has also worked as Test Development Officer with the Mathematics at Key Stage 2 Assessment Project. He was previously a teacher in primary and special schools, and worked for five years as an Advisory Teacher for mathematics. His research interests include children's learning of simple arithmetic and mental arithmetic, and formative assessment.

Sue Waring is a secondary school mathematics teacher. Her research interests are largely focused on developing teaching methods to improve students' learning. Her doctoral study was entitled 'Learning and teaching proof and pattern in mathematics in the age range 14–16 years'.

Preface

It is not easy to define what we mean by 'pattern', even in mathematics. One of the difficulties is that the word has a variety of different meanings. On the one hand, 'pattern' can be used simply in relation to a particular disposition or arrangement of shapes, colours or sounds with no obvious regularity. Indeed, sometimes the arrangement might form a recognizable representation or picture. On the other hand, it might be required that the arrangement possesses some kind of clear regularity, perhaps through symmetry or repetition. In mathematics, we more often than not use the word 'pattern' in relation to a search for order, so regularity is more likely than not. In writing about the place of music in human society and culture, and in connection with the relationships between pattern and music, Storr (1992, p. 64) claims that 'What is universal is the human propensity to create order out of chaos'. An attractive melody written in a predictable rhythm is an arrangement of sounds in a regular pattern, which is somehow more memorable and appealing than most random sequences of noises. When we involve or appeal to pattern in teaching mathematics, it is usually because we are trying to help pupils to extract greater meaning or enjoyment, or both, from the experience or learning environment with which they are occupied, and perhaps also to facilitate remembering. In all walks of life, it seems we are attracted to regularity, and often try to interpret situations by looking for, or even imposing, pattern. Gestalt psychology embraces the view that it is a human quality that we constantly seek to 'interpret incoming sensations and experiences as an organized whole and not as a collection of separate units of data' (Orton, 1992), which suggests that it should be positively helpful to pupils if they can be encouraged to perceive, comprehend and then use patterns whenever possible in mathematics.

Mathematicians and educationists have long been enthusiastic about the importance of pattern in mathematics. Sawyer (1955, p. 12) claimed that 'Mathematics is the classification and study of all possible patterns'. Williams and Shuard (1982, p. 330) suggested that 'the search for order and pattern ... is one of the driving forces of all mathematical work with young children'. Biggs and Shaw (1985, p. 1) wrote: 'Mathematics can ... be thought of as a search for patterns and relationships'. Mottershead (1985, p. vii) simply described mathematics as 'the study of patterns'. Such views of mathematics have been perpetuated by repetition and reformulation, certainly from the middle of the twentieth century onwards. To my knowledge, they have never been contradicted. In other words, no justification is needed for making pattern the unifying theme of a collection of specialized studies in children's learning. Yet there is a further justification in our case. The Pattern in Mathematics Research Group was set up at the School of Education of the University of Leeds in early 1992, 'to provide structure and support to our developing studies of children's perception, conception and use of pattern in learning mathematics' (A. Orton, 1993, p. 39). A wide variety of studies have now been completed, or are nearing completion, embracing work across the whole curriculum, and through all the years of compulsory schooling. Many local teachers and their pupils have helped us with our work, and to them we accord our grateful thanks.

Each chapter of this book relates to a different study, and thus the chapters are to a large extent independent and can be read in isolation. However, there is the consistent recurring theme of pattern binding the separate studies together, and there is also continuity. The early chapters concern very young children, subsequent chapters are more firmly based within primary and middle school age ranges, and the later chapters are based in secondary school work, so there is progression in that sense. Several of the chapters follow through the important content theme of number leading to algebra. Other chapters are concerned with shape and space, with probability, with proof, with assessment and even with what is sometimes termed the process side of mathematics. All the chapters include original elements based on recent research carried out at Leeds, but this is always set against the background of prior knowledge from earlier studies, and with the implications for teaching mathematics firmly in mind. One chapter is entirely devoted to providing ideas for pattern work in classrooms, because one strand of the work of the Pattern Group was to do just that, partly through a regular newsletter. Thus, in this one volume, we describe our work so far, discussed in the context of attempting to provide guidance for teachers of pupils of all age groups. Naturally, our hope is that the book will be a useful contribution towards further improving the progress of all children in learning mathematics.

Tony Orton
March 1998

Chapter 1

Pattern in the Nursery

Rosalind Garrick, John Threlfall and Anthony Orton

In every early years classroom, there are many children who are highly motivated to work with mathematical apparatus such as pegs, beads, tiles and magnetic shapes, and it is almost inevitable that when doing so they will notice and create patterns. Children also often choose to work with a range of other play materials which provide opportunities for pattern-making, including wooden blocks, collage materials and construction sets. Sometimes it is in social group activities that children notice and make patterns – for example, when building a fire engine with large wooden blocks – when they may strive for pattern effects such as symmetry. Other pattern-related thinking occurs in more solitary activities; for example, when painting. On the whole, children only occasionally try to verbalize their pattern-related perceptions and intentions during such play activities, and so for the most part children's thinking about pattern is shown only by what they do.

In any nursery class during any session, the children notice patterns of different kinds and make patterns in a variety of different ways. A typical scene may have two children picking up objects from a colourful pattern display table. 'Our Nan does patterns', says Lisa to her friend, handling an attractive crocheted blanket. Close by, two three-year-olds have started to play with wooden threading beads. They sit contentedly, threading long strings of beads that trail on to the floor. 'I'm making a big pattern', says Sara, as she proudly lifts her string and shows it off to the teacher. 'Mine's a doggie', says her friend, Tom. 'I'm taking it for a walk now.' Alongside, a new child, Jonathan, sits quietly by himself on the floor, placing pegs in a pegboard. Later, Angela, aged four years, nine months, and soon to start in the school's reception class, seeks out the teacher. She wants to show off her elaborate pegboard pattern. 'It's a pattern. Can I put it on the table?' She finds a label, confidently writes her name and then writes the sentence, 'I md a pttn.' Angela places both the pegboard and its label on the pattern display table. Jonathan's and Angela's patterns are shown as Figures 1.1 and 1.2 (see colour plates).

DEVELOPMENT IN PATTERN WORK

In early years classrooms, there does seem to be a gulf between the apparently random arrangements of materials made by such children as Jonathan and the complex structuring of

Angela's work. In many ways this parallels the gulf between early mark-making and confident early writing, which is also noticeable in nursery settings. However, while much is known about developmental sequences in children's acquisition of literacy skills and in some aspects of mathematical learning, particularly number, relatively limited attention has been given to pattern as a particular aspect of mathematical learning. The HMI document *Aspects of Primary Education: the Education of Children under Five* (Her Majesty's Inspectorate (HMI), 1989a) gives an influential perspective on an effective curriculum for the early years, and provides a description and discussion of a wide-ranging and stimulating mathematics curriculum, based on 'practical activities and play experiences'. However, the references to pattern are few and far between. There is one reference to the way in which 'playing games and singing number songs and rhymes help children to begin to see sequences and patterns in number and encourage their interest in mathematics' (HMI, 1989a, p. 21). Many interesting examples of teaching and learning in the area of space and shape are described in the document, but in all the examples there are no specific references to pattern. Among a set of interesting photographs of children's practical work, just one photograph of a display about time includes pattern-making work, using mark-making materials. The document shows children in successful schools making significant progress in a number of areas of mathematical learning during this period of their education. However, there is little in the document to suggest that children can make significant progress in the development of knowledge, understanding and skills in the area of pattern or to detail how development might proceed.

Some early years educators working with four-year-olds in nursery and reception classes may turn for guidance to another 1989 report, *Aspects of Primary Education: the Teaching and Learning of Mathematics* (HMI, 1989b). In contrast to the emphasis in the report cited earlier, HMI here highlights work with pattern as a particularly significant feature of successful mathematics teaching with four- and five-year-olds. It praises teacher-led work, focused on identifying and continuing patterns that involve many different elements. Additionally, it praises work led by children, in which children create and record their own patterns.

> Throughout the work with this 4 and 5 year old age group, pattern was one of the most significant and common features ... The children showed they could confidently create and continue quite complex patterns ... Children in many schools consciously imposed pattern on exploratory play activities. (HMI, 1989b, pp. 30–1)

HMI provides varied examples of children engaged in challenging pattern-making activities with pegboards, construction sets, 2D shapes, duplo tiles and linking cubes. There is an emphasis on young children exploring and creating with such materials and this is seen as a significant feature of successful early mathematical learning.

Several examples of work with pattern described and illustrated in HMI (1989b) are explicitly included as the work of five-year-olds. Thus it is possible that a great deal of the work that so impressed HMI was the work of five-year-olds rather than four-year-olds, but this is not made clear in the report. There may in fact be significant differences between the achievements we can expect from three-, four- and five-year-olds. Whatever these differences are, however, there seems to be a lack of consensus about what can be achieved by three- and four-year-olds and what kinds of learning opportunities should be provided in this important area of the mathematics curriculum.

RESEARCH ABOUT YOUNG CHILDREN AND PATTERN

There is a large body of research (Askew and Wiliam, 1995) into children's developing concepts of number, the knowledge and understanding about number that young children bring with them on entry to formal schooling at four or five years of age and the counting skills that develop in the pre-school years. In contrast, the research into the developing concepts of pattern and the pattern-making skills that we would expect to be developing concurrently is harder to find. Nevertheless, there are some relevant studies that can be used to chart developmental pathways in children's early pattern work, using some of the materials detailed above. Research evidence provides insights into the sequence of children's development in terms of their developing knowledge and understanding of pattern, as well as their pattern-making skills, leading towards skilful pattern-making. Further research evidence provides insights into children's early competence in recognizing patterns. The insights gained from these studies can enable early years educators to provide the most appropriate contexts and support to enhance children's mathematical learning, and to design the detail and style of a mathematics curriculum that can most effectively support this development.

The research studies in pattern have between them employed a range of approaches. Some researchers working in the area have used observational techniques, working in the naturalistic setting of the nursery class to look at the kinds of knowledge and abilities developing as children engage with the range of materials and equipment with potential for pattern-making activity, such as wooden bricks, threading materials, pegs and pegboards, construction sets, mark-making and collage materials, a variety of natural materials and more. In *The Teaching and Learning of Mathematics* (HMI, 1989b), HMI highlight the way in which the child who is highly motivated to explore aspects of pattern will impose a patterned structure on almost any play materials. Observation of children doing so has provided rich and detailed accounts of the competences of pre-school children. For example, Gura (1992), working with the Froebel Blockplay Research Group, focused solely on children's self-initiated play with wooden blocks. She found that young children vary in their motivation to explore pattern when working with blocks. Some children are primarily interested in the use of blocks to make configurations or patterns, whereas other children are far more likely to use their blocks as story props or individual representations of objects. Gura refers to the tendency of children to fall into three distinct groups: a group of 'patterners' or 'visualizers'; a group of 'dramatists'; and a group of children who are happy to mix the two. Because of the focus on a single material, however, this research cannot tell us whether 'patterners' and 'dramatists' will sustain these distinctive styles of play during their interactions with a variety of classroom materials. If styles of play are in fact sustained, it may be necessary for educators to support the 'dramatists' in developing more varied styles of play to enrich their mathematical development.

Athey (1990) also employed an observational approach, working with a teacher in a small nursery class. Athey offers detailed insights into the ways in which the structures or 'schemas' of early motor and perceptual behaviours can be identified in young children's play. She uses a classification of action into types of 'graphic schemas', 'space schemas' and 'action schemas' to represent many salient experiences.

> Peter ... struggled to draw a discrete enclosure instead of his habitual circular scribble. When he had achieved a fairly good form he named it 'Bubble'. Five days later he used his new form to represent 'Hat'. At that time he could not be parted from a white bowler hat. (Athey, 1990, p. 98)

This study shows how pre-school children impose structure on a wide variety of play materials. It may be possible to take Athey's findings in a new direction and show how the varied early structuring behaviours she details could be significant behaviours in a developmental journey towards mature work with patterns.

In contrast to researchers using naturalistic observation, some researchers in the field have used specific assessment tasks in more formal settings. For example, Pierrault-Le Bonniec (1982) assessed pattern on a set of increasingly complex pattern-making tasks at three, four and five years of age, focusing on progress towards 'operatory reversibility', in the Piagetian tradition. Pierrault-Le Bonniec provides some evidence of the cognitive advances that children can be expected to make over periods of time, in that the older children in the study were more successful in tackling the more complex pattern-making tasks, showing greater confidence in working with alternating structures, inversions of alternation and, in some cases, cyclic organization. A limitation of the Pierrault-Le Bonniec account, however, is that the elicited behaviour of the three-year-olds is characterized largely in deficit terms. The challenge for researchers working with this age group is to see how such simple, early-appearing behaviours as the stacking, in-filling and enclosing evidenced in the work of Pierrault-Le Bonniec's three-year-olds can be interpreted as positive steps on a developmental journey towards the mature pattern-making abilities evidenced by his most successful five-year-olds.

Aubrey (1993), in more wide-ranging research, focused assessment tasks on pattern-making abilities as one aspect of children's wider mathematical abilities at the point of entry to formal schooling. One interesting finding of this research is the relative difficulty experienced by children working with assessment tasks which incorporate some element of pattern when compared with their achievements in other aspects of the number curriculum. Fewer than half the group were successful in both copying and continuing simple repeating patterns. In a more open-ended task, children were asked to make a simple pattern with plastic forms, and no children at all were successful, although it is possible that the assessment underestimated the children's pattern-making abilities because the assessment materials were not the familiar materials of previous pattern-making work. Flavell *et al.* (1993) discuss the inconsistencies that we can expect from children's responses to varying assessment techniques. It may be that the materials selected for use in pattern-making assessments constitute a significant variation that will affect children's performance. The nature and extent of any such variation will need further clarification.

THE OFFICIAL VIEW

In 1996, the School Curriculum and Assessment Authority (SCAA) produced the document *Nursery Education: Desirable Outcomes for Children's Learning on Entering Compulsory Education.* The desirable outcomes outlined are intended as the goals for the learning of pre-school children in a variety of educational settings. It is proposed that children in all such settings have access to a curriculum that will support their progress towards these goals. The document sets up the expectation that most children will be able to achieve these goals by the time of entry to compulsory education, in the term following their fifth birthday. Mathematics is, of course, included as one of six key areas of learning.

The goals outlined for mathematical learning are to be achieved through a focus on practical activities and on the use and understanding of mathematical language. Among the goals it is stated briefly that children should 'recognize and recreate pattern' (SCAA, 1996). No more specific contexts than the 'practical activities' of the introduction are suggested. 'Recreate' is an unusual word to use, and seems to indicate an intended curriculum in which young children are to be encouraged to recognize and copy, but not primarily to make up patterns on their own. A parallel curriculum in English would be one in which children were encouraged to recognize and copy print but not necessarily to explore the features of print independently. The apparently simple statement about activities related to pattern is embedded in a list of mathematical activities and experiences which are familiar and valued by most early years educators. It is likely to be accepted by many in its intended audience as unremarkable. However, implicit in this stated goal of early mathematical learning, there seems to be first a particular view about how children learn mathematics and second an assumption about the sequence in which knowledge, understanding and skills are developed in relation to pattern. The particular view is one where adults are firmly in control of the direction of practical activities, there to provide the necessary models for pattern-making and probably to approve or correct the children's early 'recreations'. The assumption about a sequence of development is highlighted by SCAA's inclusion of National Curriculum Level 1 description within the nursery education document. Where children's achievements exceed the desirable outcomes, they should be taught to 'recognize and make repeating patterns' (SCAA, 1996). The assumed developmental sequence is one in which young children develop skills in recognizing and copying patterns before going on to develop skills in making patterns. However, it seems to us that the research evidence available raises serious questions about this assumption. There is in our view more to children's pattern than what they are taught. For that reason, it was decided to examine the issue in more detail.

A DEVELOPMENTAL STUDY OF YOUNG CHILDREN'S PATTERN

A doctoral research study was set up by one of the authors to look in detail at the way in which three- and four-year-olds structure play materials and develop early pattern-making skills. The research was carried out in a large inner-city nursery where the ability range of children was wide, including a significant number of children from socially disadvantaged backgrounds showing generalized developmental delay. The research included a longitudinal study of 24 children, followed through from three and a half to four and a half years of age. Data collected in a variety of play contexts have been used to chart a developmental journey towards the mature pattern-making skills evidenced in the work of children like Angela, with their elaborate pegboard patterns, created before anything of the kind is explicitly taught.

When children are given an opportunity to explore varied materials, they structure their pattern-making using a variety of attributes, including shape, size, orientation, colour and position. Thus the development of pattern-making incorporates a number of strands. In an attempt to simplify the demand, it was decided to restrict the materials used in the study to pegs, beads and mosaic tiles, in which children can be seen to structure their patterns both spatially and in terms of colour organization, but which do not offer the means to consider shape, size or orientation. The aim of the study was to trace two strands of the development towards mature pattern-making: patterning with colour and patterning by position.

In presenting the findings in the following pages, we must acknowledge that although there do seem to be important commonalities in the developmental sequences, there are also many opportunities for more individual explorations along more personal routes. In other words, the developmental journey for each child should be considered unique.

SPATIAL ORGANIZATION

Children's early spatial structuring of materials can be categorized as a series of single-element characteristics, which later on can be seen to occur in combination in more mature pattern-making. It seems reasonable, therefore, to identify them as the 'basic elements' of spatial organization. At first, children's patterning does not seem to have any spatial organization at all. Jonathan, in the opening scene, plays in a way that is characteristic of the earliest stage of exploratory play. He works contentedly, placing pegs into the holes of his pegboard, but with no form of spatial organization evident from either the order in which materials are placed or the completed configuration. Figure 1.1 is a placement typical of many three-year-olds first working with pegs or similar materials. Very young children are likely to lose interest in the activity after perhaps a dozen pegs have been placed. Occasionally, however, young children will persist and gain a sense of achievement from, for example, filling a complete square. With just a little experience, in the work of most children, a simple form of organization, 'proximity placing', appears. On one or more occasions during the placement of materials, two tiles or pegs are placed in adjacent positions. Figure 1.3 shows the placement order of tiles along a strip as an example of 'proximity placing'. The third and fourth tiles have been placed next to each other. This can be seen to be a step towards the spatial organization of making lines.

Figure 1.3 *Tile placement with 'proximity placing'*
(a = first tile placed; b = second tile placed; and so on)

A further stage in this development towards the marking of a single line is given in Figure 1.4. With experience, the child shows increased skill in controlling the unidirectional proximity placing in marking a single line. At these earliest stages, the main thrust of spatial development seems to be towards marking a line, and at around three and a half years of age many

Figure 1.4 *'Proximity placing' towards creating a line*

children already show such a competence. Once young children have mastered the unidirectional proximity placing of materials to create a line with tiles or pegs economically, they are able to use pegboards to investigate different kinds of lines, such as 'horizontal' and 'vertical' lines, and then, as a later development, 'diagonal' lines. In the nursery, diagonal lines are seen in the work of only a small number of four-and-a-half-year-olds. There are, however, exceptions to this 'thrust' towards lines. A minority of the youngest children seem to show a greater interest in the symmetrical placing of materials, as in Figure 1.5.

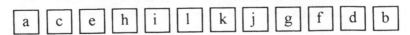

Figure 1.5 *Symmetrical placement*

In children's work with pegs, there are other early-appearing basic elements which are not towards making a line. An example of a 'non-linear' basic element of spatial organization is 'marking a square'. A special case of this, 'marking the centre', is shown in Figure 1.6. Another

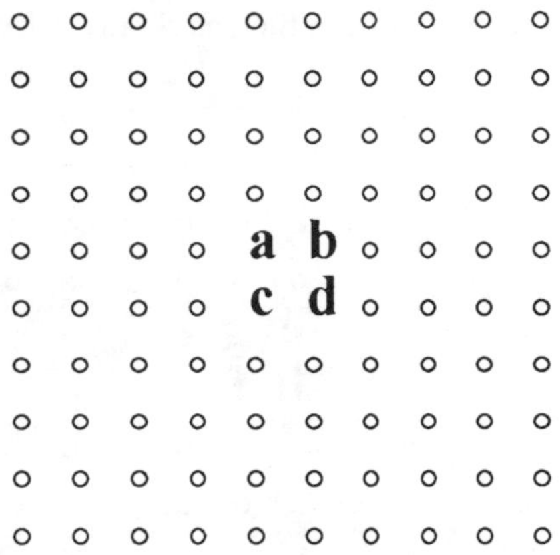

Figure 1.6 *Marking the centre*

early-appearing non-linear basic element is 'marking the corners'. 'Marking midpoints', seen in Figure 1.7, is yet another non-linear basic element, one with significant potential for later patterning. Non-linear basic elements appear in the early work of some but not all children.

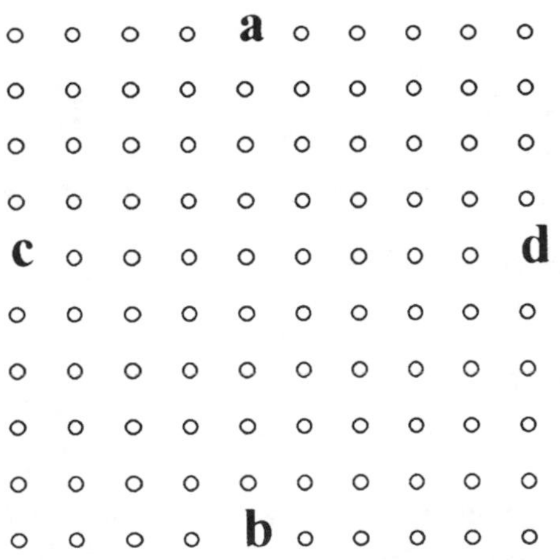

Figure 1.7 *Marking midpoints*

Once established, the non-linear and linear basic elements categorized above function as building blocks of spatial organization in children's work with pegs and pegboards. They can be combined in a variety of ways, making it possible for children to create more varied and complex forms of spatial organization. Children go on to collect, repeat, connect or intersect particular elements in a variety of ways. Angela's mature work with pegs, shown in Figure 1.2, provides evidence of how such early-appearing 'non-linear basic elements' as 'marking the corners' and 'marking the centre' are used as the building blocks of later pattern-making work.

Collecting basic elements is the earliest-appearing and simplest form of combination. In Figure 1.8, for example, the basic elements of 'marking the corners' and 'marking the centre' are collected together. At around the same time as children begin to collect basic elements,

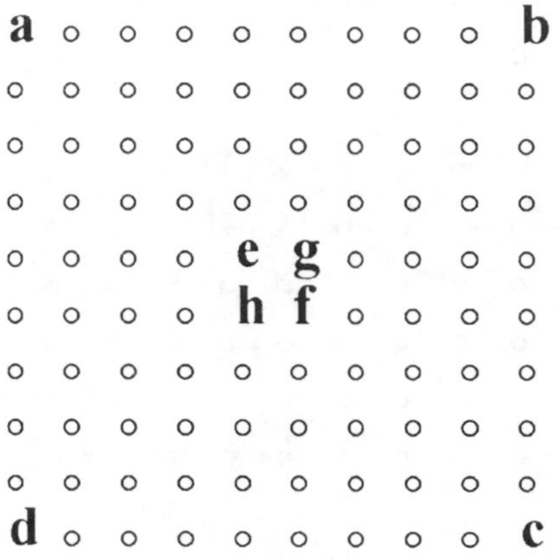

Figure 1.8 *Combination of marking the corners and marking the centre*

or shortly after, they also begin to repeat basic elements. Early repeated work is likely to include partial lines and sometimes multi-directional placing. With practice, however, children are able to repeat sustained lines, as in Figure 1.9.

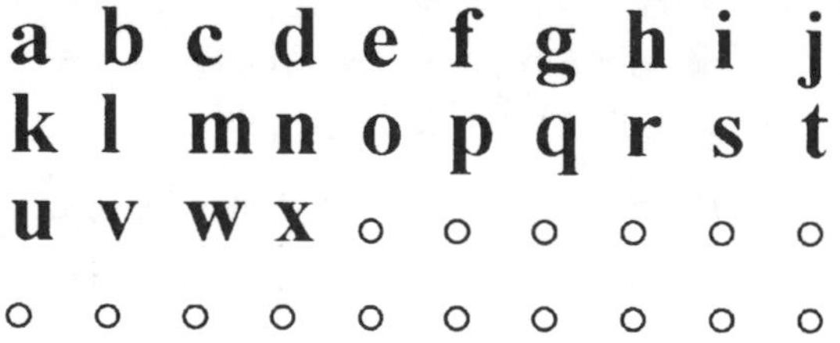

Figure 1.9 *Connected lines*

Alongside the collecting and repeating of basic elements, children also begin to connect the basic elements of spatial organization, starting with 'horizontal' and 'vertical' lines. Initially, they are likely to make simple connections, as in Figure 1.10. Some children then go on to explore spirals, and most children then go on to make rectangles and most frequently squares.

The intersection of basic elements of spatial organization seems to appear later in development than the collection, repetition or connection of basic elements. The intersection of midpoint lines is particularly significant in its potential for mature pattern-making. Intersecting diagonal lines are an even later development, observed only occasionally in the work of the four-year-olds in the nursery study. Figure 1.11 shows the work of Steven, aged four years, six months, and shows just how difficult it can be for the young child to master this

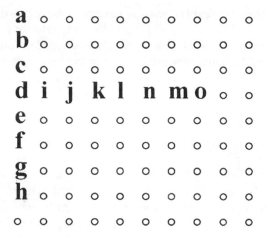

Figure 1.10 *Repeated sustained lines*

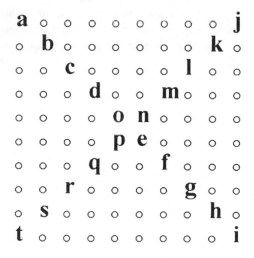

Figure 1.11 *Steven's intersecting diagonals*

intersection. Steven seems to plan ahead, leaving an empty hole after peg 'd' to allow for his expected intersection point for the second diagonal line. Steven in fact looked most surprised on placing peg 'n', suggesting that the actual point of intersection was unexpected.

The sequence above seems to be the main pathway followed by young children in developing control of the spatial elements of pattern-making. However, children do vary greatly in the rate at which they progress towards control of these basic elements. At three and a half years, some children will be engaged in the random placing of materials, while others will already be making and repeating sustained lines of pegs. At four and a half years, the least mature children in the nursery sample may still be working towards multi-directional placings, where others are attempting the intersection of diagonal lines, as with Steven in Figure 1.11.

In summary, it seems that significant development takes place in children's spatial structuring of materials during the years of nursery education. Between three and four years of age, children gain control, to varying degrees and at varying rates, of a number of 'linear' and 'non-linear' basic elements of spatial organization, which between four and five years of age they utilize in more complex pattern-making.

COLOUR ORGANIZATION

While children are working with pegs and mosaic tiles to master the basic elements of spatial organization, there are parallel developments taking place in their attempts to master the basic elements of colour organization, which is developed alongside spatial organization. In work with beads and other threading materials, however, children are able to focus on colour organization alone. There are no possibilities for the child to structure materials spatially, since the act of threading necessarily creates a linear arrangement of materials.

Young children first show awareness of colour in their work with play materials by remarking on the colour of individual items of equipment. For example, they comment 'I got purple', 'Like this red one?' and 'I'm looking for orange'. Several three-and-a-half-year-olds in the nursery sample show this level of awareness of colour during some aspect of their work with play materials. Soon this awareness is manifested in action, when a group of two or more units of play equipment from a single colour category are placed consecutively. Tom commented on his sequence of red beads, shown in Figure 1.12 (colour plate), by saying 'Got 2 reds. One more red.'

Children sometimes sustain the single colour for a longer sequence, perhaps for a complete necklace or for a complete line of pegs. On other occasions, the same children can be equally interested in colour differences, evidenced by children's comments on specific or general colour contrasts: 'Red, blue and yellow', for example, and 'Doing all different colours'. In pattern-making, this is shown by a grouping of units of play equipment placed consecutively, where each unit is from a different colour category compared with the colour of the units adjacent to it. (Of course, this can occur incidentally, as a result of not paying attention to colour. Children's commentary is needed to identify which is which in particular cases.)

A later development of this preoccupation with relationships of difference is shown when a grouping is made of one unit from each available colour category, as shown in Figure 1.13 (colour plate). This is far less likely to have occurred as a coincidence, so can be inferred from the outcome alone, but the child's comment 'Doing all different colours' in this case is further confirmation of his intention.

The basic elements of colour organization are thus the purposive creation of similarities and differences by colour. They appear relatively early in development and function as the 'building blocks' of play with beads, tiles and pegs in terms of colour organization. Once established, these basic elements of colour organization can be developed and combined in a variety of ways, leading to more complex forms of colour organization. The basic elements are 'chained', 'repeated', 'alternated', 'multiplied' and 'symmetrically placed'.

'Chaining' is the simplest combination of the basic elements in terms of the child's colour organization, and the first to be seen in children's work. 'Chaining' refers to the successive placement of groups or series, and has different forms. The simple chaining of similarity groups, in Figure 1.14 (colour plate), is an example of chaining which is among the first that children display. Figure 1.15 (colour plate) shows a more mature development, with the child successful in sustaining the chaining of groups of equivalent size. In that he or she is following several self-imposed rules for the selection of materials, the child doing this seems to be showing an early awareness of some key features of pattern.

The alternation of basic elements is closely related to chaining and seems to follow closely in development. 'Alternated' refers to the alternation of groups in two colours. The first successes in sustaining alternating patterns are with single units, as in Figure 1.16 (colour plate). Alternating larger similarity groups is a later development. Often, when children first attempt to copy a simple repeated pattern, they are successful in alternating the appropriate colours, but are unable to sustain an exact repeat of the size of the groups. Figure 1.17 (colour plate) shows an example of an attempt at alternated similarity groups, produced in the context of copying a two-colour repeated pattern.

At a more advanced level than either chaining or alternating, the basic elements of colour organization can be repeated. In the example shown in Figure 1.18 (colour plate), a 'difference series' (Figure 1.13) is repeated. In another relatively late-appearing form of colour organization, the units of a 'difference series' can be 'multiplied' as in Figure 1.19 (colour plate), a two-unit difference series.

SPATIAL/COLOUR ORGANIZATION

After the basic elements of spatial and colour organization are established, not only do they appear in more complex forms, they also occur in combination, with patterns that sustain elements of organization in both criteria. For example, Figure 1.20 shows a symmetrically placed difference group, in one line made across a pegboard.

a	c	e	g			h	f	d	b

Figure 1.20 *A symmetrically placed difference group, using pegs*

In other examples of the confluence of colour and spatial organization, a line of the material in one colour serves as the basic element of colour organization. Figure 1.21 shows a section of a pegboard in which a colour difference series is being made from lines of pegs. There are even rare examples in the nursery study of 'chained' patterns made from lines, such as

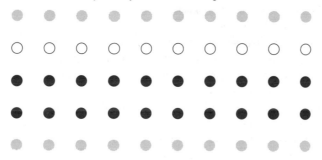

Figure 1.21 *Difference series of line groups, using pegs*

that in Figure 1.22. Along with other examples of repeated, alternated and multiplied line units, these are found more frequently in the work of slightly older children. Lines made from single colours may be placed 'horizontally', 'vertically' or 'diagonally' to make new kinds of

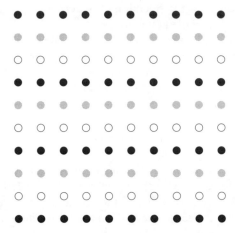

Figure 1.22 *A rare nursery example of a chained difference series of line units*

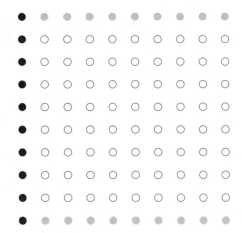

Figure 1.23 *Differently oriented pegboard line groups*

patterns, as in Figure 1.23. There were also, within the nursery study, a small number of examples of patterns made from lines of alternating units, as shown in Figure 1.24. This complex work corresponds to the 'cyclic organization' elicited by Pierrault-Le Bonniec (1982) during assessment tasks with five-year-olds.

Another form of organization mixing colour and spatial features which was observed in children's work with pegs in the nursery study was that in which there are regular or irregular blocks of colour. In the example in Figure 1.25, two colour blocks are divided by a single colour line unit. This form of organization seems to be a relatively late development, found only among four-year-olds in the nursery study.

It seems, in summary, that significant developments take place in children's ability to structure materials, using colour as the varying attribute, between three and four years of age. These developments seem to parallel the developments in spatial structuring taking place during the same period. To varying degrees and at varying rates, children gain control of a

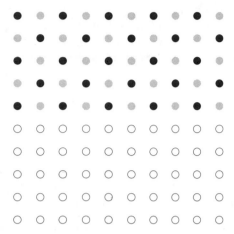

Figure 1.24 *Pattern made from lines of alternating units*

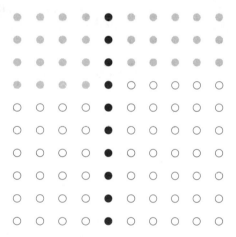

Figure 1.25 *An example of block organization in peg work*

number of basic elements of colour organization with significant potential for pattern-making. During this period, some children begin to integrate spatial and colour structuring in simple linear patterns, working with beads, tiles or pegs. A smaller number begin to integrate spatial and colour structuring in relatively complex ways, particularly in pegboard work based on 'line-unit' and 'block' organization.

ADULT AND PEER MODELS IN PATTERN WORK

In the light of the apparent assumption by SCAA (1996) of the predominance of modes where adults provide models for children to recreate as a key feature of early work with pattern, it seems important to consider the nature and significance of models for children's work with pattern. Most children in the longitudinal study, working with beads, tiles and pegs, made significant progress along the pathways to pattern-making outlined above. The assessment tasks for work with beads and tiles did include adult models of pattern-making. Pegboard work, however, was supported by adults only in terms of regular encouragement and appreciation of children's efforts. No adult models of pegboard work were provided. Many children, particularly the three-year-olds, worked alone with these materials and showed little awareness of the work of their peers. Many older children, however, regularly chose to work alongside friends. There are several examples of children's work being influenced by the observed features of the work of friends. The evidence from the nursery study suggests that the influences of models on children's pattern-making work are complex. For example, the influence of models seems to vary significantly with variations in presentation. The influence of models may also vary in relation to the level of the child's self-initiated structuring of materials.

Adult-initiated models of pattern-making may be unnecessary, and helpful only to a minority of children. There seems also to be a danger that too heavy a diet of adult-led work will undermine and limit children's individual explorations. Working with three- and four-year-olds in nursery and reception classes, it seems to be more important for early years teachers to provide varied opportunities for children to structure materials; opportunities for children to self-initiate work and follow personal routes towards pattern-making; and encouragement to children to share their work with interested adults and peers.

RECOGNIZING, DESCRIBING AND DISCUSSING PATTERNS

As well as development in pattern-making, there is development in the competences of young children in recognizing, describing and discussing patterns. Of the available research evidence relating to young children's work with pattern, there is particularly limited evidence relating to pattern perception. One interesting study by Rawson (1993), however, has focused attention on pattern perception in four- to six-year-olds. The youngest child in this study was four years, eleven months. The children in the group were asked to sort a varied collection of patterned objects into two bags, a 'pattern' bag and a 'not pattern' bag. Discussion with the children about their sorting established that a number of common criteria were used both to accept and to reject items as examples of pattern. The frequently mentioned criteria for pattern included: the repetition of a shape or motif; directional change of a repeated motif; the repetition of a sequence of numbers or shapes; symmetrical balancing of shapes or motifs; and colour as an element of change. While some children commented on features of materials that were not relevant to the sorting, many children successfully found words to describe the patterned materials. Rawson comments on how hard it is for young children to verbalize such observations effectively. He suggests that it is particularly hard for young children to comment on the interrelationship of features within a pattern.

Our research complemented the focus on children making patterns with a study of pattern perception in the younger age group of three- and four-year-olds. It is interesting to compare the responses of this younger group with the responses of Rawson's children. A pattern perception activity was the first task in a series centred on a group of four teddy bears, three of which were wearing necklaces. All three necklaces were made of green and yellow threading cubes, with one a random arrangement of beads, one a symmetrical arrangement of beads, and the last an alternating sequence of beads, as shown in Figure 1.26.

Having been introduced to the bears, the children were then invited to look at each bear's

Figure 1.26 *Three necklaces for teddy bears*

necklace in turn. They were asked which necklace they liked best and what they liked about this necklace. This was a difficult task for both three-and-a-half and four-and-a-half-year-olds. Although the task did not assume familiarity with the word 'pattern', the language demands of the task proved difficult for several of the children at both ages. In fact, 22 per cent of the three-and-a-half-year-olds and 10 per cent of the four-and-a-half-year-olds were unable to make sense of the first question and did not indicate a choice of necklace. Although there seemed to be a clear preference for the repeated pattern among three-and-a-half-year-olds, the random arrangement of beads was the preferred choice of four-and-a-half-year-olds. It seems likely that only a minority of children used the characteristics of colour organization as a criterion for choice. In the play context of this task, some children may have found the characteristics of particular bears to be more salient than the characteristics of the necklaces. Baby bear wore the necklace with the random arrangement of beads and one child made explicit reference to baby bear in the explanation of her choice: 'I like it 'cos he's like baby bear'.

Many children did attempt to provide explanations for their choice, and these explanations can contribute to our understanding of children's engagement with the task. However, 45 per cent of the children at three and a half years and 35 per cent of the children at four and a half years gave no response, a 'don't know' response or an inappropriate response to the question about choice of necklace. Of the positive responses, there is a clear increase in those responses which involve children making specific reference to colour. At three and a half years, 18 per cent of the children refer to the use of one or two specific colours; for example, 'It's nice 'cos it's got yellow and green', and, 'Because it's got all the green colours on it'. At four and a half years, 45 per cent of children make reference to colour. Children may well find it difficult to make meaningful choices among necklaces even at four and a half years because perception is still focused on the use of a particular colour or the contrast of two colours. Only a few older children provide evidence of perception focused on the interrelationship of colours within a necklace. Many children who showed confidence and creativity in devising repeating patterns with two or more colours showed little attention to patterning in this task. In fact, no child spontaneously referred to 'pattern' as a significant feature of the choice, even though many of the same children were referring to their own work as 'pattern'.

There is, however, a small number of children at both ages who provide some evidence of attending to elements of pattern in the necklaces. At three and a half years, Joel and Luke pointed to the single yellow bead at the centre of the symmetrical arrangement as explanation of their choice. Kirsty at three and a half years seemed to be attempting to describe the repeating structure of her chosen necklace, 'Cos it's got green, yellow, green, yellow, green, yellow, green'. Her intonation was suggestive of an awareness of structure. At four and a half years, Matthew struggled to express his perception of the organization of the symmetrically patterned necklace: 'All the yellows and greens are in different colours'. Usually a highly articulate child, Matthew could not communicate his likely perception satisfactorily. Only Steven, at four and a half years, was able to express his perception of the symmetry of this arrangement successfully: 'Because it's got two yellows there, two yellows there and a yellow there'.

It seems to be difficult for many three- and four-year-olds to 'recognize' pattern and even more difficult for them to talk about the significant features of patterns. Rawson (1993) stressed how difficult this was for the slightly older children in his study. Although many children in this younger age group can enjoy looking at and talking about pattern in a variety of contexts, early years educators do need to take care to ensure that such activities engage with children at an appropriate level. Many children may find it more interesting and meaningful to talk about the features of their own pattern-making activities before moving on to focus on patterns created by others.

The recommendations for appropriate work in this area in the SCAA nursery education guidelines, which place recognizing and copying the work of others before making patterns of their own devising, may well have underestimated the cognitive demands of this apparently simple activity of recognizing patterns, as well as failing to acknowledge the spontaneous pattern-making that often occurs without models.

CONCLUSION

Children entering nursery or reception classes at three or four years of age will show evidence of widely differing skills and abilities with patterns, as with all other aspects of learning. Whatever the starting point, however, it seems likely that all children will make significant progress during this period. As children engage in self-directed investigations with a variety of mathematical apparatus and other play materials, they show a gradually developing control over both the spatial and colour organization of materials. Initially, spatial and colour organization seem to develop independently, although often concurrently. There is, in this development, a degree of similarity between children and across the different kinds of organization, although it is important to acknowledge that each child's developmental journey will be unique. The 'typical' development shows the children first acquiring a repertoire of 'basic' elements of organization. These are then explored in combination, and finally elaborated by repetitions. There also comes a point when different kinds of organization begin to be integrated, in pattern-making which anticipates the pattern skills of older children.

The social context of learning seems to be important in this development. Some children, who are sometimes characterized as a type called 'patterners', are highly motivated to develop thinking and skills in this area of mathematics, and can act relatively independently in creating new kinds of patterns, whereas other children are more dependent on adult encouragement or peer group support, learning in part from the spontaneous activity of the 'patterners'. The different approaches to pattern-making between children are reflected in different ways in which children make use of the social context for learning. Yet in the guidance available to schools at this time such complexity is not acknowledged, and the advice given, which isolates the teacher as the only source of pattern, seems from the research evidence to be misleading, and to miss the potential that exists.

Similarly, the difficulty which young children have in recognizing patterns made by others relative to the facility with which they create their own patterns needs to be acknowledged. The evidence reported in this chapter suggests that the development of children's colour and spatial organization in spontaneous pattern-making is considerably more advanced than their capacity to recognize and copy the patterns of others. This conflicts directly with the implications of the current curriculum guidance for the early years.

The way to promote learning about pattern in young children is not to offer a diet of prescribed exercises to 'copy and continue' adult-devised patterns. Young children need opportunities to work with a wide variety of materials; they need opportunities to follow personal routes towards pattern-making and opportunities to create individual patterns of increasing complexity. At the same time, early years educators need to ensure that young children are encouraged to appreciate the varied work of their friends and given opportunities to share ideas, learning from each other. Educators themselves need to provide ongoing support to young children engaged in pattern-making activities. Their well timed interventions can help children to develop an awareness and appreciation of some significant features of pattern and an appropriate language to talk about these. Many children are highly motivated to work in this area and excited by their own achievements at whatever level. It is crucial that we support and provide for the development of this early-appearing fascination with an important aspect of mathematics.

Chapter 2

Repeating Patterns in the Early Primary Years

John Threlfall

INTRODUCTION

The rich and multifaceted pattern-making of the pre-school child is naturally continued into the school years. However, whereas in the pre-school setting the best approach for adults seems to be to nurture the inclinations of individuals, the challenge for schooling is to find a way of shaping the development of children in particular directions, corresponding to strands of curriculum. Work in school also has to face up to the possibility that some children may be less attracted to patterns, and less inclined to make patterns than others, as Rawson (1993) suggests. The different forms of pattern work in school are often taken to presage different kinds of later learning. In this chapter we shall be concerned only with the linear, or 'one-dimensional', repeating patterns, which represent, to some, the first step towards number patterns and algebra, and not with any kind of two-dimensional patterns, some of which may be called 'wallpaper patterns', and which may be supposed to lead on to tessellation and transformation geometry.

As suggested in Chapter 1, any pre-school setting will be characterized by young children spontaneously creating simple repeating patterns in a variety of media, including not only pegs in pegboards and tiles on strips but also, to give some examples arising from observation in a local nursery classroom, a string threaded with alternate discs and tubes (Figure 2.1), an

Figure 2.1 *A string threaded with alternate discs and tubes*

egg box containing small pieces of material – strips and 'rounds' – placed alternately in the depressions (Figure 2.2) and a drawing of a striped jumper, in a repeating pattern (Figure 2.3).

Ideas for different contexts suitable for developing children's repeating pattern work in school abound in mathematics books for young children and their teachers. Richards and Jones (1990), for example, describe how to help children to generate patterns with sticky

Figure 2.2 *An egg box containing small pieces of material – strips and 'rounds' – placed alternately in the depressions*

Figure 2.3 *A drawing of a striped jumper, coloured in a repeating pattern*

shapes, building bricks, beads, pebbles and in wet sand, or by using sound such as clapping patterns, or movement such as a repeated hop, step and jump pattern. Other possibilities include:

- arranging objects (shells, shapes, teddies, etc.);
- making pictures (painting, printing, drawing);
- using musical instruments;
- iconic and symbolic representations (coloured dots, letters, numbers, etc.).

Repeating patterns can be within one attribute (for example, the colour or size or shape or orientation of objects, where the other aspects either stay the same or are varied in an arbitrary way) or more than one, and might involve number as an additional dimension; for example, using two of each kind of element in a repeat. As a result, there can be very complex patterns using simple materials, such as the pattern in Figure 2.4, which uses shapes of different sizes.

Figure 2.4 *Complex repeating pattern using two shapes in two sizes*

PURPOSES FOR REPEATING LINEAR PATTERNS

Repeating linear patterns are the kinds of pattern for young children which have been most strongly emphasized in the National Curriculum for England and Wales, and repeating patterns occupy a relatively exalted status as a point of specified competence at Level 1 of the Attainment Target for Number and Algebra. Nevertheless, the purpose for repeating patterns given in the Programme of Study for Key Stage 1 is relatively modest: 'Use repeating patterns to develop ideas of regularity and sequencing' (DfE/WO, 1995, p. 3). This purpose seems to consider repeating patterns mostly as examples of cyclical structures, familiar to children from life events such as days of the week, and the significance of the development of these ideas to number and algebra is not made clear. Other authors have been more ambitious and more explicit about the purpose of repeated pattern work, in two distinct ways: first, suggesting how repeating patterns can be used in teaching; second, suggesting what significance the learning of repeating patterns has to later work.

Repeating patterns as a teaching reference

According to some authors, the role of work with repeating patterns is as a useful basis for teaching about other matters, with the pattern-making acting as a concrete and familiar experience, which can be meaningfully referred to in talking about new ideas. In these cases, the value of repeating patterns is as a context for teachers to draw attention to helpful aspects of experience, rather than as a conceptual precursor. HMI (1989b, p. 17), for example, suggests that perceptive teachers should use activities to create patterns with pegs, beads, bricks and so on as a starting point for analysis and development: 'Children's attention was drawn to recurring sequences and valuable number work ensued'. Another example of this kind of claim would be the link Liebeck (1984) makes between repeating pattern and ordering, with repeating patterns being used as a context for looking at 'what comes next' by reference to the pattern itself, as a prelude to the use of comparison. Doing repeating patterns does not develop ideas of ordering, but the ordering aspect can be drawn out of the experience. Similarly, Matthews and Matthews (1990) suggest that repeating patterns made when threading beads can lead into ideas of length. It is not that repeating patterns concern length, but that as they are made the length of the concrete context does increase, and this can be pointed out.

In other words, the repeating patterns work itself is not necessary for subsequent development, but it can be exploited in these ways if the children are doing it. As such, the significance of repeating patterns to learning mathematics is not general. The opportunities for exploitation of repeating patterns may be taken up or not by each teacher, and even though repeating patterns can be valuable as a teaching context, other contexts might be equally good for similar teaching.

Repeating pattern as thinking that is important to learning

Other authors claim that repeating pattern work may be valuable in itself as a form of thinking that leads towards further mathematics. In this view, there is the notion of an inherent worth in the activity, where the thinking involved in doing repeating patterns leads on in some way to more advanced ideas. It is mostly in the area of algebra (or 'pre-algebra') that repeating pattern work is seen as a conceptual stepping stone, rather than just a teaching opportunity. Owen (1995), for example, suggests that repeating patterns offer a vehicle for learning to interpret symbols. Clemson and Clemson (1994, p. 68) claim that 'Algebra is all about establishing and recognizing general statements about numbers and shapes', and repeating patterns can be seen as offering an early opportunity of doing just that. Similarly, Resnick *et al.* (1987, p. 172) state that 'Algebraic expressions can be viewed as statements of the relationships that hold between numbers and operations on them *in general*', and it can be argued that repeating patterns prepare children for the algebraic enterprise, since

> During the course of elementary schooling ... children link their knowledge about situations in which amounts are changed, combined, compared etc. to their growing knowledge of how to quantify collections of objects and perhaps to their knowledge of certain spatial arrangements. (Resnick *et al.*, p. 175)

Going even further, the National Curriculum Council (NCC, 1993, Unit E3, p. 1) suggest that 'Working with repeating patterns helps to develop an appreciation of the power of generalization'. Owen (1995) argues that it is the very familiarity of cyclical structures from real events that gives children an affinity with and understanding of repeating patterns, and through them offers younger children access to 'elements of mathematical thought which are not available to them through any other medium in mathematics' (p. 126), including recognition and prediction, and the generalization and communication of rules.

By being able to operate with patterns with which they are comfortable, young children may be able to work at a higher level than would otherwise be the case. As soon as number patterns are introduced, for example, the basic skills and knowledge have to be well established before there is any possibility that the children will be able to generalize or formulate rules about the patterns made. In this way, the purpose of repeating patterns work is established, in theory at least, as a foundation for subsequent development in algebra. How does this correspond to what children actually do with repeating patterns?

CHARACTERISTICS OF REPEATING PATTERN PERFORMANCE

As was suggested in Chapter 1, the 'official' view on the nature of repeating pattern work is that children copy adult models of patterns as a necessary precursor to devising patterns of their own. This assumption seems to have a particular view of pattern-making behind it, which is seen most clearly in NCC, 1993 (Unit E3, p. 1), in which it is stated: 'To devise a repeating pattern requires the creation of a rule and its consistent application.' Observation of children making repeating patterns can suggest a different story, however. For example, in making a pattern with pegs, children may be seen to arrange in a line two or more boxes of pegs, each with a different colour, and take a peg for their pattern first from one and then from the next in a cycle which generates a repeating pattern. They may print, holding one print stamp in each hand, and alternating them, and by so doing make a repeating pattern. The self-consciousness implicit in the phrase 'creation of a rule' is not evident in such examples.

Greeno and Simon (1974) adopt an information-processing perspective to ask how a sequence is generated. The process, they say, must hold information from previous inputs and have a place-keeping mechanism for relating items to adjacent ones. This feature is common to both repeating pattern sequences and number sequences. Greeno and Simon offer different suggestions for the generation of a number sequence, which are the equivalent of the following three ways of generating a repeating sequence:

1. A procedure that relates items to adjacent items by remembering all the relationships, then constructing the sequence by making 'pattern action pairs', e.g. for the pattern ACABACABA and so on, to say, 'If it is an "A" and the last one was a "C" it must be a "B" now', and so on.
2. A memory of the unit of repeat ('ACAB' in the given example), which is rehearsed each time to decide the current position in the repeat by comparison.
3. A rhythm or counter system, e.g. a chant with emphasis, through which the person knows the point in the sequence that has been reached by the 'value' it has. Thus, for the sequence given one might adopt a rhythm moving slightly to the left and right, with 'C' at the left, 'B' at the right and 'A' when moving.

Of these, only (2) may be thought to be a process for the creation and application of a rule. The first has a set of conditionals that may count as rules, but not a single rule to be applied, and the third, rhythmic, approach is not dependent on rules at all.

Observation of children making patterns suggests in addition that some repeating patterns in some physical contexts may be produced by 'filling in'. A sequence of coloured bricks or pegs on a board need not be made by starting at one end, but may be made as in the following example:

First	R	R	R	R
Then	R B	R B	R B	R B
Then	R B G	R B G	R B G	R B G
Then	R B G G	R B G G	R B G G	R B G G
Finally	R B G G R R B G G R R B G G R R B G G R			

In other words, the creation of a rule and its consistent application may be what is desirable in repeating pattern work, but is not all that can happen, and the existence of a repeating pattern as a product of children's work is no evidence at all that a rule has been created and applied. The existence of such alternatives does beg the question of development, of course.

DEVELOPMENT IN CHILDREN'S REPEATING PATTERN WORK

Any pattern-making can be approached from several theoretical positions on perception, such as feature analysis, template matching and Gestalt psychology, yet there is not a great deal of relevant research on repeating pattern as such. However, there was a spate of studies in the late 1960s and early 1970s, when 'the crucial importance for psychology of understanding serially-patterned actions' (Greeno and Simon, 1974) was perceived. There seem to be two approaches to research in the area:

1. Attempts to discern inherent differences of the patterns themselves, to suggest a hierarchy of performance that can be compared with real performance;
2. Empirical studies of young children's work with repeating patterns, to locate any developmental distinctions.

The structure of patterns

As an example of the first strand, Vitz and Todd (1967, 1969) offer models of ordering repeating patterns by their complexity in terms of runs of similar events, or by coding into larger and fewer elements until the pattern is predictable. Using this approach, Vitz and Todd propose the following example of an order of difficulty, with the least complex first:

```
ababababababab
aaabbbaaabbb
aabbaabbaabb
aabaabaabaab
aaabaaabaaab
abcabcabcabc
aaabbbcccaaa
aabbccaabbcc
acccbcccaccc
aaabcaaabcaa
aabcaabcaabc
aabbcaabbcaa
```

Vitz and Todd claim that the orders generated by their approach have a good correlation with judged complexity and Sternberg (1974), for example, found that the pattern abcabc was indeed harder for young children to handle than aabaab. However, Simon (1972) criticizes such approaches, saying that success in echoing actual difficulty ratings does not mean that there is anything in the approach that can claim to represent a model of what people actually do to deal with repeating pattern, and as such the approach is sterile and unproductive.

Simon himself proposes a theoretical 'information-processing' approach to the prediction of relative difficulty, suggesting, for example, that the length of the pattern portion which is repeated is bound to be related to difficulty, because

> the more relations it is necessary to induce from the sequence to find the pattern the more symbols it is necessary to fixate in order to store the pattern in long-term memory and the more working memories are necessary in order to produce the sequence from the pattern. (Simon, 1972, p. 381)

It is possible to use a variant of Simon's own argument to retort that even if the size of the pattern portion being repeated does turn out to relate to relative difficulty, that does not mean that his model is what people actually do to deal with repeating pattern. There are alternative ways to explain how a sequence is generated, such as the rhythmic approach or the 'filling in' approach which were described earlier.

Empirical studies

From a study of the ability of three- to five-year-olds to complete set tasks, Rustigian (1976) found a developmental hierarchy of responses for the extension of repeating patterns. As well as finding that physical movement (enactive) was easier to deal with than pictorial representations (iconic), and that form was easier than colour, Rustigian found a progressive reference to prior elements:

1. No reference to prior elements at all, and a random choice of new elements.
2. A phase of repeating the last element (perseverance).
3. Use of the elements used previously but in any order.
4. A symmetrical approach, reproducing the sequence to date but in reverse.
5. A deliberate continuation of the pattern, involving glances back to the start (to check).

Rustigian also points out a difficulty for some children who are otherwise successful if the spaces for the extension of the pattern do not allow the completion of the final repeat; for example, if there are 16 spaces yet the pattern is red blue blue, red blue blue, etc. In these cases, the last few elements may be treated differently: left blank or filled with the last one used, or with the last one in the pattern, or with something else entirely.

Similar results occurred in an exercise conducted by the author in local schools, in which a total of 119 children aged three to nine were asked to 'make a nice pattern' by colouring in a line of spots in a 'snake', as in Figure 2.5. Many of the youngest children (and a few of the

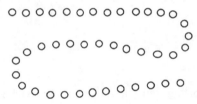

Figure 2.5 *A snake of dots for colouring in*

older children) created sequences corresponding to the second stage in Rustigian's progression, the tendency to 'perseverance', such as the example in Figure 2.6 by Amy (three years, eleven months). The large majority of the children (60 per cent) – including some as young

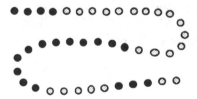

Figure 2.6 *A perseverance pattern*

as three years, ten months – made a simple repeating pattern, alternating colours in groups of fixed size; for example,

	R G R G R G R G R G R G
or	R R G G B B R R G G B B
or	R B Y G R B Y G R B Y G
or	R R R R G G G G R R R R

Only six children attempted more complex patterns, such as

	R R R B B Y R R R B B Y
or	B R R B Y Y B R R B Y Y

and all these were from the same class, perhaps showing the benefits of recent teaching.

Such studies suggest that there are two strands to development in repeating patterns. One is in the complexity of the patterns with which the children can work. The simplest alternating elements type can be seen to be more common among younger children than patterns which include more complex elements, or a repeating pattern utilizing more than one characteristic of the material (colour and size and shape, for example, rather than just colour). The second strand is in how children are 'seeing' the repeating patterns. In this there seems to be a major developmental threshold, concerning whether or not the children are aware of the pattern as a whole being related to a unit of repeat. In the context of children's recognition of repeating patterns, the question of whether or not the child is aware of the unit of repeat can be shown by asking children how given repeating patterns 'work'. Children seem to answer in one of two ways. They may set up a chant, or refer to the unit of repeat. For example, in patterns of coloured dots children may say 'Red green yellow yellow red green yellow yellow ... .' Or they may describe the patterns in terms of what is repeated: 'It is one red, one green and two yellows.' Both approaches enable the prediction of subsequent items in the sequence, but in different ways. Although the unit of repeat can be detected in the rhythm of the chant, there is in the other approach evidence of a qualitatively different level of awareness, with completely different implications for mathematical understanding.

This contrast is indirectly related to the ways in which a repeating pattern can be created. As was seen above, making a repeating pattern can arise from different kinds of thinking. The pattern action pairs procedure – following through relationships of what is next to what – and the filling in strategy illustrated above generate repeating patterns in the concrete sense, but do not actually involve repetition, and the child doing it need not be aware of having made a repeating pattern. The rhythmic approach does involve something repeating, but this does not in itself seem to bring an awareness of a repeat in the pattern which results – although of course such an awareness might be there. The recognition and use of a small sequence as an element to be repeated does, however, bring an awareness of a relationship between a part of the pattern and the whole as a repeat of it.

The two strands of development, the degree of complexity and the kind of understanding seem to be relatively independent; that is, one can find children who handle very complex patterns in a rhythmic way, and others who see the simplest alternating patterns as a unit repeated. The pedagogical question must therefore be which if any is more important. Should schooling be aimed at increasing the complexity of pattern with which children can cope, and ignore how the children actually go about making the repeating patterns, or should it give priority to trying to get children to see patterns as repeated units, and not worry so much about how complex the patterns are?

THE VALUE OF REPEATING PATTERNS WORK

In an earlier section, the contribution repeating patterns work is felt to make to developing mathematics as one element of 'pre-algebra' was described in terms of it being a context for generalization. Seen in this way, the importance of unit repeat perception in repeating patterns may be as an early example of the algebraic principle of generalization. Dienes (1963, p. 98) describes this as follows:

> The most frequent form of generalization is extending the class of cases where a certain thing can be done from a finite to an infinite class. When children learn that they can do a certain operation for certain values of the variable, there comes a moment when they suddenly realize that the value of the variable is irrelevant and the operation may be carried out for any value of the variable.

Dienes suggests that progress occurs when the rules that children have perceived become 'the objects of manipulation' (p. 23), as a result of which 'the situation is open again at a higher level'. In a repeating pattern context, seeing the unit of repeat enables the pattern to be changed easily and in a controlled way – that is, manipulated.

Gray and Tall (1994) argue that in many aspects of mathematics both procedure and concept are relevant, and the child who can alternate at will between the procedural and conceptual aspects is advantaged compared to one who cannot. They term this forming a 'procept'. Seeing a repeating pattern in terms of a unit of repeat involves both a conceptual aspect and a procedural aspect, in that it is a way of understanding the pattern, yet still offers a way of creating a pattern, and could be seen as a form of 'procept'.

In terms of the claims made about the potential of repeating patterns work for mathematical development because of the thinking that is involved, the conceptual element, which enables conscious examination and reflection, seems to be critical. A rhythmic or purely procedural approach, however complex the pattern, does not represent the recognition of a 'general statement about numbers or shapes' (Clemson and Clemson, 1994); nor is it an *idea* about regularity or sequencing (SCAA, 1995). Only the 'proceptual' approach, which 'sees' the unit of repeat within the procedure of generating the pattern, can enable the comparison of patterns, for example, or the manipulation of patterns to get a desired effect.

In this way the 'creation of a rule and its consistent application' promoted by NCC (1993) may not be needed for devising repeating patterns, but is the more valuable way to do so. As a particular example, consider an activity suggested by Straker (1993) for repeating patterns. With a repeating pattern such as the one in Figure 2.7, questions such as 'What colour will the

Figure 2.7 *A repeating pattern with ordinal values*

25th be?' or, 'What would be the position of the 13th black?' or even 'If there were 32 squares in the pattern, how many of each colour would there be?' could be asked.

A child with a unit of repeat perception, who would be thinking of this pattern in fives, could approach the questions in a way that related features of parts to questions about the whole, and this could be seen as an early example of the process by which algebra can be 'abstracted from more concrete situations like relationships and patterns with numbers' (Orton, 1992, p. 178). But how would children with a procedural or rhythmic approach deal with the demand? Elaborate and convoluted counting strategies would have to be invoked, with many opportunities to slip up and no method for checking other than to repeat the procedure. As Gray and Tall (1994, p. 132) suggest, 'emphasizing procedures leads many children inexorably into a cul-de-sac from which there is little hope of future development'. Seen from the point of view of mathematical thinking which leads on to further development, the way repeating patterns are seen seems to be more important than the complexity of what can be copied, continued or devised. The next question to ask is then: is it possible to teach the more valuable perception of repeating pattern as a repeated unit?

TEACHING REPEATING PATTERN

How to get another person to 'see' in a particular way is one of the challenges of education at all levels. However, it seems worth persevering with repeating patterns work beyond the point when children can make up repeating patterns, and aim to develop in them the ability to operate 'proceptually' – with a perception of the unit of repeat. Dienes (1963, p. 23) feels that the shift from one form of perception to the other may occur quite naturally:

> Manipulative play may quite imperceptibly move over to a search for regularities. When ... rules are found, play may occur which uses these rules. Children delight in regularities and the formulation of a rule structure is a kind of closure which ties up all the loose ends of past experience.

However, this does presume certain kinds of experience, and certain attitudes in the learner. It could not be expected to occur 'naturally' in all classrooms, and would have to be taught more actively.

A study was undertaken by the author of the inclination of children of an older age group to create repeating patterns, by asking 276 children, aged nine and ten, to make repeating patterns out of shapes, numbers and letters, using given elements in a paper and pencil format. The results reveal the tendency of children to reflect experience in their pattern perception. Over 75 per cent of the children made a simple repeat: e.g. when the elements were three shapes, the most common response was to cycle through them, as in Figure 2.8. When

Figure 2.8 *A three-shape repeating pattern*

different responses did occur, they were not more complex repeating patterns, but different kinds of pattern altogether. There were, for example, arrangements in the shapes patterns in which each group of three is different in order from the previous three (7 per cent), as in Figure 2.9. In the shapes and numbers patterns there were symmetrical arrangements (8 per

Figure 2.9 *A cyclic shapes pattern*

$$3 \quad 5 \quad 7 \quad 9 \quad 9 \quad 7 \quad 5 \quad 3$$

Figure 2.10 *A symmetrical pattern from the elements 3, 5, 7 and 9*

cent), as in Figure 2.10. In the numbers and letters patterns there were sequences (9 per cent) developed by extending the elements given. The example in Figure 2.11 was quite common. It is the result of 'counting' the letters in the alphabetic sequence between 'b' and 'h' and then b   h   n   t   z   f   l   r

Figure 2.11 *A sequence developed from the given elements of 'h' and 'b'*

carrying on through the alphabet in similar sized steps, starting again at 'a' after 'z'. The diversity of pattern possibilities in sequences means that any universal trend to impose structure (Frith, 1970) may not manifest itself in repeating patterns at all, and if schooling offers alternative methods of looking at patterns, the step to seeing repeating patterns as a unit of repeat seems unlikely to occur as a result of any natural process of imposing order. Consequently, for many children, the awareness of repeating patterns as repetitions of units of repeat has to be taught.

In seeking to find ways to guide children towards a particular way of thinking about the familiar context of repeating patterns, a brief 'teaching experiment' was conducted in local schools, involving 76 children from six classes, with an even age distribution from four to nine. The aim was to guide the children towards a unit of repeat perception by dividing up the lines of dots on which the pattern was to be made, in three ways: (a) by spaces; (b) by lines; and (c) with boxes, as in Figure 2.12. Compared with the outcomes of the 'snakes' pattern activity,

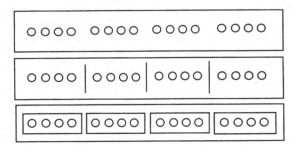

Figure 2.12 *Three ways to suggest units of repeat*

undertaken by children with a similar distribution of ages in the same schools, the approach with lines and boxes did seem to promote a greater complexity in the patterns, as summarized in percentage terms in Table 2.1.

Table 2.1 *Quality of colour pattern by children colouring rows of dots*

	Patterns on 'snakes'	Separated into fours	Lines between	Boxes around
Alternating colours (e.g. three of one, eight of another, four of the first, etc.)	11	11	12	14
Pattern of colours without a sustained repeat	23	38	25	29
Simple repeating pattern, e.g. B R B R B R B R	60	40	36	28
More complex repeating pattern, e.g. B R R R B R R R	6	11	27	27

In a second 'experiment', twelve children (aged six or seven) were asked to make a colour pattern on a 'snake', after some experience with making complex repeating musical patterns on chime bars which were labelled with colours rather than as notes in a scale. In this case, several of the children again made more complex colour patterns after such an experience, for example

R G G B G G R G G B G G R G G B G G

However, the fact that children are making more complex patterns does not necessarily mean that they have done so on the basis of perception of the unit of repeat. For that reason, some of the children who had made a more complex pattern of dots were asked to explain the pattern they had made. All but one did so by a chant of the rhythm (e.g. 'It goes red red green red red blue red red green red red blue red red ...'), rather than making a statement of the unit of repeat. This suggests that the complex patterns were often being achieved on the basis of a rhythmic approach.

It is also possible that the children were 'seeing' the pattern as units of repeat but chose to articulate their perception in a rhythmic way. How children describe things is not in itself sufficient for reliable assessment of their understanding. It is sufficient, however, to throw doubt on the use of complexity as evidence of unit of repeat perception, and in turn this leaves open the matter of whether the two teaching approaches used might contribute to a less rhythmic, more 'unit of repeat' way of thinking about repeating pattern. In the case of patterns made on dots that had been separated into groups, it had been supposed that the spaces, lines and boxes might promote the perception of the unit of repeat, but it seems they may actually offer an improved way to establish a rhythm, with the lines showing where to take breaths.

Another approach to change the perception of patterns is by going further in terms of what is done with them. This could be by talking about them in an appropriate way, requiring the children to articulate what the unit of repeat might be and exposing children to the descriptions of repeating patterns by others, preferably other children in their class. A complementary activity would be to generate a pattern just by defining what the unit of repeat is to be, as can happen within the computer program *Tiling* (National Council for Educational Technology). Building on these, a further activity would be to compare patterns in terms of their units of repeat, and to manufacture patterns by deliberate step-by-step alteration of the defined unit.

Other suggestions for activities helpful to this ambition include 'translating' between media – taking a peg pattern, for example, and making a bead-threading version, or taking a musical pattern and making an equivalent version using coloured tiles. This leads to a notion of representing patterns symbolically, and creating patterns from representations, and this in turn leads to attempting to operate on pattern by associating elements of the patterns with ordinal values, as in the example of Figure 2.7.

Unlike the usual activity of making repeating patterns, these activities depend on seeing the patterns in the 'right' way, and rhythmic, procedural approaches will not be enough. The children who do not at first see the patterns in the appropriate way will need to be supported by the teacher, but in time all children should become able to do these things on their own as the perception of units of repeat develops. It follows that the activities involving manipulation of patterns, when done unsupported, could be seen as a form of assessment of the ability to see the unit of repeat in a repeating pattern.

DEVELOPMENTAL DIMENSIONS

Generally, in any school, younger children are asked to work with or create repeating patterns far more than are older children, and, as has been reported, they are by and large very successful in creating patterns, and soon learn to copy and continue them. As a result of developmental factors, however, it may be that younger children cannot do so with the desirable understanding of the perception of a unit of repeat. Sternberg (1974) found that children of four and five years of age were generally unable to manipulate patterns by reversal or changes to elements while retaining the pattern, which may be taken as indicative of how the pattern is being seen. Phillips (1969) and Wood (1988) suggest that from a Piagetian perspective, 'pre-operational' children are limited in how they can think about repeating patterns. If a child under the age of approximately seven cannot see an element as a constituent of two configurations at the same time, he or she will be unable to have repeated unit perception, which consists of seeing the elements of the pattern as part of a part as well as the whole. In this view, young children are able to generate a repeating pattern, using rhythmic methods perhaps, but they cannot understand it in the way an older child or adult would, and the 'proceptual' perception of repeating patterns is precluded in young children by developmental factors.

Phillips (1969) also offers a reminder that children can seem to be operating with a strategy when they are not, and false hopes may be being raised about the value to mathematical development of repeating pattern work on the basis of successful performances which are assumed to have a certain kind of thinking behind them. If repeated unit perception relies on deep-seated developmental factors (which could apply even if a Piagetian view is denied), teaching would not bring young children to it. It would follow that teaching around repeating patterns aimed at the kinds of perceptions that have been posited as the most helpful to later development would be unproductive if done too early. However, repeating patterns work seems rarely to occur with older children. In the published mathematics materials and books of teaching suggestions for teachers, the patterns for older children have mostly become number patterns, and explicit references to repeating patterns are rare. Repeating patterns are not mentioned in the Key Stage 2 Programmes of Study in the National Curriculum for mathematics in England and Wales. If the developmental factors do apply, therefore, the full contribution of repeating patterns work to learning mathematics would seem unlikely to be achieved.

CONCLUSION

Work on repeating patterns can be a rewarding activity, generating aesthetically pleasing outcomes and offering a valuable context for the teacher to bring out mathematical perceptions. For the whole of its mathematical potential to be realized, however, and to deserve its comparatively exalted status in 'pre-algebra', the approach of the child to the recognition and creation of repeating patterns needs to be developed to a 'proceptual' one, in which the unit of repeat is 'seen' and can be processed both as a part of the pattern and as a composite of parts. As in many other cases in mathematics, a procedural approach to repeating patterns can bring short-term success relatively quickly, but is limited in its value to later progress.

The potential to mathematical development of repeating patterns is not fully realized if repeating patterns work is abandoned at the 'Level 1' stage, when they are merely 'recognized and made'. It is only realized if the repeating patterns are done through a conscious awareness of the unit of repeat – which needs additional work after the ostensible performance level has been reached.

Chapter 3

Primary School Children's Knowledge of Odd and Even Numbers

Len Frobisher

INTRODUCTION

The National Curricula for England and Wales, Scotland and Northern Ireland include in their Programmes of Study for primary schools statements such as this example from the Department for Education /Welsh Office: 'Pupils should be taught to ... recognize sequences, including odd and even numbers' (DfE/WO, 1995, p. 3). In the curriculum for England and Wales this is translated into assessment 'criteria' in the Level 2 descriptor of the 'Number and Algebra' Attainment Target as requiring that children 'should recognize sequences of numbers, including odd and even numbers' (DfE/WO, 1995, p. 25).

Thus, in the United Kingdom, learning about odd and even numbers is a required part of the curriculum. It is also possible to find reference to the teaching and learning of odd and even numbers in the mathematics curricula of many other countries across the five continents. Why these particular numbers are singled out for special treatment in preference to other types of number involving multiples is seldom stated. One reason may be that odd and even numbers have a long history in the development of mathematics, dating back at least to the time of the Greeks and, perhaps, even longer. Little, however, is known about how children perceive odd and even numbers, and whether they understand:

- that every natural number is either even or odd;
- that the odd or even nature of the unit digit can be used to determine whether a number is odd or even, irrespective of the number of digits the number may have;
- that the number zero can be considered to be an even number.

This chapter gives a brief history of odd and even numbers, describes how children meet the numbers in the mathematics classroom and considers each of the above three issues in the light of recent research conducted by the author.

A BRIEF HISTORY OF ODD AND EVEN NUMBERS

The two volumes of *History of Mathematics* by D.E. Smith (1958) are considered by many mathematicians and educators to be classics. Smith claims that 'the distinction between odd and even numbers is one of the most ancient features of the science of arithmetic' (Vol. 1,

p. 16). One of the first recorded distinctions between odd and even numbers is to be found 'in the Chinese Canon known as the "I-King", believed to have been written about 1150 BC' (Willerding, 1967, p. 108). The Chinese divided whole numbers into male and female, male numbers being the odd numbers and even numbers female. Ancient civilizations appear to have attached a mystical character to numbers. 'In Chinese mythology, odd numbers symbolized white, day, heat, sun, and fire; even numbers, cold, night, matter, and earth' (*ibid.*, p. 108).

The Greeks, whose main interest in mathematics was geometry, represented numbers in geometrical forms called *polygonal* or *figurate* numbers. They referred to odd numbers as *gnomonic numbers*, as a square number when represented by dots can be partitioned into gnomons or carpenter's squares. Thus an interesting property of odd numbers is that the sum of a given number of consecutive odd numbers starting with 1 is always a square number.

Figure 3.1 *A square number and its gnomons*

Figure 3.1 illustrates this property for the fourth square number, which is the sum of the first four odd numbers. When symbolized, this becomes

$$1 + 3 + 5 + 7 = 4^2$$

The generalization of this pattern can be expressed as

$$1 + 3 + 5 + 7 + ... + (2n - 1) = n^2$$

The fact that the sum of successive odd numbers starting at 1 produces square numbers as illustrated in the gnomonic pattern was evidence to the Greeks that odd, male numbers had a purity and goodness that was absent from the human, earthly and even evil female numbers, which were lacking in goodness. This was supported by the non-square rectangular patterns produced where even numbers are added in the same way, starting at 2.

$2 + 4 = 2 \times 3$, which can be represented by

and $2 + 4 + 6 = 3 \times 4$, which can be represented by

These patterns generalize as

$$2 + 4 + 6 + 8 + ... + 2n = n(n + 1)$$

The expression $n(n + 1)$ cannot be a square number for any natural number values of n.

Like the Chinese, the Pythagoreans, a group of philosophers and mystics who developed many ideas in mathematics around the period 700 to 500 BC, regarded even numbers as being feminine, in that they had earthly associations, while the odd numbers were masculine, having a god-like nature (Dantzig, 1954).

Reference is also made to odd and even numbers in Euclid's Book VII of the 'Elements'. Some historians of mathematics suggest that Euclid obtained many of his ideas directly from the Pythagorean School, who in turn may well have gathered their knowledge from the Egyptians or Babylonians. Like the Chinese before them, the Pythagoreans believed that 'the distinction between evenness and oddness was of mystical significance' (Wilder, 1978, p. 73). It is unlikely that the mystical nature of the two classes of number is ever experienced by children, but there appears to be something special about odd and even numbers that fascinates children of all ages; this in itself may be a justification for their inclusion in a mathematics curriculum, as well as their place in the history of mathematics.

Euclid's 'Elements' was a set of thirteen books which systematically and logically organized what was then known of geometry and attempted to link ideas of number with geometry, thereby raising the study of number to a higher plane. Euclid provided a definition of number and extended it to odd and even numbers. This can be summarized as:

- an **even number** is divisible into two equal parts;
- an **odd number** is not divisible into two equal parts, or differs by one from an even number (Smith, 1958).

The definitions of even and odd numbers are worthy of further examination, particularly in relation to the methods used to introduce children to the two classes of numbers. Euclid's definition of an even number involves the partitioning of a natural number into two equal parts. This is illustrated in Figure 3.2 with the natural number 8. The first part of the definition of

Figure 3.2 *Partitioning 8 into two equal parts*

an odd number stands in its own right independent of that of an even number. The second, alternative, definition relates an odd number to an even number, overlooking the fact that an odd number differs by 1 from two even numbers, just as every even number differs by 1 from two odd numbers. To many this would not be considered a definition, but a relationship that is the outcome of the definitions of even and odd numbers.

Although odd and even numbers are found in most curricula, seldom are the numbers explored to unearth their true richness. Eagle (1995, p. 23) suggests that there are many propositions about odd and even numbers that Euclid listed in Book IX of the 'Elements' 'which are quite accessible' to children. 'Pupils can investigate for themselves what rules exist and try to justify them'. She lists just a few:

If you add together as many even numbers as you like, the total is even.

If you subtract an odd number from an even number ...

If you multiply an odd number by an odd number ...

If an odd number divides exactly into an even number, it will also divide exactly into half of it.

Even and odd numbers recur throughout the study of mathematics and it is important that they are immediately recognizable by children, whatever their magnitude. A variety of possible approaches is suggested here, aimed at developing this competence.

TEACHING ODD AND EVEN NUMBERS

Very young children are able to construct their own meaning of odd and even numbers. Clarke and Atkinson (1996, p. 55) quote the experience of Derek (age six) when using cubes. His teacher suggests that he should draw circles around pairs of cubes (see Figure 3.3), and he responds:

Figure 3.3 *Derek divides 8 into 2s*

> I know what an odd and even number is now because you made me draw circles around the pictures, dividing into twos and if there are none left that's an even number and I am finding out by counting in twos.

Derek's teacher, perhaps unknown to herself, provided him with a working definition of an even number that he can apply to any concrete or pictorial situation. The definition his teacher gave Derek is not the one that Euclid stated, but is equivalent to it. Herein lies a danger, as Derek, at some later stage, may be presented with an alternative rule or algorithmic approach to finding even and odd numbers and not understand the equivalence of the new approach and his previous experience with pictures. If dividing a number equally into sets of 2s produces an even number, what happens when the number is divided into two equal parts? The latter is Euclid's definition, the former Derek's. Should a young child be able to recognize their equivalence given that the equivalence of the concepts of sharing and grouping is rarely dealt with below the age of nine?

Derek appears to have generalized his thinking so that it has application to all whole numbers. We have evidence, however, that young children make such generalizations in relation to a restricted domain of numbers, which is often only the domain of 'small' numbers, believing that 'large' numbers sometimes behave differently. It would be wrong, therefore, to conclude that Derek knows about even and odd numbers in general.

Caine (1970, p. 4) proposes that odd and even numbers are observable by their 'shape': 'If we use drawings of small squares to represent numbers we can show the shapes which odd and even numbers take'. He then provides four examples of each (see Figure 3.4). Reference

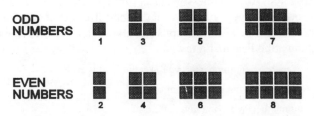

Figure 3.4 *Representing odd and even numbers*

is made to the squares being arranged in pairs, with even numbers making rectangular shapes and odd numbers making more irregular shapes. Caine then provides a 'definition' by stating: 'An odd number of squares cannot be arranged in pairs' (p. 4). To some children, it may not be at all obvious how the idea of pairs relates to each of the shapes, as it very much depends on whether one perceives the squares in terms of pairs of columns or rows, as shown in Figure 3.5.

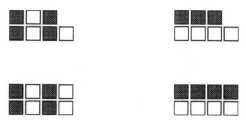

Figure 3.5   *The numbers 7 and 8 in sets of 2s*   *The numbers 7 and 8 in two sets*

The 100 counting square is used by Glenn and Sturgess (1977, p. 35) to introduce odd and even numbers: 'Thus to begin at 1 and to cross out every second number thereafter gives a column pattern of the odd numbers', as shown in Figure 3.6. In a similar way, 'to start at 2

1	2	3	4	5	6	7	8	9	10
11	12	13	14	15	16	17	18	19	20
21	22	23	24	25	26	27	28	29	30
31	32	33	34	35	36	37	38	39	40
41	42	43	44	45	46	47	48	49	50
51	52	53	54	55	56	57	58	59	60
61	62	63	64	65	66	67	68	69	70
71	72	73	74	75	76	77	78	79	80
81	82	83	84	85	86	87	88	89	90
91	92	93	94	95	96	97	98	99	100

Figure 3.6 *The 100 counting square showing the odd numbers*

gives the pattern of even numbers and also the multiples of two'. This is illustrated in Figure 3.7. Both approaches are based upon counting on in 2s, differing only in the start number. The production of the odd numbers in the 100 counting square is also founded on the assumption that 1 is an odd number and that all numbers produced by counting on from 1 in 2s are themselves odd numbers. Thus, to use this approach as an introduction to odd numbers presupposes knowledge that is much more than many children are capable of understanding at an early stage of number learning. The relationship between counting on in 2s and dividing into 2s is a difficult one for many children to understand. The 100 counting square, incorporating shaded and unshaded numbers, establishes conclusively that every whole number is either even or odd, as when the odd numbers are shaded the even numbers are not, and when the even numbers are shaded the odd numbers are not. Every whole number from 1 to 100 is in one or other of the even or odd set, as are numbers greater than 100.

The format of the counting square is based upon having ten numbers in each row. This

1	2	3	4	5	6	7	8	9	10
11	12	13	14	15	16	17	18	19	20
21	22	23	24	25	26	27	28	29	30
31	32	33	34	35	36	37	38	39	40
41	42	43	44	45	46	47	48	49	50
51	52	53	54	55	56	57	58	59	60
61	62	63	64	65	66	67	68	69	70
71	72	73	74	75	76	77	78	79	80
81	82	83	84	85	86	87	88	89	90
91	92	93	94	95	96	97	98	99	100

Figure 3.7 *The 100 counting square showing the even numbers*

helps to focus children's attention on the unit digit of each of the shaded numbers in a column, thus assisting the development of a general rule for testing whether any number is odd or even. The rule that a number is even if it has a unit digit that is 0, 2, 4, 6, or 8 is arrived at inductively by considering numbers 1 to 100 in the counting square. If this approach is used it is essential that children discuss the applicability of the rule to numbers larger than 100, including those with more than three digits.

'Peak Mathematics' (Brighouse *et al.*, 1981, for example), a popular series of textbooks in the United Kingdom through the 1980s and 1990s, introduces odd and even numbers already partitioned using circles as the unit shape. Figure 3.8 illustrates this approach. Before they are

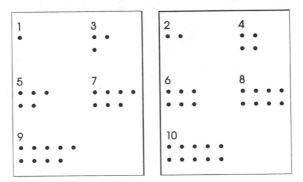

Figure 3.8 *Odd and even numbers already partitioned*

introduced to this kind of pictorial representation, children are normally given opportunities with apparatus, such as counters or linking cubes, to share collections of objects into sets of 2s, or to partition objects into two equal subsets, thus attempting to establish the difficult relationship referred to earlier. Such activities are intended to lead to the development of the concepts of 'divisible into two equal parts' and 'divisible into two equal parts with one left over', mirroring Euclid's definitions of even and odd numbers.

An alternative approach is described in *HBJ Mathematics Year 1* (Kerslake *et al.*, 1990). This is based upon jumping in 2s along a number line to produce the sequences of the odd and even numbers, as in Figure 3.9. The jumping in 2s from different starting points collects together the set of even numbers when the starter number is 0, an interesting place to start

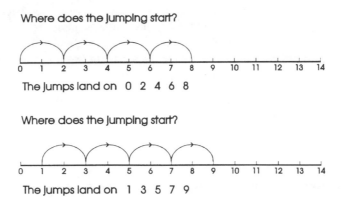

Figure 3.9 *Jumping in 2s*

given pupils' difficulties with zero, and the set of odd numbers when the starter number is 1. This activity is similar to the use of the counting square, but because of the linear nature of the number line the numbers that can be shown are limited. Nor is it as obvious that a pattern exists in the unit digit of the even numbers and of the odd numbers as it is when the two sets of numbers are shaded in the counting square.

Apart from the 100 counting square activity, many illustrations of odd and even numbers in textbooks use a very restricted domain of whole numbers, usually single-digit numbers, and occasionally numbers in the 'teens'. This has the distinct disadvantage of assuming that children can infer the unit digit pattern from a very limited experience of the pattern. Caine and Peak Mathematics both show only the set of whole numbers 1 to 10, while the HBJ textbook has on the number line the numbers 0 to 15. While it is expected that practical activities and discussion would extend the domain to much larger numbers, it is the early experience with smaller numbers that provides children with an introduction to the concept of odd and even. The issue is whether activities restricted to small numbers do lead children to an understanding of the concepts of odd and even that enable them to generalize to larger numbers. It was this concern, together with empirical evidence from talking to children, that prompted our initial study conducted with nearly 400 seven-year-old children (Frobisher and Nelson, 1992). The results of the study suggested that seven-year-old children were most successful in recognizing the odd or even nature of single-digit numbers but that, in certain cases, they were influenced in their decision about two-digit numbers by the odd or even nature of the ten digit.

It is frequently believed by teachers that children's knowledge of odd and even numbers is based upon the recognition of the odd or even nature of the unit digit. The evidence provided by the 1992 study suggests that for a significant number of children this is not the case. Although the evidence from the survey is very strong, suggesting that many children apply inappropriate rules when determining the odd or even nature of two-digit numbers, the following limitations were immediately acknowledged.

- The study does not reveal the actual processes children used, and the results were also based upon children having a 50:50 chance of getting the correct answer (indeed, they may have been guided to guess, as no opportunity was given for them to make any decision other than that a number was either even or odd).

- The number of numbers chosen for use in the study was restricted because of the one-to-one interview method adopted, and thus a selection was made from the whole numbers 0 to 100, excluding numbers with which children may have behaved differently.
- Only seven-year-old children were used in the study, and so it is not possible to draw conclusions about the behaviour of other ages of children.

A further empirical study that adopted a different methodology has now been undertaken, and this addresses the same issues more thoroughly.

THE EMPIRICAL STUDY

In the light of the findings of the preliminary study, a further investigation was conducted on 481 children across Years 1 to 6 (ages five to eleven) in primary schools. Three schools were chosen to reflect the mathematics achievement of children across the attainment levels.

Each child was given, on two sides of A4 paper, the numbers 0 to 99 randomly presented, with five choices for every number, namely 'odd number', 'even number', 'neither odd nor even', 'both odd and even' and 'don't know'. In this way, it was hoped that the limitations of the preliminary study would be overcome, where only the two possibilities odd or even were provided. This proved to be the case, as some children chose to tick boxes other than the 'odd number' box or the 'even number' box. No time limit was placed upon the children. Interviews with children were conducted after the survey to throw light on the reasoning behind their decisions.

Tables 3.1 and 3.2 list the percentages of children in Years 2 and 6 ticking the correct boxes for the numbers 0 to 99. The facilities for children in Years 1, 3, 4 and 5 show very similar trends to those in the tables, with, as might be expected, higher facilities in general for any particular number as the age of the children increases. The outcomes across all six year groups are analysed in greater detail by considering different categories of numbers.

Table 3.1 *Percentages of correct responses for Year 2 children*

	Unit digit									
Ten Digit	**0**	**1**	**2**	**3**	**4**	**5**	**6**	**7**	**8**	**9**
0	32	64	56	59	60	59	59	63	60	55
1	48	59	41	55	43	52	48	63	48	55
2	47	40	51	47	54	45	51	49	51	56
3	36	59	34	59	40	51	41	62	39	56
4	37	51	49	51	48	51	48	49	45	48
5	34	58	41	60	41	52	37	55	38	55
6	52	49	34	47	49	44	52	53	45	51
7	33	59	52	52	37	59	44	58	41	67
8	38	51	51	53	48	44	52	48	52	52
9	29	59	43	59	36	62	39	51	43	67

Single-digit numbers

As with the earlier study, the responses to single-digit numbers were used as standards to compare how children had performed with two-digit numbers. The means of the facilities for the nine numbers 1 to 9 for each year group are shown in Figure 3.10 (there was little

Table 3.2 *Percentages of correct responses for Year 6 children*

					Unit digit					
Ten Digit	0	1	2	3	4	5	6	7	8	9
0	47	84	84	83	84	86	86	87	86	91
1	84	82	82	82	78	84	79	85	76	85
2	86	47	88	71	86	69	84	69	81	69
3	71	80	72	81	70	81	74	86	68	80
4	87	68	82	69	79	70	83	75	86	76
5	74	85	69	86	71	76	70	81	66	84
6	79	79	83	65	80	67	82	75	82	71
7	67	84	67	84	71	80	68	82	64	85
8	84	69	84	67	83	62	87	72	84	66
9	67	88	68	82	62	78	69	86	68	85

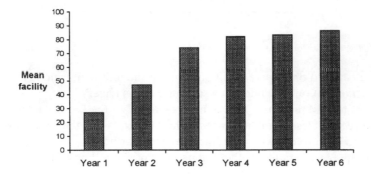

Figure 3.10 *Mean facilities of the numbers 1 to 9 for each year group*

variation from the mean of the facility for each of the numbers 1 to 9 within each year group). The facilities are disappointingly low for every age group of children. As was mentioned at the start of the chapter, odd and even numbers appear in the National Curriculum Level 2 descriptor, yet in Year 6 only 86 per cent of the year group successfully recognized the odd or even nature of a single-digit number. The poor level of performance is more starkly observed when the percentage success rate out of the total for the nine numbers is considered. These results are shown in Figure 3.11.

If children are to use the odd or even nature of a single-digit number to determine the nature of larger numbers that are not multiples of ten it is essential that they know the nature of every single-digit number. This is obviously not the case with many of the 481 children in this study. However, it is possible that a child does not use this knowledge, but considers whether a number is divisible by 2 or not, in order to decide if a number is even or odd. In that case, not knowing the nature of each of the single-digit numbers is not important, but this approach places a greater demand on the child than the use of the much simpler 'rule'. The children interviewed showed a variety of strategies for deciding on the nature of a single-digit number.

Joseph (Year 2) had developed a strategy based upon the odd, even, odd, even ... sequence. When presented with the number 7, he used his fingers to match the odd-even sequence to numbers until he reached 7. This enabled him to say that 7 was an odd number. When shown the number 58 he said, 'I just work on the 8.' He was unable to explain why he could ignore

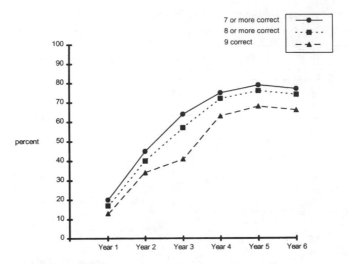

Figure 3.11 *Percentage of children with 7 or more, 8 or more, or 9 correct*

the ten digit, but showed obvious recognition of using the unit digit 'rule', always, however, needing to match one-to-one the odd–even sequence to his fingers.

Carly (Year 5) related the single-digit numbers 4 and 7 to the 2 times table. When asked why 7 was odd she said, '7 is not in the 2 times table.' She explained that she knew this always worked as she had been told it when she was in Year 2. For her it was a piece of knowledge she was able to apply successfully without apparent understanding of the reasons why her 'rule' worked.

Leigh (Year 5) related the number 7 to a count of the single-digit even numbers, adopting an elimination strategy. Her response was '0, 2, 4, 6, 8. So 7 is odd.' Jonathan (Year 4) also related 7 to the even numbers, but operated on 8 to decide 7 was odd: '8 is even. Go down 1 to 7 – it's odd.' His strategy is in effect Euclid's alternative definition of odd numbers, recognizing them as differing by 1 from an even number.

Richard (Year 4), who was about to be statemented, decided that both 4 and 7 were odd numbers because they were small. He spoke of high and big numbers being even.

Kurt (Year 4) used Euclid's definition of an even number. He said, 'Can split 4 out of 2 people, get 2 each.' He also applied Euclid's first definition of an odd number when presented with 7. 'Goes like this: 1, 3, 5, 7. Can't split it into 2 people.' He reinforced his conclusion by adding, 'Not like this 2, 4, 6, 8', indicating that he had eliminated 7 from the set of even numbers, so inferring that it must necessarily be odd. Ben used a similar approach expressed differently. 'Can't share 7: won't get the same amount.'

The number zero

In the earlier study, the number zero was chosen as an even number by 45 per cent of the seven-year-olds. However, this may be unreliable, as the children had only to decide whether zero was an odd number or an even number, there being only two choices available to them. The more recent survey offers children five choices, including the possibility that a number may be considered to be both even and odd, or that it is neither even nor odd. The percentages of children making the different choices are listed in Table 3.3. The percentage of Year 2 children deciding that zero is an even number is much lower than in the previous study, 32 per cent as opposed to 45 per cent.

Table 3.3 *Percentages of children making different choices for zero in each year group*

Year	Odd number	Even number	Neither odd nor even	Odd and even	Don't know	Missing
1	20	10	0	3	53	13
2	25	32	1	5	19	18
3	22	57	0	5	5	12
4	30	48	2	8	6	6
5	22	59	2	7	6	3
6	24	46	5	17	5	2
Mean	**25**	**46**	**2**	**9**	**11**	**8**

The success in deciding that zero is an even number did not continue to rise with age, with approximately one in two children in each of Years 3 to 6 putting a tick in the 'evens' box and more than one in five deciding that zero is an odd number in every year group. Zero is well known as a number that creates difficulties for children in every way that it is used. Although zero is not specifically mentioned in the mathematics National Curriculum, it is implicitly required by children when 'developing an understanding that the position of a digit signifies its value' (DfE/WO, 1995, p. 3). It is, however, unlikely that children younger than eleven years old will have considered dividing zero by 2, which is the only way that they can reliably decide on the odd or even nature of zero.

In the interviews, '0' was expressed as 'zero', 'nought', 'none' and 'O' (the sound of the letter O) by the eight different children. It would appear that the name given to the number symbol '0' may influence how children think about and operate with zero. Joseph (Year 2) was quite convinced that 0 (he called it 'zero') was odd, as 'it is the first number you count'. Richard (Year 4) decided that 'none' was neither odd nor even, as 'it's not a number'. Jonathan (Year 4), who gave 0 the name of the letter O, worked down from 1 using the sequence odd/even to conclude that zero is even, saying '1 is odd and if I go down it's even'. Kurt and Ben, both in Year 4, decided that zero was even and operated on it using Euclid's definition to justify their decision. Kurt referred to '0' as 'zero', saying, 'can't split it out, because you haven't got nowt'. This was replicated by Ben who claimed that 'no one gets owt if it's shared out'. Carly (Year 5) used her knowledge of the 2 times table, including 0 in it, saying, 'it is even because the 2 times table it goes 0, 2, 4, 6, 8'.

Multiples of ten

As the 'unit' digit of every multiple of ten is zero, knowledge of the odd or even nature of the numbers 1 to 9 is not of help in determining whether a multiple of ten is even or odd. If children do not know that all multiples of ten are even then two strategies are available to them. First, they may use their knowledge that zero is an even number; second, they may divide the multiple of ten by two to test if it has a remainder. Joseph (Year 2) confidently explained, 'Ignore the 9; 0 is odd, so 90 is odd'. Although he was unable to say why he could ignore the 9 he knew a rule that 'worked' and was only let down by his misunderstanding of the nature of 0. Leigh (Year 5) claimed that both 90 and 60 were even as they had 'nought on the end', later confirming that she knew that 0 was an even number.

Ben (Year 4) also remarked that '9 does not count', after saying 'no one gets anything because it is nought'. He repeated this approach with 60, using the very same language to describe his thinking. Ben had previously made reference to sharing between two when dealing with other numbers and used this knowledge on the unit digit of 90, namely 0.

Table 3.4 *Facilities of multiples of ten in each year group*

Multiple of ten	Year 1 (*n*=30)	Year 2 (*n*=73)	Year 3 (*n*=83)	Year 4 (*n*=102)	Year 5 (*n*=94)	Year 6 (*n*=99)	Mean (*n*=481)
10	33	48	65	70	80	84	**68**
20	20	47	67	71	82	86	**69**
30	23	36	58	59	72	71	**58**
40	23	37	70	74	78	87	**68**
50	20	34	59	58	67	74	**57**
60	13	52	66	75	81	79	**68**
70	13	33	59	54	69	67	**55**
80	13	38	73	73	82	84	**68**
90	13	29	66	58	65	67	**55**
Mean	**19**	**39**	**65**	**66**	**75**	**78**	

The 1992 study suggested that seven-year-old children were able to recognize the even nature of 10, and the even multiples 20, 40, 60 and 80, much more readily than the odd multiples 30, 50, 70 and 90. The percentages of correct responses in Table 3.4, from the later study, confirm that the lack of relative success with the odd multiples of ten, other than 10 itself, continues through the succeeding years.

Kurt (Year 4) responded to the number 60 by saying very quickly, 'It is even: goes up 2, 4, 6', ignoring the 0 and concentrating on the ten digit. He later said that 90 was odd, as '80 is even, goes 2, 4, 6, 8, 12, for ever', again ignoring the relevance of the 0 unit digit.

Both Carly (Year 5) and Jonathan (Year 4) used their knowledge that 60 and 90 were multiples of ten to decide that they were even. Carly merely said, 'Because 0 is one of the numbers in the 10 times table; 10 is an even number.' Jonathan was much more explicit, 'Like number 10, number 10 is an even number and go up in another 10 – even and so on, 4 more 10s.' Most of Jonathan's explanations for his decisions about the nature of two-digit numbers were based on his understanding that 10 was even. For 58, his strategy was built around multiples of 10 and the odd/even sequence of numbers: '10 is even. Add another 4 tens – still even. Every 10 is even. Add another 10, get 60 even. Take away 2, still even: go down odd, even to another even number.'

The facilities for each of the multiples in Year 2 are much less than the corresponding facilities in the earlier study. This might be explained by the times in the year when the two studies were conducted. The 1992 survey took place in the mid-summer term, while the more recent study was held in February, some three to four months before. It is possible that teachers do not introduce children to odd and even numbers until late in the year, nearer to the time of the national tests.

The number of children in Year 1 who participated in the most recent study was only 30, all from the same school, the other two schools feeling the task was inappropriate for very young children. The very low facilities for Year 1 children for the higher multiples of ten – 60, 70, 80 and 90 – may be due to the very small numbers of children involved, or to the size of the numbers, which are beyond the requirements of Level 1 (England and Wales) or Level A (Scotland) in the National Curriculum.

Multiples of eleven

The numbers less than 100 that are multiples of eleven, namely 11, 22, 33, 44, 55, 66, 77, 88 and 99, are particularly interesting, in that they use the same digit twice. Thus, it might be expected that children who use their knowledge of single-digit numbers apply that knowledge to the corresponding multiple of eleven. In general, this appears to be what happens, as the corresponding facilities are very close, irrespective of the age of the children. Table 3.5 illustrates this for the numbers 1 and 11, 4 and 44, and 9 and 99. The facilities for the double-digit numbers are on the whole slightly lower than for the corresponding single-digit numbers. This

Table 3.5 *Comparison of facilities for single-digit numbers and double-digit numbers*

	1	11	4	44	9	99
Year 1	30	27	27	23	23	20
Year 2	64	59	60	48	55	60
Year 3	78	75	77	68	71	63
Year 4	82	82	79	78	83	86
Year 5	83	82	86	82	84	80
Year 6	83	82	83	79	90	85
Mean	**76**	**74**	**75**	**69**	**75**	**73**

suggests that there are some children in each year group who, although they have knowledge of the nature of the nine single-digit numbers, are unable to use this knowledge when confronted by the larger corresponding two-digit number that uses the same digit twice. This is supported if the facilities for the whole population of children are compared for nine pairs of corresponding numbers, such as 6 and 66. These are shown in Figure 3.12.

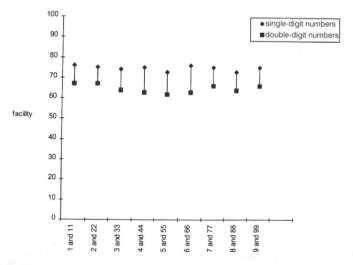

Figure 3.12 *Facilities for single-digit and corresponding double-digit numbers*

When interviewed, Richard (Year 4) showed very little understanding of odd and even numbers, saying that 55 is even, 'because it's a big one', and 22 is even, 'because it is going down'. Kurt's strategy involved considering both the ten and the unit digit when faced with multiples of 11. Although his strategy was incorrect, it produces correct outcomes. For 55 he said, '5 is odd, 50 is odd, so it's got to be odd'. He used a similar approach with 22, which he said was even: '20 is even and 2 is even'. He then added a supporting strategy counting up in 2s, 'goes up 2, 4, 6, 8, up to 22 and higher'.

Two-digit numbers that are not multiples of ten or eleven

The use of single-digit numbers may suggest to children that the odd or even nature of numbers with more than a single digit is determined by only one of the digits in a number, and this may not necessarily be the unit digit. Indeed, it could be that a child constructs, from limited experience, a rule that uses, for example, the larger of the two digits in a two-digit number to decide whether the number is even or odd. If the numbers 11 to 19 are the only ones considered, then every such number has a unit digit that is equal to or larger than the ten digit. In subsequent decades of numbers there are progressively fewer numbers having this property, but overall many numbers do. Those numbers having a unit digit larger than the ten digit are shaded in Figure 3.13.

1	2	3	4	5	6	7	8	9	10
11	12	13	14	15	16	17	18	19	20
21	22	23	24	25	26	27	28	29	30
31	32	33	34	35	36	37	38	39	40
41	42	43	44	45	46	47	48	49	50
51	52	53	54	55	56	57	58	59	60
61	62	63	64	65	66	67	68	69	70
71	72	73	74	75	76	77	78	79	80
81	82	83	84	85	86	87	88	89	90
91	92	93	94	95	96	97	98	99	100

Figure 3.13 *Numbers having the unit digit larger than the ten digit*

There are 36 numbers from 1 to 100 which have the unit digit larger than the ten digit. Experience of numbers chosen solely from this set of 36 numbers could lead to the observation and incorrect generalization that *an even number is one that has the larger of its two digits even and an odd number is one that has the larger of its two digits odd*. In order to explore this possibility in greater depth, the set of all two-digit numbers that are not multiples of ten and eleven has been broken into smaller categories for analysis.

Ten and unit digit both odd or both even, and different

In the domain of two-digit numbers there are twenty numbers with both digits odd and different: 13, 37, 59, 75 and 91 are examples of such numbers. In the same domain there are twelve numbers with both digits even and different: 26, 48, 62 and 86 are examples of this set of numbers. The twenty numbers with both digits odd and the twelve numbers with both digits even generated similar behaviour in each of Years 1 to 6. The distribution of the means and ranges of the facilities for the twenty odd-digit numbers and the twelve even-digit numbers are shown in Figure 3.14. The means for each number for the whole population of

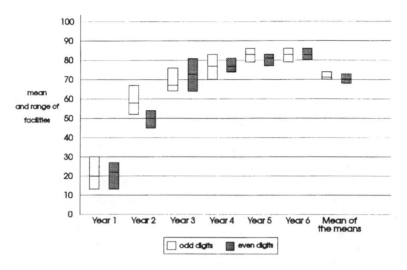

Figure 3.14 *Mean and range of facilities of numbers with both digits odd or even, but different*

children ranged from 68 to 74 per cent, showing a remarkable consistency of response, with little variation from the mean. Children are able to respond correctly to numbers in this category using an incorrect strategy because both digits have the same nature. Thus a child using the nature of both the ten and the unit digit to determine what a number is arrives at the same conclusion as a child who uses only the unit digit or only the ten digit. Kelly (Year 6), when interviewed, explained that 37 was odd, 'because they are both odd numbers', referring to the two digits 3 and 7. It would be interesting to observe children who operate this strategy with two-digit numbers deciding what the nature of 437 is.

The ten digit less than the unit digit and with a different nature

In the preliminary study only the numbers 38 and 49 were used. In the follow-up survey all twenty such numbers were included. This provides the opportunity to partition the set into the ten numbers with an even ten digit and an odd unit digit (it is convenient to represent this set as 'set E < O'), and the remaining ten numbers that have an odd ten digit and an even unit digit (set O < E). Table 3.6 lists the means of the facilities in each of the years for set E < O and set O < E.

Table 3.6 *Mean facilities for each year for numbers with ten digit less than unit digit*

Set	Year 1	Year 2	Year 3	Year 4	Year 5	Year 6	Overall facility for 481 children
E < O	23	50	62	69	78	71	64
O < E	18	42	62	64	75	73	61

The lower mean facilities for the whole population suggest that, in general, the odd nature of the ten digit has a slightly greater influence than an even ten digit on children's decision-making when it comes to determining whether a number is odd or even. Despite the ten digit being less than the unit digit, our evidence reveals that nearly 10 per cent of the children appear to decide on the odd or even nature of numbers in these two sets by considering the nature of the ten digit.

Carly (Year 5), when interviewed, used her familiar '2 times table' strategy that she adopted for every number. Her response to 29, which is in set E < O, was '9 is not in the 2 times table', indicating her knowledge that only the unit digit was important when deciding on the odd or even nature of a number.

Kurt (Year 4) combined his knowledge of the nature of 20 and of 9 for 29 saying, '20 is even and 9 is odd', and concluding that 29 was both odd and even. He repeated this approach with the numbers 63, 74 and 58.

The ten digit greater than the unit digit and with a different nature

The numbers 72 and 87 were used in the 1992 study, which suggested that children were likely to be influenced by the nature of the ten digit as it was the larger of the two. The set of twenty numbers in this category has been partitioned into the ten numbers with an even ten digit and an odd unit digit (set E > O), and the remaining ten numbers that have an odd ten digit and an even unit digit (set O > E). Table 3.7 lists the means of the facilities in each of the years for set E > O and set O > E.

Table 3.7 *Mean facilities for each year for numbers with ten digit greater than unit digit*

Set	Year 1	Year 2	Year 3	Year 4	Year 5	Year 6	Overall facility for 481 children
E > O	21	49	63	68	78	69	63
O > E	21	41	60	62	74	69	59

In each of the six years the facility for set O > E is less than or equal to that for set E > O, and the overall mean also suggests this relationship. The number 72 in the 1992 study also had a lower facility than the number 87. Thus it appears that when the ten digit is larger than the unit digit it is the odd digit that again is slightly more influential on children's decision-making. On average, one in ten of the 481 children chose 'odd' when the number was 'even' and chose 'even' when the number was 'odd'. These children were, perhaps, using the nature of the ten digit as their 'rule'. Interestingly, as many as 15 per cent of children decided that a number such as 54 was both odd and even. This percentage was reasonably consistent for all numbers in this category. The interview with Kurt (Year 4), who claimed for the number 63 that '60 is even and 3 is odd', and concluded that 63 was, therefore, both even and odd is an example of how such children think.

A comparison of the mean facilities for the four sets suggests that, where the ten and unit digits are different, children are most successful when the even ten digit is *less* than the odd unit digit, set E < O, and least successful when the ten digit is odd and *greater* than the even unit digit, set O > E. This pattern is consistent across all six age groups. For some children, the odd nature of a unit digit appears to be slightly more dominant than the even nature of the ten digit. It is difficult to explain why this occurs. Joseph (Year 2) was always confident that it was the unit digit that decided the nature of a number. He responded to 63 by saying, 'I worked on the 3; the last number gives you a clue.'

No direct evidence was collected in the interviews to confirm that the ten digit, when greater than the unit digit, influences children's odd/even decisions. However, the facilities suggest that this is likely, particularly when the facilities for numbers in these two categories are compared with those in the other eleven categories listed in Table 3.8.

A comparison of the mean facilities in each category

Table 3.8 lists, in descending order of the means, the mean facilities of Year 1 to 6 in each category of number.

Table 3.8 *Mean facilities for each year for each category of number*

	Year						
Categories of numbers	1	2	3	4	5	6	Means of the Years 1 to 6 facilities
Odd single digit	40	59	74	82	82	85	75
Even single digit	26	59	74	82	85	84	75
Ten and unit digits both odd and different	22	58	67	77	83	83	71
Ten and unit digits both even and different	20	50	67	77	81	83	70
Even multiples of ten	17	44	69	73	81	84	68
Odd multiples of eleven	21	58	69	80	80	81	65
Even multiples of eleven	23	51	69	78	81	83	64
Even ten digit less than odd unit digit	23	50	62	69	78	71	64
Even ten digit greater than odd unit digit	21	49	63	68	78	69	63
Odd ten digit less than even unit digit	18	42	62	64	75	73	61
Odd multiples of ten	20	36	61	60	71	73	59
Odd ten digit greater than even unit digit	21	41	60	62	74	69	59
Zero	10	32	57	48	59	47	46

With a few exceptions, each of the year groups behaves in the same way, having approximately the same order of difficulty across the twelve categories. As one would expect, irrespective of their evenness or oddness, the single-digit numbers have the highest mean facility in every year group. What is surprising is that there appears to be a limit on the highest mean facility one can expect from a sample of primary school children, even with single-digit numbers, this facility being in the region of 85 per cent. In other words, at least one in ten primary school children in Year 6 do not have the knowledge that would enable them to apply the unit digit rule to numbers that have more than one digit. Most of those children who are skilled at distinguishing between odd and even single-digit numbers, irrespective of their year group, appear able to apply this skill to two-digit numbers where the digits have the same nature, to even multiples of ten and to both odd and even multiples of eleven. However, fewer and fewer of them are capable of consistently using their 'rule' when the two digits are of a different nature and when odd multiples of ten are involved.

IMPLICATIONS FOR TEACHING

It is obviously insufficient for children to consider only the odd or even nature of the numbers 1 to 9, as the evidence quite clearly indicates that children do not readily transfer this knowledge to larger numbers. The partitioning of numbers greater than 9 into two equal sets and into sets of 2s should continue for two-digit numbers beyond the 'teens'. It is important that the patterns that exist in the partitioning of like numbers, those that end in the same unit digit, are established with children using concrete or pictorial representations to support their search for relationships. For example, children should successively partition the numbers 2, 12, 22, 32, etc. in order that they can generalize inductively that all numbers with a 2 in the unit position are even. This should be repeated with other related numbers, such as 7, 17, 27, 37, 47, etc. Children can record all the numbers that they discover are even on both a 100 counting square and a number line. In this way the relationship between counting on in 2s and even and odd numbers can be established. This approach is a reversal of that to be found in textbooks which assumes that children will recognize odd and even numbers having jumped in 2s on a number line or shaded in numbers on a counting square.

Odd multiples of ten are obviously causes of error in young children in relation to their evenness. As with other two-digit numbers, odd multiples of ten should be partitioned into two equal sets or into sets of 2s, as a teacher cannot rely on children using the rule that such numbers are even because they end with a zero; this assumes that children know that zero is itself even, which the evidence clearly shows they may not.

What appear to be two relatively simple concepts, odd and even numbers, are clearly not as straightforward and as uncomplicated as placing them at 'Level 2' suggests. Much more quality time needs to be spent developing the idea of partitioning into two equal sets and the equivalent activity of dividing into sets of 2s in order that children are able to observe the patterns in odd and even numbers whatever the size of the numbers.

Chapter 4

Patterns in Processing and Learning Addition Facts

John Threlfall and Len Frobisher

INTRODUCTION

An adequate and acceptable level of numeracy requires competence in the four operations with numbers. This includes the ability:

- to calculate mentally when small numbers are involved;
- to call upon and use accurately written methods of calculating with large numbers;
- to use a calculator effectively when appropriate.

At the heart of proficiency with the manipulation of numbers is knowledge of number facts – knowing or calculating the answer to, for example, $7 + 8, 9 - 4, 3 \times 5, 8 \div 2$, without having to think for a lengthy period of time. Accounts of the processes involved in, or necessary for, the development of a high level of expertise with numbers are diverse (Van Lehn, 1990). All, however, agree that children are more able to reach a conclusion if:

- they have to think less about the sub-components in a procedure;
- they are more able to focus their attention on the overall picture of how to calculate;
- they are aware what stage of the procedure they have reached.

At the very start of their formal education, young children know (i.e. can recall from memory) few number facts; they calculate the answers to $2 + 3, 4 - 3$ and the like by counting. In general, children's knowledge of addition facts increases through the primary school years, with many eleven-year-olds replacing counting as a method of calculation by one based upon the structure of the number system.

It is reasonable to conclude that the sooner such knowledge acquisition occurs the more a child grows in confidence and, in addition, becomes able to work with ideas in mathematics that would otherwise be beyond him or her. The mechanisms by which the earlier amassing of knowledge of number facts may occur are less clear. Should there, for example, be a conscious attempt in primary schools to place a strong emphasis on memorization of number facts by using rote exercises such as recitation and by frequent use of routine testing? Alternatively, would it be sufficient, and preferable for reasons related to attitude and understanding, to increase knowledge by exposure to number facts in meaningful contexts? We argue, in this chapter, for a third approach: that children's recognition and use of pattern is central to their development of number fact knowledge and brings about a greatly accelerated acquisition of these facts. The study of pattern in number facts both develops a child's understanding of numbers and extends that understanding to include a broader awareness of mathematical structure, improving number competence along the way. It is only possible in the space available to consider the use of pattern in the learning of addition facts. We leave the reader to extend the ideas we describe to those facts associated with the three remaining operations of subtraction, multiplication and division.

The chapter begins with a consideration of the structure of the number system, suggesting reasons why number patterns exist and why they contribute to a child's development of addition knowledge. We then examine evidence of how knowledge of addition facts develops in primary children. It is notable that this process is a natural one, in that, unlike multiplication facts, there is seldom a concerted effort in schools to encourage children to commit addition facts to memory. The means by which the process occurs may be seen, therefore, as a reflection of children's cognitive inclinations and strengths that have potential for exploitation more extensively than in current practice. We go on to consider how patterns may be drawn on in working with addition facts, and offer teaching suggestions about how the approach could be developed.

THE STRUCTURE OF THE NUMBER SYSTEM

Relationships between numbers exist because of the structure underlying the system in which the numbers reside. Observation of pattern in numbers is the manifestation of these relationships. The Hindu-Arabic number system that is now in almost universal use provides untold opportunities for exploring relationships and observing patterns in number symbols which are the consequence of its structure.

The fundamental concept upon which most number systems are based is the set of counting numbers. There is an infinity of counting numbers, but in the Hindu-Arabic system the first nine provide the foundation upon which the rest are built. Here are the first nine:

1 2 3 4 5 6 7 8 9

Although dissimilar in appearance, there is an order to the numbers based upon a convention which gives an interpretation to each symbol. Each number has a meaning independent of, yet related to, the other numbers; together the meanings allow the numbers to be placed in the order shown above. The order is a consequence of the 'one more than' relationship. This is sometimes illustrated as follows:

$$1 \xrightarrow{+1} 2 \xrightarrow{+1} 3 \xrightarrow{+1} 4 \xrightarrow{+1} 5 \xrightarrow{+1} 6 \xrightarrow{+1} 7 \xrightarrow{+1} 8 \xrightarrow{+1} 9$$

Over a period of time, children come to view the counting numbers as having a pattern. They mean by this that they 'go up in 1s'. A consequence of the order of the counting numbers is the relationship between a number and its predecessor. This is described by the relationship 'one less than', the additive inverse of 'one more than':

$$1 \xleftarrow{-1} 2 \xleftarrow{-1} 3 \xleftarrow{-1} 4 \xleftarrow{-1} 5 \xleftarrow{-1} 6 \xleftarrow{-1} 7 \xleftarrow{-1} 8 \xleftarrow{-1} 9$$

The operations of addition and subtraction may be seen by children initially as extensions of the 'one more than' and 'one less than' relationships for counting numbers. There are many interesting and thought-provoking consequences resulting from applying the operations of addition and its inverse, subtraction, to numbers. The first of these is known as the commutative principle of addition.

a + b = b + a for all numbers a and b

A second feature is the associative principle of addition.

(a + b) + c = a + (b + c) for all numbers a, b and c

A third outcome results from the relationship between addition and subtraction, the inverse of addition.

(a + k) − k = (a − k) + k = a for all numbers a and k

Evidence is clear that many children have an intuitive grasp of these three ideas and apply them successfully when appropriate to the addition of numbers.

These relationships apply to numbers however they are represented, but the system of representation in the Hindu-Arabic number system gives rise to further relationships that manifest themselves as patterns. The essence of the Hindu-Arabic number system that sets it apart from other number systems is that it combines the collective unit of 10 with the multiplicative and additive relationships. There is nothing unique about each of these aspects of the system, as they can be found in separate use in more primitive and less efficient number systems. The Roman number system, for example, used the concept of a collective unit. In fact, it employed many different collective units, such as V to represent 'five ones' and X to represent 'ten ones'. However, the way a collective unit and the multiplicative and additive relationships are combined in the Hindu-Arabic system gives it a power in calculation that is well beyond that of the Roman system.

There is also nothing numerically special about 'ten' as a collective unit, it being the result of the number of fingers on our two hands. However, the fact that 10 *is* used gives its two factors, 2 and 5, an important role in mental calculations. Some of the relationships between 2, 5 and 10 are listed below.

5 + 5 = 10
2 + 2 + 2 + 2 + 2 = 10
2 × 5 = 10
5 × 2 = 10
one-half of 10 is 5
one-fifth of 10 is 2

Happily, these relationships are in a sense readily accessible to children, as they can be 'read off' their hands.

As the collective unit of our system is 'ten', it has only ten symbols, or digits, 0, 1, 2, 3, 4, 5, 6, 7, 8 and 9. Numbers greater than nine require two or more of the ten symbols combined according to the rules of the system. The first number to require two symbols is the collective unit 'ten'. Written in its expanded form it becomes

10 = (1 ten) + (0 ones)

which children meet more usually when developing their understanding of the structure of the number system with the symbols placed in 'place value' columns (see Figure 4.1).

The column headings are the values attached to the digits 0 to 9 which appear in the columns. Initially with children it is more sensible to use words to describe the value of the

tens	ones
1	0

Figure 4.1 *Place value columns*

columns, position or place, as there is confusion in writing both ten as a number and ten as the value of a position, e.g. $10 = (1 \times 10) + (0 \times 1)$. The use of position to give value to a digit immediately gives rise to a very useful number pattern where each single digit is matched to the number which uses the same digit in the tens position and has a 0 in the 'ones' place, as in Figure 4.2. This is particularly useful when adding multiples of 10 as $20 + 50$ behaves like $2 + 5$, in that each is the addition of the same set of digits, differing only in the unit involved.

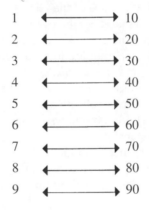

Figure 4.2 *Matching single-digit numbers to multiples of 10*

This is perhaps more easily seen if $20 + 50$ is written as 2 tens + 5 tens, the unit here being 'ten'. The idea extends naturally to other multiples of the collective unit of the system. Thus, if children have command of addition of pairs of single-digit numbers, and also understand the number system, then they should be readily able to transfer their knowledge to the additions of multiples of 10, 100, 1000, etc. The only other knowledge that children need to know in order to add any numbers is how to partition a number, e.g. $27 = 20 + 7$, and what to do if the addition equals or exceeds the value of the unit immediately to the left of that in which the addition is taking place.

   The addition of pairs of single-digit numbers with an answer up to 10 (the collective unit) is processed without resorting to the structure of the number system, although it does often utilize the patterns of 5 and 2 implicit in its derivation from two hands. When the sum of the digits is greater than 10, however, an understanding of the system becomes very useful in suggesting possible strategies for arriving at answers. For example, the closeness of single-digit numbers to 10 is often used by children to develop a strategy for the addition of single-digit numbers where the answer exceeds 10. Thus, as $9 + 1 = 10$, or $9 = 10 - 1$, the addition of 9 and 8 can be performed by adding 10 and 8 to give 18, and then subtracting 1 to give 17. Such transformations rely on:

- knowledge of the 'one more than' and 'one less than' relationships, and other knowledge of number facts;
- understanding of the role of the collective unit, 10, including an understanding of the way numbers are expressed in the number system in that 10 + 8 is written as 18.

Strategies of this kind considerably reduce the memory load of addition facts, and can be developed as strategies for the addition and subtraction of larger numbers. It can be seen that they are based on knowledge and understanding of relationships within the number system. These relationships become apparent through the study of observable patterns, and are understood and available for use when the structures within the number system that have brought about the patterns are reflected upon.

To a certain extent, this process seems to occur 'naturally' as children learn how to calculate, as is explored in the next section. It is likely, however, that there is also genuine potential for the promotion of numerical competence through teaching focused on discussion of the structural relationships manifested in patterns.

THE DEVELOPMENT OF ADDITION FACTS IN PRIMARY CHILDREN

There are two main approaches to determining the ways children calculate number facts. The first is by interview, by discussing with children the methods they use, before, during or after their actual attempts to compute, combined with observation to detect the use of fingers or other forms of recording. The second is by measuring the time it takes children to calculate facts, in 'latency' or 'time delay' studies. Evidence from the literature of both kinds of study is drawn on here to provide an account of children's 'normal' development in knowledge of addition facts, including a study by the authors which focused on single-digit addition and utilized both approaches (Threlfall *et al.*, 1995).

In the beginning, children use counting procedures to calculate addition facts. However, within the counting procedure there are three different strategies that children adopt, which may vary from fact to fact. Baroody and Ginsburg (1986) refer to these as counting all from first (CAF), counting on from first (COF) and counting on from larger (COL). These are exemplified using the addition 4 + 9:

CAF: count all starting from 1, '1 2 3 4 5 6 7 8 9 10 11 12 13'
(13 steps).
COF: count on from the first addend, '5 6 7 8 9 10 11 12 13'
(9 steps).
COL: count on from the larger addend, '10 11 12 13'
(4 steps).

The strategy of counting on from the larger addend, sometimes called the min strategy, was found by Ginsburg (1977) to be widely used by children. Siegler and Robinson (1982) believe that the min strategy is adopted by most children when they are five or six years old, even though it is not usually explicitly taught in schools. At that age, however, it may be restricted to use with smaller addends (addition up to 10). Gray (1991) found that one or other of the two 'count on' strategies has completely replaced the 'counting all' strategy in all 'above average' children by age seven, and in most 'below average' children by age ten.

A clear demonstration of the use of counting strategies by certain children is given when latency study response times for answers to individual questions are plotted against the size of the addends. One such graph is given as Figure 4.3. In this and subsequent similar figures, each point on the graph represents a fact answered by the child. On the 'horizontal' axis it is plotted by the size of the smaller addend (4 for 4 + 9; 5 for 7 + 5; and so on). This means that, for example, the points plotted in the vertical line above '4' are all the questions asked for which 4 was the smaller addend, i.e. 4 + 5, 7 + 4, 4 + 7, 8 + 4, 4 + 8, 4 + 9 and 9 + 4 (although the datum is omitted if the child was incorrect).

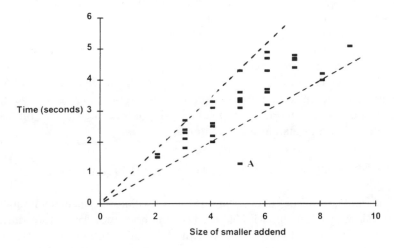

Figure 4.3 *Response times on addition questions answered by 'W', aged 10, plotted against the size of the smaller addend*

Figure 4.3 shows the response times for a particular child, 'W'. The graph has a band of points on a clear slope from the bottom left to the top right, indicating that the larger the size of the smaller addend, the longer it took for W to answer. This slope is strongly indicative of two things: first, that W used counting to find the answers to the questions, because with each step in counting taking a certain amount of time, the more steps are taken the longer the whole process takes; second, that W used the COL strategy (or min strategy), since the time taken is directly proportional to the size of the smaller addend. If W had used a 'count all' strategy or a COF strategy, the timings would not have been proportional to the size of the smaller addend. For example, if the COF strategy had been used the timing for 2 + 9 would have been much longer than that for 9 + 2, whereas in fact they are almost the same.

'Counting bands' of response times are common among children in the primary age range. Even where there is evidence that a counting strategy is extensively used by a child, however, it is not unusual to find that a few addition facts are retrieved from memory. Most of the evidence for this comes from interview data, but complementary evidence is available in the latency studies. In the graph for child W in Figure 4.3, for example, there is one exception to the COL trend. The point marked as A which stands well away from the slope is the time given for the fact 5 + 5, which W answered much more quickly than the other facts with 5 as the smaller addend. W said in interview that she just knew the answer to 5 + 5.

The evidence indicates that the first addition facts to become knowledge retrieved directly from memory are the 'ties', where both addends are the same, e.g. 3 + 3, 6 + 6, 8 + 8. The studies by Groen and Parkman (1972) and Svenson (1976), with early years children, found that on average ties are answered considerably faster than those in which the addends are different. The graph of time against smaller addend for child 'K', Figure 4.4, shows this effect.

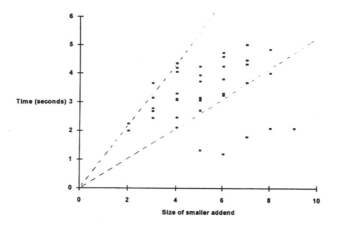

Figure 4.4 *Response times on addition questions answered by 'K', aged 9, plotted against the size of the smaller addend*

The exceptions to the clear counting band correspond to the times for 5 + 5, 6 + 6, 7 + 7, 8 + 8 and 9 + 9 (all of the ties used in the study), which in interview K claimed to 'just know'.

In addition to counting strategies and knowledge of facts, there is evidence from interview studies that as children move into the middle primary years they begin to use knowledge of some addition facts to 'derive' other facts. Carpenter and Moser (1983) describe strategies in which children derive new facts from known facts. For example, children may say that 7 + 6 is 13 because 7 + 7 is 14 and 6 is one less than 7. Other derivation strategies include bridging ten, either by 'seeing' the smaller addend as a composite, e.g. 8 + 6 = 8 + (2 + 4) = (8 + 2) + 4 = 10 + 4 = 14, which involves the associative principle, or by changing both addends in complementary directions to create an equivalent form that is easily processed, e.g. 8 + 6 = (8 + 2) + (6 − 2) = 10 + 4 = 14, which uses the idea of the additive inverse. It can be seen that these derivation strategies utilize other forms of knowledge, such as knowledge of the place value aspect of our number system, as well as knowledge of facts, in this case those which total 10. Gray (1991) found extensive use of derived facts in children from eight years of age upwards, especially among those children identified as above average.

Evidence in latency studies for the use of derivation strategies is in the spread of timings between the counting band of points and the points for the few facts which are clearly known. Figure 4.5 shows the timings for child 'G', with several examples of facts which fall in the range described. There are many addition facts with timings that are less than those in the counting band, yet which are not answered as quickly as might suggest use of 'instant recall'. In interview, G referred to her knowledge only of ties (indicated as T on the graph), but described how she works out facts from this, such as 6 + 5 and 5 + 6 from 5 + 5. The points marked as N on the graph shows these 'near ties'. It is interesting that 7 + 6 is answered more slowly than 6 + 8, which might be taken to have been counted, while 6 + 6 shows the slowest time for a tie. This suggests perhaps that G is less secure with 6 + 6 as an item of knowledge, yet perseveres with the strategy, as she claimed to do in interview, and as a result takes longer to answer than she might have done if she had counted.

In other cases, where interview data are not available, it must be said that the timings in this range would not be sufficient in themselves to draw the conclusion in any particular case that derivation strategies had been used. Such times could equally well result from

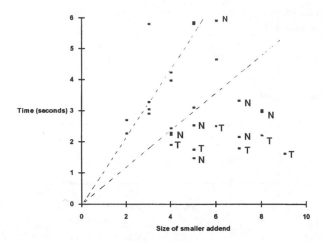

Figure 4.5 *Response times on addition questions answered by 'G', aged 11, plotted against the size of the smaller addend*

knowledge that takes longer to recall than the ties (Ashcraft, 1982). However, the correspondence between response times and interview data reinforces the general conclusion that derivation strategies for addition are widely used by children in the middle to later primary years.

In a further example, child 'S', aged nine, admitted to counting in some cases, such as for 7 + 4, and claimed to know the ties, but described how he works out 7 + 6, 8 + 7 and 9 + 8 by changing ties, and how he works out other facts with 8 or 9 by operating over the 10. His latency graph is shown as Figure 4.6. The ties, marked as T, run across the bottom of the graph,

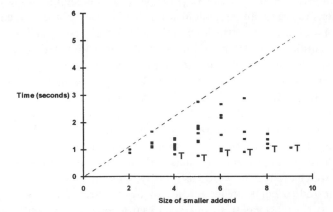

Figure 4.6 *Response times on addition questions answered by 'S', aged 9, plotted against the size of the smaller addend*

with the timings for each of the six ties being nearly the same. There is no clear counting band as such, but a slope has been added, consistent with the lower range of the counting band on the other figures, which suggests that a few facts may have been worked out by counting. However, as most of the timings come between this and the times for the ties, the graph offers some evidence of his use of derivation strategies.

The calculation of addition facts using such derivation strategies seems to be more widely used by children than teachers normally acknowledge. In partial explanation of this, Gray (1994) reports that during an observed assessment of seven-year-old children, the class teacher was unable to distinguish between children who used covert counting actions and children who knew or derived solutions.

Although deriving facts does seem to continue to an extent into adult life (Baroody, 1985), there is also a gradual expansion of the addition facts which are retrieved from memory. A review of interview data in the study conducted by the authors suggests that the most common of the non-tie facts to be claimed as known are 5 + 6 and 6 + 5. It is also notable that among the first facts of the non-tie range to be derived are 5 + 6 and 6 + 5, as interviews with younger children confirm. This extract is from an interview with 'D', aged 6.

I: Which ones do you know?
D: *Five and six is eleven.*
I: How do you know that?
D: *Well, 'cos five and five is ten and if you add another one on one of the fives it makes eleven.*

This leads us to suggest that children can come to know new addition facts through the automatization of a previously used derivation strategy. With use, the derivation of facts becomes increasingly automated and quick, apparently by-passing a central step in processing, so that in the end it is possible to say that the derived facts are effectively 'instant recall' without them ever having been consciously committed to memory.

The evidence for this process is inferential and not conclusive, but indirect evidence is offered by Gray (1991), who found in his two samples that the number of known facts increases only slowly when there is no use of derived facts, and more quickly when there is. Gray and Tall (1994, p. 135) suggest that, over a period of time, 'Simpler facts become known facts (or perhaps instantaneously derived facts).'

New addition facts seem to become known also through automatization of the counting process. To 'just know' that 7 + 1 is 8 and so on is the common first example of this. Indeed, there is evidence (Campbell, 1987) that the facts with at least one small number addend – up to 3 – remain counted in preference to the use of other strategies, because counting can be just as quick, but here too, in time, the quickly counted facts become known facts (or perhaps instantly counted facts).

ROTE LEARNING OF ADDITION FACTS

Rote learning is seen by many educators and teachers as the only method by which facts can become memorized. Under the influence of ideas drawn from behaviourist psychology, such as Thorndike's 'law of exercise' (1922), there has been a widespread belief that the only route to learning facts is by repetition. Now that the development outlined in previous pages has shown that facts can be learned in another way, through automatization of derived facts, the case for rote learning has to be made on the basis of it being *preferable* to promoting learning of facts by developing derivation strategies. Compared with such an approach, the appeal of rote learning is that it is simple and efficient – that is, the same amount of teaching produces better results in a rote approach.

However, we argue that the short-term gains that give rote learning its appeal are illusory and are less efficient in the longer term. Facts learned by rote do not endure without a wasteful amount of 'reinforcement'. The total amount of time spent in learning by rote and frequent practice overall is greater than in the approach we advocate, even though the time spent in initially learning the facts is less.

In the short term, a new fact can be learned quite quickly by a number of repetitions combined with a conscious effort to commit it to memory. If such facts, once learned, were then always correctly remembered, the argument for rote learning would be conclusive. However, what occurs in practice in the domain of number facts is the phenomenon known as 'interference' (Zbrodoff, 1995), in which errors occur in remembering by accidental association with other similar knowledge. For example, it is very common for children and adults to give the answer 54 rather than 56 to the problem 7×8. This is because of the 'interference' between the knowledge of 6×9 and 7×8. It is believed that children's apparent heightened ability to learn 'ties' is a direct consequence of the much reduced interference in these cases, because each single input is unambiguously associated with an output. Campbell (1991, p. 197) describes the mechanism of interference as follows:

> When a familiar problem (e.g. 4×7) is initially presented, a set of potential responses is activated that includes both the correct answer and incorrect answers that are associated with features of the problem.

These include:

- answers to other problems with the same operands, such as 24 (4×6) or 21 (3×7) or even 11 ($4 + 7$);
- answers of roughly the same magnitude that are known from other facts, such as 25 and 27;
- answers with parallel features, such as 18, with the same 'units' digit.

Errors then occur because 'the evidence ... accumulated for an incorrect answer can temporarily exceed the evidence for the correct answer' (*ibid.*).

'Evidence' in this context is the strength of the memory, in relation to the memory of wrong answers. The corollaries of this, which are supported by experimental findings on rote-learned facts, include the following features.

- Facts which have been remembered wrongly are more likely to be remembered wrongly in future (called 'error priming' by Campbell, 1991), which is to do with the 'evidence' for acceptance.
- Facts with a greater potential for interference, with more similarities to other facts, are more likely to be remembered wrongly – which is bad news for addition facts, where all facts (except ties!) have many similarities to many others.
- Interference increases as one learns more. Lemaire *et al.* (1994, p. 256) have observed this in relation to age: 'with increasing age, children experience interference effects on a wider range of problems'. If one only knows a few facts it is easier to keep them as separate items of knowledge. The more one learns, the greater the chance that different known facts will be similar, and provoke greater 'interference'.

These three features bring one shared conclusion: if facts have been learned by rote, there is an unavoidable need to continue rehearsing known facts at the same time as accommodating and assimilating new facts into long-term memory.

If, on the other hand, facts have become known by automatization of inferential derivation strategies, the 'evidence' for the correct answer comes from a different source. It is not just a matter of whether the memory is stronger; there is a logic to it. Equally, if one is not sure, there is a fall back position of working through the derivation again explicitly. For rote-learned facts the only option is to revert to a counting strategy. If, for example, 8 + 6 is learned by automatization of a bridging 10 strategy, and 8 + 7 by automatization of an adjusted tie, the risk of interference between them would seem to be considerably reduced. However, the extent to which facts learned in this way suffer less from 'interference' is not yet tested empirically.

For these reasons, we wish to promote here an approach to learning number facts which starts with pattern in the number system. We desire that children use patterns within counting numbers together with their knowledge of numbers in these patterns to generate new information. Eventually, the new information becomes known facts. The relationship between pattern and the derivation strategies is therefore, we believe, of crucial importance in deciding how to promote children's improved mastery of addition facts.

TEACHING DERIVATION STRATEGIES THROUGH PATTERN

The teaching of addition of 1 and 2

If children are to develop knowledge of addition facts, through either recall or deriving facts from known facts, it is essential that they are able to add and subtract 1 and 2, accurately and speedily, from any given number. This knowledge arises from the arrangement of the counting numbers in the number system, with the 'one more than' and 'one less than' relationships. In order to establish the arrangement and the relationships, time has to be spent by children adding and subtracting 1 and 2. Concrete representations of adding 1 or 2 to counting numbers may be necessary for some children, but most should be able to use symbolic representations from an early age. The operation diagrams shown in Figures 4.7 and 4.8 are useful for

Figure 4.7 *Operation diagrams for adding and subtracting 1*

Figure 4.8 *Operation diagrams for adding and subtracting 2*

children to work with as a prelude to creating mental pictures. Children write a number in the left-hand box and calculate the number that should go in the right-hand box. This is extended to adding and subtracting 2. Each of the operation diagrams illustrates the inverse nature of addition and subtraction.

Cards that contain addition facts for adding 1 and for adding 2 provide opportunities for children to explore patterns relating the facts. One way of sorting and ordering addition facts is illustrated in Figure 4.9. The idea of strategy diagrams can be introduced to children using

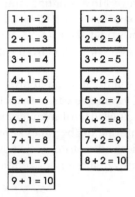

Figure 4.9 *Cards for adding 1 and adding 2 sorted and ordered*

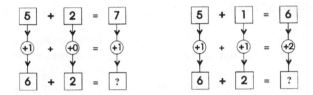

Figure 4.10 *Two strategy diagrams to derive 6 + 2*

adding 1 or 2. A strategy diagram models the derivation of a number fact from another known number fact. Figure 4.10 illustrates how the answer to 6 + 2 can be obtained from the known 5 + 2 = 7 or from the known 5 + 1 = 6. The strategy diagram provides opportunities for children to explore different strategies for obtaining answers to addition facts using a variety of known addition facts. Not only are children able to see relationships and patterns between different addition facts, they are provided with a visual model which assists the development of a mental model for operating on number.

The teaching of ties through pattern

All the research on children's recall of addition facts points to ties as the combination of pairs of numbers which are most readily known and are also the starting point for the derivation of many other facts. In order to improve each child's ability eventually to memorize all single-digit addition facts, and to increase the rate of the learning of the facts, emphasis should be placed on the learning of ties from an early age. This should begin as soon as a child has understanding of the concept of addition as a putting together of objects from two sets to make a third set. It is essential that ties are singled out for special treatment and that they are not submerged within the total domain of learning addition facts. The first five ties (1 + 1, 2 + 2, 3 + 3, 4 + 4 and 5 + 5) give answers 10 or less. These are the ones that children should explore and come to know before moving to 6 + 6, 7 + 7, 8 + 8 and 9 + 9.

Although linking cubes tend to encourage counting, they are a good starting point for very young children working with ties. Figure 4.11 shows three ways in which rods of two colours

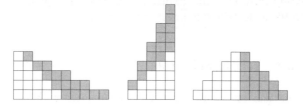

Figure 4.11 *Visual patterns relating ties using rods*

representing number pairs highlight visual patterns relating successive ties. Children should be given the opportunity to construct number rods and produce visual patterns. In discussion, the emphasis in the patterns should be placed on the numbers which the rods represent.

Number strips, Cuisenaire rods or similar materials place emphasis on the cardinality of each of the numbers in a tie rather than on their unit nature. They also allow for numbers to be represented by symbols, as shown in Figure 4.12. The pattern in ties should also be

Figure 4.12 *Pairs of number rods showing ties*

explored symbolically. Children can use ties recorded on cards to sort them into an order and discuss the patterns they observe, as shown in Figure 4.13. Figure 4.14 shows two strategy diagrams for finding the answer to 4 + 4 from two known ties. When it is felt that children

| 1 + 1 = 2 |
| 2 + 2 = 4 |
| 3 + 3 = 6 |
| 4 + 4 = 8 |
| 5 + 5 = 10 |

Figure 4.13 *Number cards for ties ordered to show patterns*

3	+	3	=	6		5	+	5	=	10
+1	+	+1	=	+2		-1	+	-1	=	-2
4	+	4	=	?		4	+	4	=	?

Figure 4.14 *Two strategy diagrams to derive 4 + 4*

understand the addition of ties 1 + 1 to 5 + 5 they should be given practice to consolidate their learning so that they become quickly recalled known facts. The extension of ties to 6 + 6, 7 + 7, 8 + 8 and 9 + 9 can follow the same approach, but may also include using other facts, such as combinations to 10, as described below.

Teaching patterns in the combinations of 10

Initially, through the use of practical apparatus and later with symbols, children should explore, understand and develop skills using the patterns related to addition to 10, often referred to as 'the story of 10', shown in Figure 4.15. It is important that children should

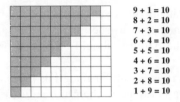

$$
\begin{aligned}
9 + 1 &= 10 \\
8 + 2 &= 10 \\
7 + 3 &= 10 \\
6 + 4 &= 10 \\
5 + 5 &= 10 \\
4 + 6 &= 10 \\
3 + 7 &= 10 \\
2 + 8 &= 10 \\
1 + 9 &= 10
\end{aligned}
$$

Figure 4.15 *Visual and symbolic patterns of addition facts to 10*

develop both the knowledge of addition facts to 10 and the skill to partition 10 into the addition of two numbers, e.g. 7 + 3 = 10 and 10 = 7 + 3. Figure 4.16 shows a strategy diagram for finding the answer to 6 + 4 using the known tie 5 + 5 = 10. Strategies for the addition of

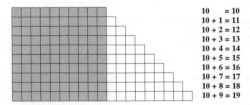

Figure 4.16 *A strategy diagram to derive 6 + 4*

single-digit numbers where the answer exceeds 10 indicate that children should consider, and come to understand and know, the patterns obtained when a single-digit number is added to 10, as shown in Figure 4.17. It should not be taken for granted that children know that the

$$
\begin{aligned}
10 \quad\;\; &= 10 \\
10 + 1 &= 11 \\
10 + 2 &= 12 \\
10 + 3 &= 13 \\
10 + 4 &= 14 \\
10 + 5 &= 15 \\
10 + 6 &= 16 \\
10 + 7 &= 17 \\
10 + 8 &= 18 \\
10 + 9 &= 19
\end{aligned}
$$

Figure 4.17 *Visual and symbolic patterns for adding numbers to 10*

addition of, say, 10 and 4 is written in the form of a two-digit number, 14. This way of writing the addition is part of the number system based upon the collective unit of ten. Much discussion is necessary with children on the visual pattern in symbolic representation to reinforce the structure of the number system.

Teaching patterns in the combinations of 5

When calculating mentally, children often make use of the number 5 by partitioning other numbers into a 5 and another number, e.g. $7 = 5 + 2$. Using number strips, children should explore the partitioning of single-digit numbers 6, 7, 8 and 9 using 5. This is illustrated in Figure 4.18 for the numbers 6 and 7. The results of partitioning 6, 7, 8 and 9 can be combined to emphasize the relationships with the number 5 and highlight the patterns to be observed, as in Figure 4.19.

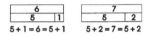

Figure 4.18 *Partitioning of the numbers 6 and 7 using the number 5*

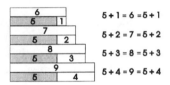

Figure 4.19 *Patterns in the partitioning of 6, 7, 8 and 9*

Teaching derivation strategies through pattern

The kinds of patterns which children may come to know, either through familiarity or as a result of developing understanding of the number system, include, as already discussed, patterns of ties, counting patterns and patterns using 5 and 10. Awareness of such patterns gives rise to some addition knowledge directly, but other knowledge can be derived by using one of the three following strategies, together with known knowledge.

● Those facts that recognize a related known fact, e.g. $8 + 7$ is one more than $7 + 7$ (or one less than $8 + 8$). This is more easily seen using strategy diagrams, such as in Figure 4.20.

$$7 + 7 = 14$$
$$(+1) + (+0) = (+1)$$
$$8 + 7 = ?$$

$$8 + 8 = 16$$
$$(+0) + (-1) = (-1)$$
$$8 + 7 = ?$$

Figure 4.20 *Strategy diagrams adjusting related knowledge for 8 + 7*

● Those that change both addends into an equivalent form, e.g. $8 + 7$ is the same as 10 (subtract 2) + 5 (add 2). Again a strategy diagram models this approach, in Figure 4.21.

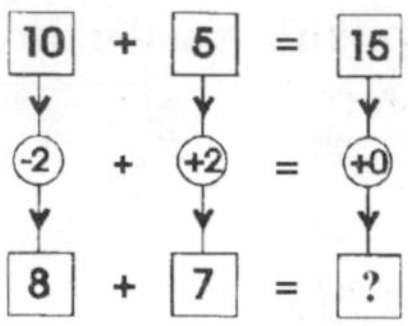

$$10 + 5 = 15$$
$$\downarrow \quad \downarrow \quad \downarrow$$
$$(-2) + (+2) = (+0)$$
$$\downarrow \quad \downarrow \quad \downarrow$$
$$8 + 7 = ?$$

Figure 4.21 *A strategy diagram using an equivalent form for 8 + 7*

- Those that break up the addends into parts that can be more easily handled, usually around 5 or 10, e.g. 8 + 7 is 5 + 3 and 5 + 2, which using the commutative and associative principles rearranges to 5 + 5 and 3 + 2. Figure 4.22 shows the strategy diagram for this approach.

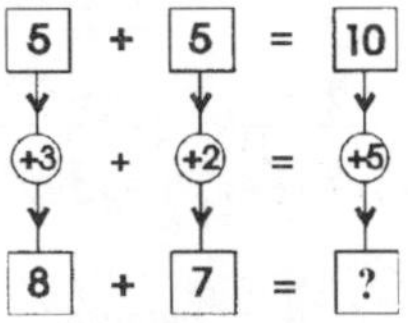

$$5 + 5 = 10$$
$$\downarrow \quad \downarrow \quad \downarrow$$
$$(+3) + (+2) = (+5)$$
$$\downarrow \quad \downarrow \quad \downarrow$$
$$8 + 7 = ?$$

Figure 4.22 *A strategy diagram for 8 + 7 breaking the addends to use knowledge of 10*

Such strategies also utilize the principles of partitioning and equivalence, and the 'analysis, rearrangement, synthesis' heuristic, which have general applicability throughout the learning of mathematics. Many facts can be worked out in any of these ways, and it is probably advantageous to be flexible enough to utilize different strategies at different times, depending on which pattern comes to mind.

In the display of addition facts shown as Table 4.1, the most likely patterns and strategies to be used for deriving facts are indicated by one or more of the following codes:

A = know as a tie
B = know as a fact to 10
C = know as counting knowledge (add 1 or 2)
D = adjust a tie
E = adjust a fact to 10
F = adjust a fact with 10 (e.g. 9 + 6 is one less than 10 + 6)
G = break smaller addend into parts
    to make ('bridge') 10 with the larger
H = break addends into parts involving 5
I = change to an equivalent tie

As can be seen from Table 4.1, there are different possibilities for deriving facts, and some facts may be considered 'easier' or 'harder' as a result. If a particular strategy is demanded of children, not all of them will necessarily understand or know that strategy. Some may know an alternative strategy which uses a different known fact. Children should be given opportunities to explore the use of different strategies for the derivation of the same addition fact using 'open' strategy diagrams, as shown in Figure 4.23 for the fact 6 + 9. Children should complete the diagrams choosing their own known facts from which to derive the answer to 6 + 9.

It appears that the three strategies described earlier – recognizing and adjusting a known fact; changing both addends into an equivalent form; and breaking the addends into parts that can more easily be handled – together with knowledge of the facts in a few patterns, are suf-

Table 4.1 *Addition facts to 18, and likely strategies for their solution*

1+1 C	2+1 C	3+1 C	4+1 C	5+1 C	6+1 C	7+1 C	8+1 C	9+1 B, C
1+2 C	2+2 C	3+2 C	4+2 C	5+2 C	6+2 C	7+2 C	8+2 B, C	9+2 C, E
1+3 C	2+3 C	3+3 A	4+3 D	5+3 I	6+3 E	7+3 B	8+3 E, G	9+3 F, G
1+4 C	2+4 C	3+4 D	4+4 A	5+4 D	6+4 B	7+4 E, G	8+4 G, I	9+4 F, G
1+5 C	2+5 C	3+5 I	4+5 D	5+5 A, B	6+5 D, E	7+5 H, I	8+5 G, H	9+5 F, G
1+6 C	2+6 C	3+6 E	4+6 B	5+6 D, E	6+6 A	7+6 D, G	8+6 G, I	9+6 F, G
1+7 C	2+7 C	3+7 B	4+7 E, G	5+7 H, I	6+7 D, G	7+7 A	8+7 D, G	9+7 F, G
1+8 C	2+8 B, C	3+8 E, G	4+8 G, I	5+8 G, H	6+8 G, I	7+8 D, G	8+8 A, G	9+8 D, G
1+9 B, C	2+9 C, E	3+9 F, G	4+9 F, G	5+9 F, G	6+9 F, G	7+9 F, G	8+9 D, G	9+9 A, G

ficient to derive all addition facts. This, however, should not preclude children from using whichever strategies they find most appropriate for a given addition fact. What cues children to use one strategy in preference to another is still an unknown.

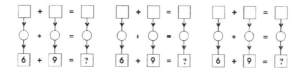

Figure 4.23 *Open strategy diagrams for 6 + 9*

CONCLUSION

At the present time, there is a demand from many directions that children should be able to respond quickly to simple number calculations. This is popularly understood to mean that they should calculate mentally in 'their heads', without the aid of pencil and paper. We have argued that rote learning does not in the long term achieve the desired aim of accuracy of recall and response to simple addition facts that we should expect of children. Competence in addition facts is attainable if children have a knowledge and understanding of the workings of the number system, of the relationships between numbers and of the principles of commutativity, associativity and inverse operations, all of which can be developed through observation and application of number patterns. There is evidence to suggest that children intuitively use such knowledge in developing strategies for calculating addition facts from known facts. We have made a case for children being 'taught' derivation strategies through pattern in numbers and, with the help of strategy diagrams, to move from deriving an addition fact to the fact becoming known and immediately retrievable from long-term memory when required.

We suggest the following teaching sequence to accelerate development of children's learning of addition facts:

1. Develop understanding of the number system through a study of pattern.
2. Look at patterns in facts, and the relationships between them.
3. Introduce children to strategy diagrams.
4. Learn the ties and the facts to 5 and 10 through their patterns.
5. Deliberately develop the strategy of adjusting a known fact to work out answers.
6. Extend the strategy using partitioning and equivalence, and develop the 'analyse, reorder, synthesize' approach.
7. Give plenty of opportunities for children to use addition facts, so that the derived and quickly counted facts become known facts by automatization.

This chapter has concentrated on addition facts. However, much of what has been discussed has applicability for children operating mentally with the addition of larger numbers, and with subtracting, multiplying and dividing numbers. This we leave for the reader to explore.

Chapter 5

Children's Strategies with Linear and Quadratic Sequences

Melanie Hargreaves, John Threlfall, Len Frobisher and Diane Shorrocks-Taylor

INTRODUCTION

Working with number sequences offers opportunities for recognizing, describing, extending and creating patterns, and is thought to have considerable value as a precursor to formal algebra (Hale, 1981; DES/WO, 1988; National Council of Teachers of Mathematics, 1989). Schoenfeld and Arcavi (1988, p. 426) suggest that, 'By asking students to observe and summarize (patterns) verbally, we may help make the transition from arithmetic to algebra'. Generalizing a pattern is considered to be a particularly important mathematical process. Thus, 'Demanding activities, such as ... the exploration of patterns leading to generalization in mathematics should be provided more frequently' (DES, 1983, p. 125), as 'Generalization is at the heart of algebra and the search for pattern is an essential step towards forming generalizations' (Jones, 1993, p. 27).

Perhaps as a result of the suggested relationship between number patterns and algebra, much of the research into how children make sense of, and work with, patterns in number sequences has been done with secondary school pupils over the age of twelve. There is little evidence available of younger children's understanding of number sequences, yet they are provided with many opportunities in primary textbooks to consider such patterns. In fact, a review of children's texts suggests that the most common kind of pattern encountered by children throughout the seven to eleven age range is that of number sequences.

In this chapter, we examine the understanding and performance of primary age children in patterns presented as a sequence of symbols (the implications of number sequences 'embedded in situations' are explored in Chapter 8). Processes that may be involved in handling number sequences include:

- searching for patterns in a sequence;
- constructing sequences;
- recognizing the existence of a pattern within a sequence;
- describing sequences orally and in a written form;
- continuing a sequence;
- completing a sequence;
- predicting terms in a sequence;

- suggesting a rule for a sequence;
- testing a rule for a sequence;
- generalizing a rule in words and/or algebraic symbols.

Evidence suggesting how children work with and operate on patterns in these different ways contributes to teaching decisions, and may suggest an optimum teaching strategy for the development of these processes. Children may, for example, find some of the processes more demanding than others; they may find that constructing a sequence is more difficult than continuing one; they may be inclined to use certain processes for some sequences and different processes for others.

TEXTBOOK APPROACHES

The most common activities for developing children's ability to deal with sequences presented in the numerical format are sequence completion questions, as in Figure 5.1, which requires the sequence to be extended, and Figure 5.2, where terms are missing from the

137   237   337   ▢   ▢

Figure 5.1 *Extending a sequence*

3   6   9   ▢   ▢   18

Figure 5.2 *Completing a sequence*

middle of the sequence. Both of these examples require children to find a relationship within the sequence, since no rule is provided, and to use the relationship to extend or complete the sequence. Sequences like these are often used to reinforce other areas of the mathematics curriculum, and it is not always possible to say whether a sequence such as that in Figure 5.2 is being used to develop sequence completion or to practise multiplication tables.

Few questions in children's textbooks for seven- to eleven-year-olds ask children to explain, describe or provide a rule for sequences, yet *Mathematics in the National Curriculum* (DfE/WO, 1995) requires that children should be taught to 'make general statements based on evidence they have produced', and 'explore number sequences, explaining patterns and using simple relationships' (pp. 6–7).

The majority of the sequences used in textbooks are *linear*, where the pattern increases or decreases by the same amount and, therefore, the difference between successive terms is constant, as in Figures 5.1 and 5.2. There are, however, occasions when children are required to work with *quadratic* sequences, where the constant difference is between the first differences. Two quadratic sequences to be extended are shown in Figure 5.3.

3   4   6   9   13   ▢   ▢

100   90   81   73   66   ▢   ▢

Figure 5.3 *Extending quadratic sequences*

In summary, the most common type of number sequence question found in primary text-books is where children are asked to continue or complete the sequence. The type of sequence does vary, but most of them focus on linear sequences including multiplication tables. Questions also vary in their format, although most are presented numerically.

A deeper appreciation and knowledge of children's approaches to and understanding of the kinds of number sequences they commonly meet is essential if we are to improve the quality of children's learning in this area. For that reason, a research study was conducted focusing on children's generalization about, and strategic approach to, common number sequences (Hargreaves, 1998).

NATURE OF THE TASKS

The number sequence questions found in textbooks formed the basis of four different tasks used in the research reported here. These were:

- a *solve* task, where the child was asked to provide a rule for a given sequence;
- a *continue* task, where the child was asked to provide the next two terms for a given sequence;
- a *sort* task, where the child had to decide if a given line of numbers was a pattern or not;
- a *create* task, where the child had to construct a number sequence.

A total of 487 children, aged seven to eleven, in primary and middle schools were involved. Every child worked with two types of sequence:

- linear sequences;
- quadratic sequences.

In each task, the children were encouraged to express their understanding of the pattern in the number sequence using a series of prompts leading from perception, to generalization, to strategy use.

1. Tell me about this number pattern.
2. What is the rule for this number pattern?
3. Tell me what thinking you did with the numbers to find the rule.

The word 'sequence' was intentionally replaced by 'pattern' because it was felt children would be more familiar with this word, since it is often used in mathematics textbooks. Data relating to children's understanding of the pattern in the sequence were collected in both an oral form, by interviewing children on a one-to-one basis, and a written form, with children reporting on a worksheet, as in Figure 5.4. Where children's written responses are reported in this chapter, they are provided in their original form, including any errors made by the children.

Most of the children's responses were in answer to the three questions above. To avoid repetition, the number of the appropriate question, i.e. (1), (2) or (3), precedes the children's responses in the examples presented later. The responses were examined to gain insights into the kinds of processes used, the strategies applied and how these might relate to generalizations. Before we examine these results, it is useful to consider the meanings of the terms 'generalization', 'process' and 'strategy', as there appears to be little agreement about their meaning among teachers and educators.

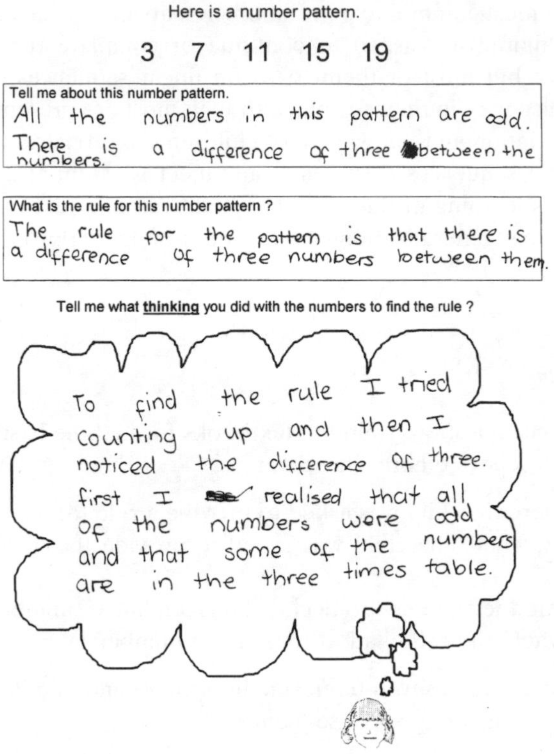

Here is a number pattern.

3   7   11   15   19

Tell me about this number pattern.

All the numbers in this pattern are odd.
There is a difference of three ⬛ between the numbers.

What is the rule for this number pattern ?

The rule for the pattern is that there is a difference of three numbers between them.

Tell me what **thinking** you did with the numbers to find the rule ?

To find the rule I tried counting up and then I noticed the difference of three. First I realised that all of the numbers were odd and that some of the numbers are in the three times table.

Figure 5.4 *Example of worksheet used in the research*

GENERALIZATION, PROCESS AND STRATEGY

When presented with a number sequence, children should be able to go beyond what is given to make sense of the pattern, in order to work with it. To operate with and on the number sequence

1   3   5   7   9

a child could notice that the numbers are all odd and/or that they increase by 2. Going beyond what is explicitly given in such ways is often referred to as 'generalization'. There are different kinds of generalization, going beyond what is given in different ways and to differing extents. Knowing that this sequence increases by 2 allows it to be worked with; for example, by extending the sequence, or by using it to help to solve more complex sequences, or by using the pattern in the sequence to help to understand more about odd numbers. However, knowing that the numbers in the sequence are all odd is a generalization about a property of the set of numbers. Thus, 'extending' the sequence may be only an extension of the set, ignoring the order of the numbers and the increase by 2 relationship; for example, 1   3   5   7   9 21   37   15. A more mathematically sophisticated generalization about 1   3   5   7   9 is to symbolize in algebraic terms the 'nth term' as $2n - 1$, which then allows the prediction of the value of any term in the sequence; for example, that the tenth term would be 19.

To arrive at a generalization about a number sequence, children must employ a strategy, a 'mode of action' (Backhouse *et al.*, 1992, p. 90) used to help reach a goal, or 'a collection of processes placed in an order in which they may be used' (Frobisher, 1994, p. 164). Strategies are always directed towards a goal, although it is not clear whether children are always conscious of this; processes, on the other hand, can include any action which a person has available to him or her, even if it is not being used or directed towards the goal at that particular time. Frobisher (1994, p. 164) notes that:

> Pupils who have decided that their first action with the problem data will be to sort it have operated a strategy. They have chosen from all the processes available to them one particular process which they see as appropriate.

Sorting is a process, but when it is the only process chosen in order to reach the goal for solving a problem, then it may be described as a strategy. Similarly, counting is a process and can be defined as a strategy only when it is used directly towards some goal, such as finding the sum of two numbers. A strategy, however, is more likely to involve the combination of two or more processes. A strategy is needed when a problem arises for a child, or when a child is presented with a problem, so that a solution can be sought and the goal attained. However, as teachers are very well aware, children frequently implement a strategy which fails to reach the goal, or achieves a different goal from that intended.

Strategies and levels of complexity

Strategies can be of relatively low complexity, such as the single strategy of counting all the items in a set to answer the question, 'How many?' Strategies can be more complex, forming 'a general plan ... that people use to solve problems' (Montague and Bos, 1990, p. 372). The complexity of a strategy may be affected by the goal the strategy is directed towards and by the characteristics of the person implementing that strategy. The strategy a child uses to attain a goal, such as forming generalizations about a sequence, may involve many processes, as in Figure 5.5. When operating on and with a sequence, a child may incidentally observe all the

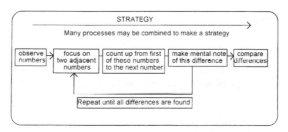

Figure 5.5 *A possible strategy for generalizing about sequences*

numbers without being conscious of doing this, and then focus on the first two. He or she may then count up to find the difference. This process may be repeated with other pairs of terms. Finally, these differences may be compared with one another in an attempt to find out if a pattern exists between the differences.

Processes, once combined to form a strategy to attain a goal, may be stored in a child's long-term memory, especially if the strategy has been used in a range of situations. These sets of processes may then be used again to reach similar goals, being retrieved from long-term memory as a collection in a given order. For example, a child may combine processes to deploy a strategy similar to that shown in Figure 5.5, and may then use the same strategy with a sequence such as 1 3 5 7 9. This has the advantage of providing, quickly, a strategy for solving common problems. However, difficulties can ensue if an inappropriate strategy choice is made or if an appropriate strategy is applied incorrectly. Thus, it is essential that a planning step precedes the implementation of a strategy.

It is useful to know to what extent children make strategy choices in their approach to number sequences, since the inclination to use the same strategy with number sequences often fails to result in a useful or accurate generalization. For example, children who always search a number sequence for a 'times table' will not get very far with a number sequence constructed using a quadratic 'rule'.

Research findings of Hargreaves (1998) suggest that seven- to eleven-year-old children have many strategies available to them when they generalize about a number sequence. These findings are now discussed in relation to linear and quadratic sequences. This discussion includes examples of children's responses to the questions (1), (2) and/or (3), presented earlier; the appropriate question number precedes each response.

CHILDREN'S STRATEGIES WITH LINEAR SEQUENCES

A linear sequence is a sequence where the difference between successive terms is constant. The sequence 1 3 5 7 9 is a linear sequence, as the difference between successive terms is always 2, as illustrated in Figure 5.6.

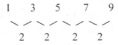

Figure 5.6 *A linear sequence showing the constant difference*

Looking for differences

The most common strategy used by children, when operating with linear sequences, involves calculating the difference between pairs of terms, usually the successive differences. For example, when Caroline was presented with the sequence 2 7 12 17 22, she responded as follows:

    2   7   12   17   22
Caroline   (3)   *2 + 5 = 7 and 7 + 5 = 12. If 2 + 5 = 7*
(age 8)   *then 12 + 5 = 17. And like 7 + 5 = 12*
          17 + 5 = 22. The pattern is it keeps adding 5.

It appears that Caroline worked systematically across the sequence of numbers from left to right. She first looked for the difference between 2 and 7. It would appear that she did this by counting up from 2 to 7, or by retrieving the information from memory, or by interpreting the relationship between the terms as 2 + ? = 7, rather than a subtraction, that is, 7 − 2. Caroline then turned her attention to the second and third terms, and found what has to be added to 7 to get 12. This process was repeated with the third and fourth terms, although to find what number was added to 12 to get 17 it appears that Caroline used her knowledge of place value: she knew that because $2 + 5 = 7$, then $12 + 5 = 17$. A similar process was used to find the difference between 17 and 22. Caroline finally compared these differences and concluded that 'The pattern is it keeps adding 5'.

The frequent deployment of strategies involving calculating the difference between terms leads to many ways of expressing the generalization about the relationships between the terms, as the following examples show.

2   6   10   14   18

David   (2)   *They're adding on four every time, they're even.*
(age 10)

2   5   8   11   14

Louise   (2)   *It's counting in threes.*
(age 8)

2   7   12   17   22

Scott   (2)   *plus five.*
(age 10)

These different ways of expressing the generalization suggest that, within the same strategy of calculating the constant difference for linear sequences, there are variations in the processes used to achieve the goal. Ben describes an alternative approach to considering the differences between successive numbers.

2   5   8   11   14
3,4   6,7   9,10   12,13*

Ben   (2)   *Add two and it makes the next number.*
(age 10)   (3)   *I added two to make the*
                  same number. I counted the numbers
                  in the middle and it went up
                  in twos.

(*The missing numbers were written in between the pattern at the top of the sheet by the child.)

The fact that Ben calls this 'adding two' may help to explain the incidence of incorrect generalizations, such as this one by Joanne.

2   5   8   11   14

Joanne   (2)   *They all go in twos.*
(age 7)

It is possible that Joanne was expressing a correct but unusual perception of the numbers between the terms of the sequence, rather than the operation required to move from one to the other. In other words the 'twos' are the missing pairs of numbers 3, 4 and 6, 7 and 9, 10 and 12, 13.

Looking at the nature of the numbers

Another common strategy used by children is to identify a quality or property applicable to the set of numbers in the sequence. For linear sequences, this was usually that they were odd or even, e.g. for 3   8   13   18   23, Rebecca responded to the questions as follows:

3   8   13   18   23

Rebecca   (1)   *The number pattern is an odd number then a even number then*
(age 10)   *a odd number.*
           (2)   *The rule of this number pattern is it goes odd then even.*
           (3)   3   8   13   18   23
                 odd   even   odd   even   odd

Rebecca adopted a strategy of identifying odd and even numbers. She appears to have processed the information across the sequence from left to right, identifying each number as either odd or even in turn, and as a result noticed that the odd and even numbers appear as an alternating pattern.

When children were working with linear sequences there were many cases where they used a strategy which involved looking at odd and even numbers, but did not make a generalization based on that observation. In the example below, Pritpal knew that some of the numbers were odd and some were even, but when asked for the rule he used a different strategy to arrive at the generalization, noting that there were two numbers between the terms. He may have recognized that his observations about the odd and even nature of the successive numbers did not constitute a rule.

2   5   8   11   14

Pritpal   (1)   *Some are even and some are odd.*
(age 9)   (2)   *That they've got two numbers in between them.*

Looking for multiplication tables

The third major strategy used by children on linear sequences was to relate the sequence to another similar one, usually a multiplication table. For example:

4   7   10   13   16

Michelle   (2)   *they are the 3 × tabuls.*
(age 8)   (3)   *4 7 10 13 16*
                  the is my 3 × tabul.

There are three possible explanations for Michelle's claim that they are the '3 × tabul':

1. She may have noticed that the unit digits of the last three terms (10, 13, 16) are the same as the start of the 3 times table.
2. She may have calculated the constant difference of 3, referring to this as the 3 times table.
3. She may have noticed that the sequence is 1 more than the numbers in the 3 times table.

It is not possible to determine which is the true explanation.

For some, it seems that their feel for multiplication table patterns can lead to quite subtle understandings, as Sarah shows.

2   5   8   11   14

Sarah   (2)   *Well it goes up in 3s, but instead of the 2, the 3 starting there it's 1*
(age 8)   *below all the 3 times table.*
         (3)   *I just noticed it then.*

Sarah arrived at the rule 'it goes up in 3s' possibly by a 'difference' strategy. To decide 'it's 1 below all the 3 times table', it appears she deployed a strategy of relating each term of the pattern to a number in the times table; that is, each term was one less than its corresponding number in the 3 times table.

Jennifer also deployed this strategy for the following linear sequence:

4   7   10   13   16

Jennifer	(2)	*Goes up in 3s.*
(age 9)	(3)	*Um, the first one I looked at the 4, but then I just decided to look at 7 and see if it went up to 10 which would be 3, then saw 10 went up to 13, 16.*
		If you started from the 3 that'd be a 3 and that would be 6 and that would be 9, so I counted one less than that.

These two examples are important because, unlike the 'difference' and 'nature of numbers' strategies, this strategy allows the sequence to be extended using its relationship to the 3 times table. For example, knowing that the sequence 2 5 8 11 14 is '1 below all the 3 times table', the twentieth term could potentially be calculated by $(20 \times 3) - 1$, which equals 59.

Thus, both Sarah and Jennifer are part-way towards developing an algebraic generalization for the nth term. The two sequences are listed below with each term related to the 3 times table.

Sarah's sequence	Jennifer's sequence
$2 = 3 - 1 = (3 \times 1) - 1$	$4 = 3 + 1 = (3 \times 1) + 1$
$5 = 6 - 1 = (3 \times 2) - 1$	$7 = 6 + 1 = (3 \times 2) + 1$
$8 = 9 - 1 = (3 \times 3) - 1$	$10 = 9 + 1 = (3 \times 3) + 1$
$11 = 12 - 1 = (3 \times 4) - 1$	$13 = 12 + 1 = (3 \times 4) + 1$
$14 = 15 - 1 = (3 \times 5) - 1$	$16 = 15 + 1 = (3 \times 5) + 1$

Both girls have intuitively made the first association with the 3 times table numbers (for example, $11 = 12 - 1$), and may be ready to record the relationship before rewriting each 3 times table number as a multiple of 3; for example, $11 = (3 \times 4) - 1$. This would appear to be an essential step towards an algebraic generalization, namely $(3 \times n) - 1$ (see Chapter 7).

CHILDREN'S STRATEGIES WITH QUADRATIC SEQUENCES

Quadratic sequences are those where the difference of the differences – that is, the second difference – is constant. The sequence 2 4 8 14 22 is quadratic because the differences between successive terms are 2 4 6 8, and the difference between these differences is always 2, as illustrated in Figure 5.7.

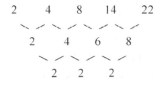

Figure 5.7 *A quadratic sequence showing the constant second differences*

Looking for differences

Laura used a strategy involving calculating the difference between the terms when operating with quadratic sequences. For example:

2   4   8   14   22

Laura	(2)	*You add 2, 4, 6 and 8.*
(age 8)	(3)	*I got 2 and 4 added 2 and*
		then got 4 and 8 added 4 and
		the same with the rest.

Laura calculated the difference between successive terms by working across the pattern from left to right. She calculated what should be added to 2 to make 4, and then what should be added to 4 to make 8. Looking for successive differences was fairly common, as the further example from Richard shows.

2   5   10   17   26

Richard	(2)	*the 1 one goes in 3 then*
(age 9)		*5 / 7 / 9*
	(3)	*I worked it out like I counted*
		it 2 to 5 is 3 5 to 10 is 5
		10 to 17 is 7 17 to 26 is 9

Richard provided each successive difference as the rule for this pattern but did not explicitly make a generalization about these differences.

Both Paul and Zoe applied an incomplete strategy of calculating the difference of only part of the sequence, using these limited data to make a generalization.

3   5   8   12   17

Paul	(2)	*Itt goes up in twoz.*
(age 10)		
Zoe	(2)	*they go up in 2s.*
(age 8)		

Thus children sometimes make a generalization about the difference relationship, but on the basis of the first two terms only. The Assessment of Performance Unit (undated) also identified generalizations which were made using only partial information about a sequence, and suggested that 'as the sequence gets more difficult, more pupils generalize from only some of the given information' (p. 419).

This use of partial information may be owing to children having only one strategy available; that is, calculating the differences. They make the strategy 'fit' the sequence, but are unable to apply it consistently when a constant difference fails to materialize. Children may not be sufficiently confident arithmetically, and when they fail to find a constant difference between the terms they put the cause down to their own calculation error. The use of partial information may be due to the belief that this is an efficient approach, as all previous sequences encountered may have had a constant difference. If children believe all number sequences have a linear structure, then there is no need to calculate all the differences as the difference between the first pair of terms is sufficient.

Looking at the nature of the differences

For some children, using a strategy involving calculating the difference between the terms was only the first step. When they noticed that the differences were not equal, this prompted a further strategy to explore a pattern in the differences. For example:

2   5   10   17   26
  3   5   7   9 *

John   (1)   *they go up in 3, 5, 7, and 9s.*
(age 8)   *all of them numbers are odd.*
             (2)   *they go up in odd numbers.*
             (3)   *I added them up.*

(*The difference between the terms was written in by the child.)

John used a strategy involving calculating the difference between terms. He then operated on these differences. He appears to have observed the odd nature of the differences and possibly recognized the differences as the sequence of odd numbers, which he saw as the rule.

Looking for differences between differences

Some children, on seeing that the differences were unequal, applied the 'difference' strategy on the differences.

2   4   7   11   16
  2   3   4   5 *

Matthew   (1)   *This number pattern is not a table. I found it*
(age 10)   *hard to do at first but I found out that you add 1*
                    on to the number in the gap each time.
           (2)   *The rule of this pattern is to add 1 on to the*
                    numbers in the gap each time.
           (3)   *At the top of the page I knew that 2 was in the*
                    gap on the first one and I used my fingers on the rest.

(* The difference between the terms was written in by the child.)

Matthew recognized that the sequence was 'not a table', indicating that he expected it might be a multiplication table. He calculated the differences and then appears to have counted on to find the difference between the other terms, as indicated by him using his fingers.

Looking at the nature of the numbers

As with linear sequences, some children used a strategy that identified a feature of the numbers, usually noting the odd and even terms within the quadratic sequences. For example:

2   5   10   17   26

Nick   (1)   *They is 3 even numbers and 2 add numbers.*
(age 10)   (2)   *it go even add even add.*
            (3)   *I looked at the numbers and sar that*
                    there is even numbers and they was a add number.

In this example, Nick identified all the numbers of the pattern as either odd or even. First, this process involved counting how many odd and even numbers there were: '3 even and 2 add'. He then appears to have observed the alternating pattern in these odd and even terms, which he then provided as the rule. It is interesting to note that children who consider the nature of the numbers in a sequence equalize the demand of linear and quadratic sequences.

Looking for multiplication tables

Again, as in linear sequences, some children adopted a strategy of using their knowledge of 'times tables', and sought to compare one with the other in order to generalize about the quadratic sequences.

3   6   11   18   27

Sophie   (2)   *3 × insept [except] for 11*
(age 7)   (3)   *I went 3 6 and 18 and 27 are in the times tables*
                     so thats how I worked it out.

Sophie focused on each of the terms in the sequence, identifying which of the terms were part of the 3 times table. She may have processed each number in this way because the pattern starts with 3 and 6. Thus, her thinking became dominated by the 3 times table relationship, resulting in the rejection of 11 which did not fit her confident conclusion.

Combining terms to make other terms

A strategy sometimes used to generalize about a quadratic sequence, but never about a linear sequence, is that of adding the terms in the sequence to make other terms. For example:

2   5   10   17   26

Simon   (2)   *The first three numbers add up to the fourth.*
(age 7)   (3)   *First I saw that 2 + 5 + 10 = 17. Then I saw the*
                    numbers even, odd, even, odd, even. I think the
                    next number is 53 because 10 + 17 + 26 = 53.

Simon observed that the sum of the first three terms gives the fourth term, although it is not clear how and why he did this. This is an interesting strategy because it led to a perfectly reasonable way of continuing the sequence. The fact that this is not the level of consistency that adults would expect (i.e. because 5 + 10 + 17 does not equal 26) does not seem to bother children. Once they have observed a relationship between terms, they are happy to apply the relationship without confirming that it holds for other terms.

DIFFERENCES WHICH OCCUR WITH TASK

Each of the four tasks described earlier included opportunities for children to express their perceptions, state rules and describe their strategies. However, the **continue**, **sort** and **create** tasks include other demands additional to the requirement to describe, offer a rule and articulate their thinking. Children's responses to these other demands offer additional sources of insight into their thinking.

The *continue* task

In the *continue* task, the children were asked to give the next two terms in a number sequence, which is a standard approach in the everyday exercises so common in textbooks. However, in this study, the demand to extend a sequence followed on from children having to explain their thinking.

The generalizations made in the *continue* task were very similar to those found in the other tasks, but there were some particularly interesting findings. There were occasions when children provided no evidence for the rule of the sequence, but went on to continue it correctly, obviously applying the rule. For example:

4   7   10   13   16

Bronwen	(1)	*it has got 5 numbers in it.*
(age 7)		*The numbers get higher.*
	(2)	*it goes odd even odd even.*
	(3)	*the number what is even is*
		4, 10, 16 and the odd numbers are 7, 13.
Teacher		What are the next two numbers in this pattern?
Bronwen		*19, 22.*

Bronwen, when asked about the rule, only talked about odd and even numbers, and the numbers getting higher. She provided no evidence that she knew the pattern increases by 3, yet the next two terms were provided correctly. It would appear that she may have been unaware of the meaning and intention of the question 'What is the rule for this number pattern?', or felt that saying 'it goes odd even odd even' was a sufficient answer, while conscious that she knew more than what she said. Alternatively, she may have been prompted to perform further calculations on the terms when asked for the next two numbers.

Some children correctly identified the rule for a sequence and expressed their thinking clearly. However, when asked 'What are the next two numbers in this pattern?', they either ignored what they had previously done or misapplied their rule, thus providing incorrect terms. It is as if the description of the rule and the explanation of thinking were not thought relevant to the demand of giving the value of the next term, and there was a reversion to the tried and tested strategy used in other similar tasks.

This raises a question about the notion of 'generalization'. A child may articulate a rule for a sequence, but seem to have no sense of the sequence continuing in that way. In other words, he or she generalizes within the sequence given, but not beyond the sequence. The need to generalize about the given terms seems to have two meanings. One meaning is to see more in the set of numbers than is given – a pattern generalization. The other is to go beyond the set of numbers – a sequence generalization. It is clearly necessary to go beyond what is given in order to do things with the sequence, but what is to be done with the sequence can vary, and some 'uses' require only a pattern generalization, while others require a sequence generalization. It will be seen in later chapters that as understanding extends towards algebra, the kinds of generalization in relation to different uses extend further, to include generalizations which permit a calculation of an extended term in the sequence.

The *sort* task

In the ***sort*** task, children were asked to decide if a line of numbers was a number pattern or not. If they thought it was a pattern, they were asked to provide the rule. Given the opportunity to make this decision about the line of numbers, some children describe sequences as not being patterns. This applied particularly to younger children.

Some children performed very well on the ***sort*** task with relatively difficult sequences, such as:

3   5   9   15   23

2   4   6   8 *

Thomas	(1)	*This line of numbers goes up in the 2 times table you add*
(age 11)		*2 then 4 then 6 then 8 this is the two times table.*
Teacher		Is this line of numbers a number pattern?
Thomas		*Yes.*
	(2)	*You add the 2 times table.*
	(3)	*I worked it out by takeing away the numbers.*
		I took away t 3 from 5 to get 2, 5 from 9 + 6 to get 4,
		9 from 15 to get 6, 15 from 23 to get 8.

(* The difference between the terms was written in by the child.)

Thomas used a strategy involving calculating the differences between successive terms, then went on to identify these differences as the 2 times table.

There were examples where children wrote correctly that some of the sequences were patterns, but for the wrong reason. For example:

3   5   9   15   23

Alison (age 8)	(1)	*Some of them are odd numbers.*
Teacher		Is this line of numbers a number pattern?
Alison		*Yes.*
	(2)	*it goes up in three.*
	(3)	*I worked it out in my head in 3 times.*

The *create* task

The ***create*** task was fundamentally different from the other tasks in that, rather than the children being presented with patterns which they were asked to explain, they made their own patterns. The examples below are from workbooks where the only restriction on the sequences the children made was that they only had space to provide five terms. The majority of the patterns created by the children were multiplication tables, as the example below shows.

11   22   33   44   55

Kirstie	(1)	*my nuber patern gose in the 11 times tables.*
(age 10)	(2)	*it gose in 11 time*
	(3)	*I worked out the 11 times in my head and i got the ansur.*

(* The numbers were selected and sequenced by the child.)

This may reflect the fact that many of the patterns found in children's texts and workbooks seem to be designed more to practise the 'tables' than to promote strategy use or generalizations about number sequences. It may also be possible, however, that the inclination to make equal difference patterns is most easily met by adding the first term successively.

Some patterns, although not recognizable multiplication tables, had the same structure, in that they increased each time by the value of the first term. For example:

*368   736   1104   1472   1840**

Jeffrey	(2)	*I keep adding 368 as I go along.*			
(age 9)	(3)	368	736	1104	1472
		+368	+368	+368	+368
		736	1104	1472	1840

(* The numbers were selected and sequenced by the child.)

Some children, however, made linear sequences which were not multiplication tables. For example:

*1   5   9   13   17**

Sally	(2)	*the rule for my number pattern is you miss three*
(age 8)		*numbers out.*
	(3)	*I did one number and missed three numbers out*
		and put the next one down.

(* The numbers were selected and sequenced by the child.)

Sally made this sequence by missing out three numbers between the terms; the difference between the terms is actually 4. This may have involved similar processes to those used by other children who, when presented with a linear sequence such as 2   5   8   11   14, gave the rule as 'it goes up 2', or 'misses 2 out'.

Most children created linear sequences with terms increasing in value from left to right. There were some examples of more unusual patterns. The example below has an elaborate rule involving a decreasing sequence.

*44   28   20   16   14 **

Andrea	(2)	*the rule for my number pattern is you can only find the*
(age 11)		*next number by dividing by 2 then adding 6.*
	(3)	*I tried to think of a number pattern that nobody else*
		would think of I had to work out what each number was
		after dividing by 2 then I had to add 6 to the nuber I got
		when I divided it by 2.

(* The numbers were selected and sequenced by the child.)

Such invention was rare enough to invite a particular explanation, of a special child or a special teacher, or a special experience, perhaps of one of the calculator explorations of 'chaining' which follow such rules, and probably all three.

CONCLUSION

Most children between the ages of seven and eleven have strategies for analysing linear and quadratic sequences, and many of them can use what they find to make generalizations. The strategies that children use include:

- looking for differences between terms;
- looking at the nature of the differences;
- looking for differences between the differences;
- looking at the nature of the numbers, usually odd and even;
- looking for multiplication tables;
- combining terms to make other terms.

The dominance of looking for differences suggests that many children are not aware of other types of number sequences where the strategy may be inappropriate. The evidence presented here suggests that some children approach number patterns in a flexible manner, but that for others it is a case of using the first strategy which comes to mind. The inflexible strategy use, of sticking with a strategy in the face of its lack of success, which is also fairly common, is additional evidence of the restricted experience provided by teachers of different kinds of sequence. Some children are aware of different pattern structures, however, and make generalizations about an appropriate relationship within different patterns, indicating both strategy choice and flexibility. The frequency of varied strategies and appropriate choices increases through the age range, but even among the oldest children there are still far too many who are reliant on a single type of strategy when working towards making a generalization about a given number pattern. This may be caused by lack of experience of any pattern structures other than linear sequences. This in turn may be the by-product of the way in which number sequences are treated at the primary stage. They are frequently viewed as number exercises for times table practice, rather than as teaching and learning contexts for the development of strategies towards effective generalizations. The extent to which children utilize a strategy of looking for multiplication tables in the sequences used in the study is further evidence of this.

Classroom implications

Even though their experience seems to be quite limited, the majority of children between the ages of seven and eleven appear to be able to make some accurate generalizations about linear sequences. Some children can even make generalizations about, or begin to describe, quadratic sequences. This suggests that there is potential for development.

In order to promote improved strategy use and better generalizing about number sequences, children should be provided with the opportunity to work with sequences covering a wide range of structures. In doing so, it is particularly important to provide children with tasks which encourage them to work with and appreciate number sequences in their own right, rather than tasks designed as a quick and easy reinforcement of other areas of the mathematics curriculum. There is evidence to suggest that there should be a variety of challenges, not just continuing sequences, but also describing and creating them. This is because the *continue* task encourages children to deploy a strategy which involves calculating the difference between terms at the expense of other strategies, thus limiting children's strategy use.

It may also be valuable to encourage children to make more than one generalization about different number sequences; for example, using tasks which provide only the first three terms of a sequence, such as 1 2 4, and asking children to continue this in as many different ways as possible, justifying each extension. It is equally important when doing so, however, not to be too prescriptive in the kinds of patterns being sought. Children should not be discouraged from using strategies which involve looking at the properties of the numbers, such as looking for odd and even numbers, since these strategies may be a precursor to looking for patterns of square and triangular numbers.

Tasks which are more similar to the *solve* and *sort* tasks used in this study may provide an especially valuable setting for work with number sequences for broadening children's strategies. The *sort* task elicited the widest variation of strategies for all the types of number sequence and may be a useful way to encourage children to use more than one strategy with each sequence, thus promoting flexible strategy use.

In summary, the results suggest that children of all ages should be provided with a much wider array of pattern structures and tasks within the classroom. Using a wide variety of pattern structures and tasks, it may be possible to encourage children to:

- be less reliant on strategies involving looking for a difference between the terms;
- use more than one strategy and choose information from an appropriate one to make a generalization;
- be more persistent in searching for patterns within data.

Pattern and making generalizations are very important in the study of mathematics, and an investment in their development during the primary years provides the necessary foundation for, and will greatly enhance, the development of the kind of strategic thinking and generalization about sequences as an ordered set which is a cornerstone of later algebraic thinking.

Chapter 6

Teaching and Assessing Patterns in Number in the Primary Years

Len Frobisher and John Threlfall

INTRODUCTION

Over fifty years ago, Brownell (1945, p. 481) claimed that 'meaning [in mathematics] is to be sought in the structure, the organization, the inner relationship of the subject itself'. The structures, organization and relationships within mathematics are patently visible in the form of patterns. As a subject, mathematics expresses itself through pattern, which pervades every aspect and topic in the curriculum. English and Halford (1995, p. 5) write of Van Engen's belief that schools for the past fifty years 'had failed to develop students' ability to detect patterns in similar and diverse situations and had been directing children to the wrong element in problem solving, namely the answer'.

In 1959, the Mathematical Association published an influential book entitled *Mathematics in Secondary Modern Schools*, in which were given five reasons for mathematics being part of the school curriculum, one of which included an implicit reference to pattern – 'Mathematics is the language of orderliness and ordered thinking' (p. 2) – and the second an explicit statement of the relationship between pattern and children's thinking: 'Mathematics develops patterns of thinking which are fundamental patterns of all thinking' (p. 2).

In the late 1960s, the Schools Council's Mathematics for the Majority project was set up with the aim of improving the teaching of mathematics in secondary schools to children of average and less-than-average ability. It published seven books, one of which was titled *Mathematical Pattern* (Schools Council, 1971). It claimed that 'Recognition of a variety of patterns, produced by or leading to a variety of mathematical situations, starts at the stage of infancy' (p. 3). How then do primary schools, through textbooks which the greater number of them use, set about introducing children to pattern in mathematics?

[handwritten note: Could link to why I think its important to teach Pattern though an embodied approach.]

PATTERN IN NUMBER IN PRIMARY SCHOOLS

Curriculum documents in many countries highlight the need to introduce young children to 'the patterns and relationships inherent in mathematics' (English and Halford, 1995, p. 17). In particular, the National Curriculum for England and Wales (DfE/WO, 1995, p. 2) requires that children, as part of the Using and Applying Key Stage 1 programme of study

(PoS), 'recognize simple patterns and relationships and make predictions about them'. This is further enlarged in the number PoS, which requires that

> Pupils should be taught to:
>
> use repeating patterns to develop ideas of regularity and sequencing; explore and record patterns in addition and subtraction, and then patterns of multiples, *e.g. 3, 6, 9, 12*, explaining their patterns and using them to make predictions; progress to exploring further patterns involving multiplication and division, including those within a hundred-square of multiplication facts. (p. 3)

The Key Stage 2 Number PoS extends the requirement to include 'using simple relationships' and progressing 'to interpreting, generalizing and using simple mappings'.

Despite the specific inclusion of the study of pattern in the primary curriculum, there is a great variation to be found in the extent of coverage of number patterns in different primary textbooks. There are also obvious differences in the ways patterns in number are treated in textbooks. At one extreme, there are those which look upon 'pattern' as a topic for children to learn; at the other end of the spectrum, there are those which attempt to highlight pattern in topics at every opportunity. There is, however, a core of work on pattern in number that can be found in the majority of textbooks. A good deal of this is on number sequences but, as this is dealt with in Chapter 5, it will not be repeated here. A few textbooks provide children with experiences of number patterns that are set in situations, which are frequently to do with patterns arising out of sequences of shapes, but again these are more extensively dealt with in Chapter 8. Much of the rest is described here, together with suggested extensions in order to show how many textbooks fail to explore the wealth of patterns to be found in activities with numbers. Textbooks seldom provide ideas for investigating beyond the superficial surface of the pattern in the structures of the number system. Some of these are described to assist teachers to take their children along with them towards a deeper understanding of mathematics.

Patterns in counting grids

The 100 counting grid is to be found in use in most primary classrooms and textbooks. It provides a wealth of opportunities for children to observe and explore patterns in number (see Figure 6.1). The simplest pattern involves the numbers along a row, as they increase from left

1	2	3	4	5	6	7	8	9	10
11	12	13	14	15	16	17	18	19	20
21	22	23	24	25	26	27	28	29	30
31	32	33	34	35	36	37	38	39	40
41	42	43	44	45	46	47	48	49	50
51	52	53	54	55	56	57	58	59	60
61	62	63	64	65	66	67	68	69	70
71	72	73	74	75	76	77	78	79	80
81	82	83	84	85	86	87	88	89	90
91	92	93	94	95	96	97	98	99	100

Figure 6.1 *A 100 counting grid*

to right by 1, and decrease by 1 from right to left, as illustrated in Figure 6.2. The numbers in a column have the same unit digit and the tens digits increase by 1; thus the numbers increase by 10 from top to bottom of a column, as shown in Figure 6.3. These are the two basic

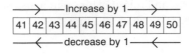

Figure 6.2 *A row from the counting grid*

Figure 6.3 *A column from the counting grid*

patterns resulting from the structure of the number system, base 10, and having ten numbers in each row. There are many others, a few of which are illustrated in Figure 6.4 by shading numbers in the 100 grid. Although the shading of the numbers produces interesting

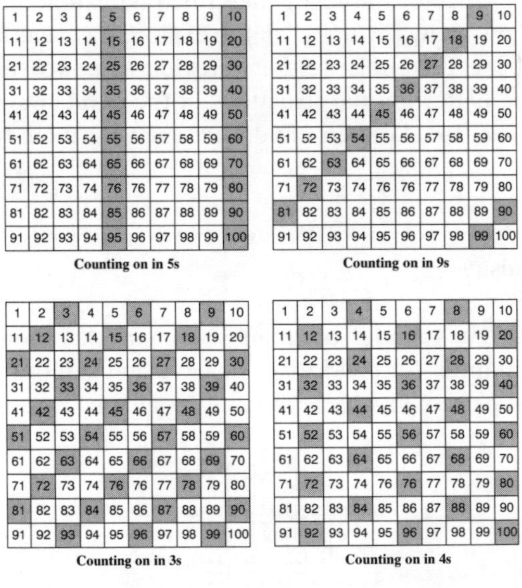

Counting on in 5s

Counting on in 9s

Counting on in 3s

Counting on in 4s

Figure 6.4 *Shading numbers in the 100 grid*

visual patterns, it is important that children consider the structure which has created the visual patterns. Each pattern is produced because of the relationship between the 'count on' number and the 'ten-ness' of each row. An investigation related to 'count on' patterns involves children considering the number of squares shaded in each row for a given 'count on' number. For example, the 'count on 6' grid is shown in Figure 6.5, with the number of shaded squares in each row listed at the end of every row. These numbers produce the sequence 1, 2, 2, 1, 2, 2, 1, 2, 2, 1. Children should be asked to explain why they think this

1	2	3	4	5	6	7	8	9	10	1
11	12	13	14	15	16	17	18	19	20	2
21	22	23	24	25	26	27	28	29	30	2
31	32	33	34	35	36	37	38	39	40	1
41	42	43	44	45	46	47	48	49	50	2
51	52	53	54	55	56	57	58	59	60	2
61	62	63	64	65	66	67	68	69	70	1
71	72	73	74	76	76	77	78	79	80	2
81	82	83	84	85	86	87	88	89	90	2
91	92	93	94	95	96	97	98	99	100	1

Figure 6.5 *The number of shaded squares in each row for the 'count on 6' pattern*

pattern occurs, and to predict, with justification, whether it continues if the grid is extended with numbers 101 to 200, and beyond.

Another interesting pattern considers how the numbers in the shaded squares are distributed in each column. In the 'count on 6' pattern, shown in Figure 6.6, the successive shaded numbers always increase by 30; at least they do on the 100 grid. Children should

Figure 6.6 *A column from the 'count on 6' pattern*

investigate if this is always the case: (a) when the grid is increased to, say, 200, and (b) when the grid has a different number of numbers, say 7, in each row. The 'counting on' activities described above assume that the counting begins at the first square, that which is labelled by the number '1'. If the counting begins at the square labelled '2', an entirely different set of numbers is shaded, but the visual pattern of the structure remains very much the same.

Figure 6.7 shows the three possible patterns produced by changing the start number for 'count on 3'. Each grid produces a sequence of numbers related in different ways to the

1	2	3	4	5	6	7	8	9	10	3
11	12	13	14	15	16	17	18	19	20	3
21	22	23	24	25	26	27	28	29	30	4
31	32	33	34	35	36	37	38	39	40	3
41	42	43	44	45	46	47	48	49	50	3
51	52	53	54	55	56	57	58	59	60	4
61	62	63	64	65	66	67	68	69	70	3
71	72	73	74	76	76	77	78	79	80	3
81	82	83	84	85	86	87	88	89	90	4
91	92	93	94	95	96	97	98	99	100	3

1	2	3	4	5	6	7	8	9	10	3
11	12	13	14	15	16	17	18	19	20	3
21	22	23	24	25	26	27	28	29	30	3
31	32	33	34	35	36	37	38	39	40	4
41	42	43	44	45	46	47	48	49	50	3
51	52	53	54	55	56	57	58	59	60	3
61	62	63	64	65	66	67	68	69	70	3
71	72	73	74	76	76	77	78	79	80	4
81	82	80	04	05	00	07	00	89	90	3
91	92	93	94	95	96	97	98	99	100	4

1	2	3	4	5	6	7	8	9	10	2
11	12	13	14	15	16	17	18	19	20	4
21	22	23	24	25	26	27	28	29	30	3
31	32	33	34	35	36	37	38	39	40	3
41	42	43	44	45	46	47	48	49	50	4
51	52	53	54	55	56	57	58	59	60	3
61	62	63	64	65	66	67	68	69	70	3
71	72	73	74	76	76	77	78	79	80	4
81	82	83	84	85	86	87	88	89	90	3
91	92	93	94	95	96	97	98	99	100	3

Figure 6.7 *Counting on in 3s starting at different numbers*

multiples of 3, as listed below. Placing the three sequences below each other enables further patterns to be observed, explored, described and explained.

3	6	9	12	15	18	21	24	27	30	33	etc.
4	7	10	13	16	19	22	25	28	31	34	etc.
5	8	11	14	17	20	23	26	29	32	35	etc.

The question immediately arises as to what to do with the numbers 1 and 2, which do not 'appear' in any of the sequences. The numbers to the right of each grid in Figure 6.7 count the squares shaded in each row. Children need to discuss the differences and similarities among the three sequences, acknowledging, it is hoped, that they have the same structure, but start at a different place. Work with patterns on the counting grid resulting from using different 'count on' numbers is an essential prerequisite to searching for patterns in the multiplication tables.

Patterns in multiplication tables

The early use of the counting grid with children is usually restricted to consideration of patterns resulting from counting activities. However, as the reader will have noticed, many of these patterns are directly associated with numbers in the multiplication tables. Thus, shading of squares based on 'counting in 6s' produces the numbers that are part of the 6 times table. This is, of course, only true if the first number counted is 1. (Many would argue that the grid should show the number '0' in the first square and count up to 99. You may wish to investigate what happens if you create this type of counting grid.)

Many textbooks introduce tables as the outcome of repeated addition. For example, repeatedly adding 3 produces the following pattern shown as an addition and a multiplication for the first few repeats.

$$
\begin{aligned}
3 &= 3 = 1 \times 3 \\
3 + 3 &= 6 = 2 \times 3 \\
3 + 3 + 3 &= 9 = 3 \times 3 \\
3 + 3 + 3 + 3 &= 12 = 4 \times 3 \\
3 + 3 + 3 + 3 + 3 &= 15 = 5 \times 3
\end{aligned}
$$

(Some would argue that the multiplications should be written in the reverse order, e.g. 3×4, not 4×3.) It is important that children build up such 'tables' themselves. They should follow their construction of each table for the numbers 2, 3, 4 and so on by discussing and recording the patterns they observe.

The 'times table' numbers are themselves full of patterns. Activities to explore patterns in 'times tables', such as the pattern in the unit digits, are to be found in many textbooks (see Figure 6.8). Most textbooks ask children to 'discover' patterns in the unit digits of 'times

| 3 times table numbers | 3 | 6 | 9 | 12 | 15 | 18 | 21 | 24 | 27 | 30 | 33 | 36 |
| unit digits | 3 | 6 | 9 | 2 | 5 | 8 | 1 | 4 | 7 | 0 | 3 | 6 |

Figure 6.8 *The 3 times table and the pattern in the unit digits*

tables', but fail to ask the children to explore the structures that bring about the patterns. It is left to the teacher to ask children to write about the relationships that may exist between patterns from different 'times tables', and to ask such questions as 'Do the patterns continue for ever?'

Opportunities for representing such patterns in a variety of ways should be given to children, since different modes of representation can provide insight into the structure that is behind the pattern. As the number of unit digits is finite, and repeats, a circular number line is an appropriate way of representing the pattern in the unit digit of any 'table' (see Figure 6.9). The arrowheads in Figure 6.9 are essential to indicate the order of the sequence of the

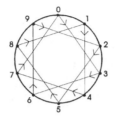

Figure 6.9 *A representation of the unit digit pattern in the 3 times table*

occurrence of the unit digits. Children should investigate the patterns produced by the remaining 'times tables' and look for relationships between different 'times tables'. For example, the '7 times table' has the sequence of unit digits shown in Figure 6.10. It may

7 times table numbers	7	14	21	28	35	42	49	56	63	70	77	84
unit digits	7	4	1	8	5	2	9	6	3	0	7	4

Figure 6.10 *The 7 times table and the pattern in the unit digits*

not be obvious from the sequence that a relationship exists between it and that of the '3 times table' unit digit sequence. However, the relationship is immediately observable when the sequence is represented as in Figure 6.11. The reader will immediately notice the similarity of

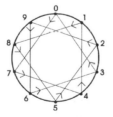

Figure 6.11 *A representation of the unit digit pattern in the 7 times table*

this visual representation to that of the '3 times table'. This is no coincidence. The difference is in the order in which the unit digits occur as indicated by the arrowheads. If the representations of the tables are matched in this way a pattern emerges as an 'n times table' pattern is paired with a '$(10 - n)$ times table' pattern. Children will be able to offer reasons why this occurs, relating their explanations to the 'ten-ness' of the number system.

Patterns between multiplication tables

The latter example of the relationship between the representations of the '3 times table' and the '7 times table' is only one of many relationships between 'tables' that show themselves as patterns. The marking of 'table' numbers on a counting grid shows that some tables are 'subsets' of other tables. This is illustrated in Figure 6.12 for the 3 and 6 tables. Shading of other

Figure 6.12 *A counting grid showing the 3 times and the 6 times table numbers*

tables on grids highlights the 'intersection' of 'table' numbers, e.g. the '2 times table' and '5 times table' have multiples of 10 in common. The concepts of multiples and factors can arise out of the exploration of patterns on grids.

Box 6.1 *A listing to show the relationships between the 2, 4, 8, 16 and 32 times tables*

$1 \times 2 = 2$				
$2 \times 2 = 4$	$1 \times 4 = 4$			
$3 \times 2 = 6$				
$4 \times 2 = 8$	$2 \times 4 = 8$	$1 \times 8 = 8$		
$5 \times 2 = 10$				
$6 \times 2 = 12$	$3 \times 4 = 12$			
$7 \times 2 = 14$				
$8 \times 2 = 16$	$4 \times 4 = 16$	$2 \times 8 = 16$	$1 \times 16 = 16$	
$9 \times 2 = 18$				
$10 \times 2 = 20$	$5 \times 4 = 20$			
$11 \times 2 = 22$				
$12 \times 2 = 24$	$6 \times 4 = 24$	$3 \times 8 = 24$		
$13 \times 2 = 26$				
$14 \times 2 = 28$	$7 \times 4 = 30$			
$15 \times 2 = 30$				
$16 \times 2 = 32$	$8 \times 4 = 32$	$4 \times 8 = 32$	$2 \times 16 = 32$	$1 \times 32 = 32$

Different representations highlight the patterns between tables in different ways, and a variety of representations should be explored by children. Box 6.1 lists some of the 2, 4 and 8 times tables to show their relationships and how easy it is to extend this to the '16 times table' and the '32 times table'.

Patterns in place value relationships

Very often primary textbooks in mathematics overlook many patterns, possibly because to adults they are simple, appear too trivial and seem to be of little interest. As teachers, this is a position and view that we should adopt with caution. What to us has little value and attraction can to children be fascinating and make a significant contribution to their learning of mathematics. Many of these apparently simple patterns explore place value and its representation in symbols. Some possibilities are shown here.

$$
\begin{aligned}
1 &= 1 \\
10 + 1 &= 11 \\
100 + 10 + 1 &= 111 \\
1000 + 100 + 10 + 1 &= 1111
\end{aligned}
\qquad
\begin{aligned}
10 - 1 &= 9 \\
100 - 1 &= 99 \\
1\,000 - 1 &= 999 \\
10\,000 - 1 &= 9999
\end{aligned}
$$

$$
\begin{aligned}
9 + 1 &= 10 \\
90 + 10 &= 100 \\
900 + 100 &= 1\,000 \\
9000 + 1000 &= 10\,000
\end{aligned}
\qquad
\begin{aligned}
10 &= 10 \\
10 \times 10 &= 100 \\
10 \times 10 \times 10 &= 1000 \\
10 \times 10 \times 10 \times 10 &= 10\,000
\end{aligned}
$$

Observing such patterns is only the beginning of children's understanding of what lies behind the patterns, the principle of grouping by tens. Children are frequently able to recognize a pattern sufficiently to extend it, without understanding why the pattern exists and the mathematical structure which brings about its existence. The importance of children talking about, describing and giving their reasons for a pattern cannot be over-emphasized, as this encourages them to find a meaning for the pattern, and consequently develops their understanding of mathematics.

Patterns involving more than one operation

There are many patterns that are the result of relationships between numbers, involving more than one of the operations of addition, subtraction, multiplication and division. Few of these are to be found in textbooks, and when they do occur seldom is the reason for the pattern fully explored, missing the opportunity for children to learn about the structure of the number system. Below are two simple patterns that most primary school children are able to observe, extend, describe and explain.

$$
\begin{aligned}
1 \times 9 &= 10 - 1 \\
2 \times 9 &= 20 - 2 \\
3 \times 9 &= 30 - 3 \\
4 \times 9 &= 40 - 4
\end{aligned}
\qquad
\begin{aligned}
1 \times 8 &= 10 - 2 \\
2 \times 8 &= 20 - 4 \\
3 \times 8 &= 30 - 6 \\
4 \times 8 &= 40 - 8
\end{aligned}
$$

There are patterns not only within each of the two sets of relationships, but also between the two sets, and children can investigate, creating other similar patterns. Both patterns can be explained in terms of the 'ten-ness' of the number system and the use of the distributive principle. Thus,

$$
\begin{aligned}
2 \times 9 &= 2 \times (10 - 1) = (2 \times 10) - (2 \times 1) = 20 - 2 \\
3 \times 9 &= 3 \times (10 - 1) = (3 \times 10) - (3 \times 1) = 30 - 3
\end{aligned}
$$

and so on. Children must always be challenged to find out and decide if a pattern 'goes on for ever'. As later examples show, this is not always the case.

The following pattern is often to be found in the 'puzzle' section of textbooks, suggesting that it is something exceptional, rather than an example of pattern that is commonplace in the study of mathematics.

$$(1 \times 9) + 2 = 11$$
$$(12 \times 9) + 3 = 111$$
$$(123 \times 9) + 4 = 1\,111$$
$$(1234 \times 9) + 5 = 11\,111$$

When patterns are as complex as this, it is essential that children check that each relationship holds true, perhaps using a calculator, before looking to extend the pattern and checking as they go along. As the above pattern is more complex than some of the previous ones, so is the explanation. Often, it is only necessary to take one of the relationships to develop a generalized 'proof'. In this case, $(1234 \times 9) + 5$ is rearranged as:

$$((1111 + 111 + 11 + 1) \times 9) + 5$$
$$= \quad (9999 + 999 + 99 + 9) + (1 + 1 + 1 + 1 + 1)$$
$$= \quad 10\,000 + 1000 + 100 + 10 + 1$$
$$= \quad 11\,111$$

The method is sufficiently general to confirm that every relationship in the pattern is true. Helping children to appreciate the general nature of such methods is preparation for further development towards the concept of proof.

The reader may wish to challenge children to extend the above pattern as far as they can to show that it is finite, having only 9 relationships in it. Children quickly discover when the pattern fails to work and are able to offer an explanation why this is so. Below are four other patterns that break down after a number of steps.

$$(1 \times 9) - 1 = 08 \qquad\qquad (1 \times 8) - 1 = 07$$
$$(21 \times 9) - 1 = 188 \qquad\qquad (21 \times 8) - 1 = 167$$
$$(321 \times 9) - 1 = 2\,888 \qquad\qquad (321 \times 8) - 1 = 2\,567$$
$$(4321 \times 9) - 1 = 38\,888 \qquad (4321 \times 8) - 1 = 34\,567$$

$$1 \times 1 = 1 \qquad\qquad 12 \times 21 = 21 \times 12$$
$$11 \times 11 = 121 \qquad\qquad 12 \times 42 = 21 \times 24$$
$$111 \times 111 = 12321 \qquad\qquad 12 \times 63 = 21 \times 36$$
$$1111 \times 1111 = 1234321 \qquad 12 \times 84 = 21 \times 48$$

Children should always be asked to discover when a pattern breaks down and attempt to give a reason why this occurs.

THE ASSESSMENT OF PATTERN

The chapter to this point has been concerned with patterns in number, and has shown how the patterns common in children's textbooks can be used to reveal the underlying structures within the number system which give rise to them. By doing so, the first part of the chapter has complemented the analyses of number pattern found in several other chapters in the book.

The chapter now takes an abrupt turn, because in considering the assessment of number patterns in the primary years the domain of concern is broadened to include not only the patterns considered in the first part of the chapter, but also the other kinds of number pattern treated in the other parts of the book. There is also a change in style. This is partly the effect of the broadened coverage, since the assessment section makes points about many kinds of pattern and is more general and less detailed. The contrast in style also reflects a difference in concerns between teaching and assessment when each is considered in isolation, assessment being by and large reactive, whereas teaching is, or should be, proactive.

In order to maximize the value obtained from teaching activities on pattern, there has to be assessment of what children know and can do. Assessment can serve a number of different purposes within the broad context of the 'educational process', but in this chapter we focus on the main one, agreeing with Gipps (1994, p. 3) that 'the prime purpose of assessment is ... to support the teaching/learning process'. The assessment of pattern should support the teaching and learning process in the kinds of activity described earlier, as well as those described in Chapter 5 and the kinds of situational patterns which occur as part of 'investigations' or 'problem-solving' in texts in the later primary years (see Chapter 8).

Assessments might be done summatively, to say what a child has learned as a result of teaching, or formatively, to give helpful information to assist teaching decisions. Either way, the assessment of pattern involves assessment of competences involved in the work children have done or will do. To say that someone has a competence to do something is to suppose that he or she will be able to do it reasonably reliably under a range of circumstances. The competences involved in pattern work in the primary years include the ability to:

- describe a pattern that has been seen or used;
- operate on a set of numbers to find a pattern;
- complete a pattern;
- extend a pattern to the next case, or a near case;
- calculate the value of specified cases in a pattern;
- extend a pattern to answer a problem;
- create a pattern with a given structure;
- use the rule for a pattern to characterize a specific case;
- locate the numbers in the situation and give them as a number pattern;
- move from a written to a symbolic expression of the perception of the pattern, or vice versa;
- explain the structure which has given rise to a pattern;
- use pattern to express relationships.

These competences develop through children working with patterns. However, the assessment of such competences often requires a very different kind of activity from that which may be used in developing them. The kinds of teaching activities outlined earlier in this chapter, for example, would not be suitable as contexts for assessment, as they are too divergent and exploratory. Assessment requires that children be set a specific task which requires one or more of the competences listed, so that a judgement might be made about it.

The assessment judgement is made by noting the children's responses and making an inference about their competence. Assessment judgements rely on there being a traceable connection between performance on an activity and underlying competence. This can be problematic, and as a result mistaken conclusions can be drawn, either by supposing from what occurred that children cannot do something which they can do, or by thinking that they are more capable than they are.

The importance of accurate assessment to the teaching/learning cycle, and to the educational process in general, is not in doubt, but it is essential to be clear about the difficulties involved. To examine this, we consider the assessment of some of the competences listed above, noting some of the issues that are raised by that example. These are reviewed to suggest a possible approach to assessing pattern in the primary years.

ASSESSING THE ABILITY TO DESCRIBE A PATTERN THAT HAS BEEN SEEN OR USED

One of the myths of assessment is that it is about whether someone can do something or not. In the case of the competence of describing patterns, this is doubtful. To make an assessment which answers the question 'Can they describe a pattern or can't they?', children's attempts at describing a pattern need to be clearly classifiable as successful and unsuccessful. Figure 6.13 gives an example of a question designed as an assessment of this competence. On this

Number of apples	Cost
1	11p
2	22p
3	33p
4	44p

Look for a pattern in the numbers.

Use the pattern to find the cost of 9 apples.

What is the pattern you used?

Figure 6.13 *'Apples' pattern context*

and the assessment question shown in Figure 6.14, data will be used which were collected by the authors from primary children answering the questions in a paper and pencil format. Some of the different responses which children gave to the question in Figure 6.13 were:

> Every time you just add one to the first and the second.
> When you times 11 by a number you get two digits which are the same, e.g. $11 \times 4 = 44$.
> I simply went $11 \times 9 = 99$.
> 11 22 33 44 55 66 77 88 99.
> Add the same number to the first number like $9 = 99$ or $6 = 66$.
> 11 time tables.

Some explanations are clearly 'better' than others, but it does not seem possible to divide them into two groups – those which are a description of a pattern and those which are not. It may be preferable to assess the competence in terms of the descriptions being at different levels – in other words the competence is not a matter of *whether* a child can describe a pattern, but *how well*. This is preferable but is still not easy. The first step is to have reasons for deciding which descriptions are better than others. Although in some cases it seems quite clear, there might be disagreement on, for example, whether 'I simply went $11 \times 9 = 99$' is a better explanation than '11 time tables' – one side may claim that the first description is explicit, concise, full and clear, where the second is vague and incomplete; the other side could then point out that what has been said is more a description of a numerical operation than a description of a pattern.

A further example is given as Figure 6.14. Here too there is diversity of response.

Write in the missing numbers to continue the patterns.

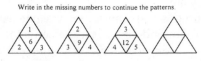

Explain how you worked out the missing numbers.

Figure 6.14 *'Triangles' pattern context*

In the middle I just $6 + 3 = 9, 9 + 3 = 12, 12 + 3 = 15$.

I looked at the numbers at the top first then I saw that one has been added so I added another one. For the middle number it went up in 3 so I added a 3.

The next number after $3 = 4.$ 6 9 12 is all the 3 × table. $12 + 3 = 15.$ 2,3/ 3,4,/ 4,5 it must be 5,6 add them together $4 + 5 + 6 = 15$ correct.

Because they all went up by times.

The middle numbers go up by 3. When some numbers swaped places two times they went to the top.

Again there is variety in quality, but it is difficult to offer a rationale for placing even these few in an order. One feasible approach may be to create distinct bands of competence, with a series of categorized levels for pattern description, such as saying that descriptions that refer to usable general qualities are in the top band, those that give a procedural method are in the second, and those that just report features are in the third. Even then, the challenge remains to determine which level of competence each reply represents.

A further complication in attributing competence to children's descriptions is deciding on their significance, because of the difficulty some children have in articulating their perceptions of pattern. The problem of interpreting what children have written is not just a matter of spelling and grammar, although naturally they present difficulties enough where descriptions (of the patterns in Figure 6.14) are like this:

On the top I + 1, on botem left I did the sam and on the botem right I did the sam in the midel I + 3.

It is also a matter of understanding intent, as shown by this example (also on Figure 6.14):

When some numbers swaped places two times they went to the top.

There is then the further issue that some children report only a portion of what they notice, and their understanding is in advance of their expression of it. As a result, assessments may come to unflattering conclusions about children's ability to describe pattern just because they did not think to write or talk about the pattern, but chose instead to talk or write about a different part of the process. In this context, it might be noted that the assessment examples given are of children not merely describing patterns, but using them to do something, and reporting on that. This differs considerably from the experiences of pattern in textbooks, and is a specific example of the difference between good teaching activity and a revealing assessment task. Children interpret the word 'pattern' in a broad, 'common-sense' way, and asking about pattern in numbers is often treated by them as asking what they notice about the numbers, rather than implying a mathematical relationship, or governing rule. Asking 'How does this pattern work?' gives a large number of observational replies of the lower level, such as 'It is odds and evens' (see also Chapter 5). That does not mean that the children are unaware of the structure of the pattern. The progressive interview technique used for the research reported in Chapter 5, which provides the possibility of follow-up, extending, questions, such as saying 'Yes, anything else?', overcomes this, but is too time-consuming for everyday assessment. We have found, however, that when children have to use what they notice to do something, they are more likely to find the mathematical pattern in it. This is therefore a preferable approach to assessing the competence, although it is not by any means foolproof. When children are asked to explain what pattern they used, they may say, for example, 'The pattern I used was the same one as on the chart'. When they are asked to explain how they worked out the answers, they may say, for example, 'I looked at the numbers and continued the pattern'.

It may be concluded that some children have a greater understanding of pattern than is evident from their descriptions. It is for this reason that assessments are formulated in terms of competences, and there are few direct attempts to assess children's understanding of pattern. Poor descriptions may arise from not understanding the pattern, or from limited powers of description, but the competence does not distinguish between these, and any action taken as a result of assessment of the competence must act to develop both perception of pattern and the ability to articulate that perception.

THE ABILITY TO COMPLETE A PATTERN

A pattern can be understood well enough for a child to describe it, but this does not necessarily translate into the ability to work with it or operate on it. In the same way as describing a pattern, the competence of using pattern perception to do something with the numbers is far from being a yes/no affair. In this case, however, it is possible to specify a series of competences to do with the different actions that can be taken when working with or operating on patterns. The competence of completing a pattern is perhaps the simplest and most basic. Figure 6.15 shows a requirement to complete a simple number pattern.

Fill in what is missing in this pattern

$$1 + 5 = 6$$
$$2 + 4 = 6$$
$$3 + 3 = 6$$
$$\square + \square = 6$$
$$\square + \square = \square$$

Figure 6.15 *'Sixes' pattern context*

An issue that arises from such an assessment concerns the matter of validity in assessment: whether the task truly calls upon the competence about which a judgement is to be made. In other words, when children answer correctly, writing 4 and 2 in the first line of empty boxes, and 5, 1 and 6 in the second line, need they have seen the sequences and relationships as patterns, and had the patterns in mind when deciding what to write? Could they not have seen the first line as a distinct number sentence question, and happen to know that 4 and 2 make six, then make the last line add to 6 by association, holding up 6 fingers and seeing that there are 5 on one hand and 1 on the other hand, and represent that as the answer? Without asking the children to describe the pattern they used it is not possible to say.

A further issue concerns the level of difficulty of the 'pattern' used in the assessment, and the assumptions that can be made about the extent to which a competence assessed using one pattern will generalize to other patterns. The assessment task shown used a pattern with small numbers, and an addition operation. The ability to complete that pattern will not indicate the ability to complete any pattern at all. Yet unless there is some sense of generalizability, unless performance on one pattern can indicate a competence which gives the means to predict performance on others, there is no point in assessment. In this regard, the matter of type of pattern needs to be considered, and also the matter of the size and nature of the numbers. To what extent does an ability to complete patterns of the kind in Figure 6.15 imply an ability to complete other patterns? Would a child who was successful in the pattern in Figure 6.15 be able to complete a pattern with subtraction operations, or one which used larger numbers, or fractions?

It is clear that the competence could not be assumed to extend to all patterns, because they are so different. This also applies to all the other competences in the list, for similar reasons.

It follows that although the competences have been expressed in general terms ('the ability to ...'), it is in fact necessary to be more specific, and to give an indication of the range of pattern which is being assumed to be 'covered' in any case. To establish this range by assessment would require a large number of tasks, so it is usual for 'common sense' to be applied, and an assumption made which seems reasonable, based on experience of children's pattern-making. Sometimes this is done implicitly, so that 'the ability to complete patterns' is understood differently when it is applied to children of different ages.

THE ABILITY TO CONTINUE A PATTERN TO THE NEXT CASE, OR A NEAR CASE

A slightly more advanced competence in the domain of the application of pattern perception is that of continuing patterns to new cases. A simple example of this would be a sequence such as:

5   7   11   17   ☐   ☐

An issue which arises in the context of pattern extensions is: what counts as the correct answer? In order to say that a performance is evidence of a competence, there have to be clear criteria of acceptable evidence. When the answer is being considered, there has to be a notion of what is accepted as showing the competence. The answer that conforms to the pattern in the mind of the teacher or question-setter must certainly count as a correct answer. However, the question is whether that is the only possibility allowed, as the 'intended' answer is commonly not the only 'logical' possibility.

The expected answers to the sequence above are of course 25 and 35, as the constant difference between differences is 2, as shown in Figure 6.16. However, as the differences are

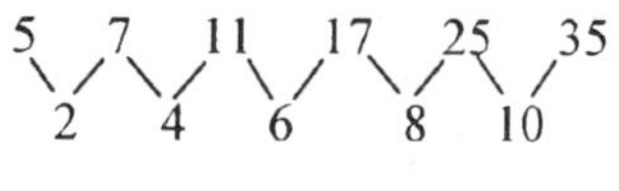

$$5 \quad 7 \quad 11 \quad 17 \quad 25 \quad 35$$
$$2 \quad 4 \quad 6 \quad 8 \quad 10$$

Figure 6.16 *Sequence showing constant differences between differences*

2, 4, 6 and 2 + 4 = 6 it could also be argued that the next difference should be 10, as 4 + 6 = 10, and the following difference should be 16, as 6 + 10 = 16, giving terms of 27 and 43 (see Figure 6.17). Alternatively, a child might see the sequence as having symmetry of differences, with the differences going 2 4 6 4 2, and the next two terms are then 21 and 23. Which of these

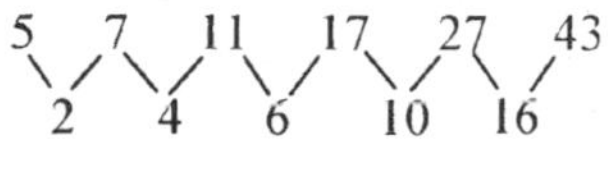

$$5 \quad 7 \quad 11 \quad 17 \quad 27 \quad 43$$
$$2 \quad 4 \quad 6 \quad 10 \quad 16$$

Figure 6.17 *Sequence showing additive differences between differences*

should be allowed? The more answers allowed as correct, the greater is the chance that some answers are given as a result of actions that do not represent the competence being assessed.

Another possible pattern perception which offers a strategy for continuing patterns is that of noticing a common property of the numbers, and using that. For example, children often see a sequence as odds and evens. In the sequence 5, 7, 11, 17, some children may notice that all the numbers are odd, and give two other odd numbers, perhaps 19 and 21. (They may even note that the numbers are all prime numbers, and give 19 and 23!) To count this as incorrect seems harsh, as what they have noticed is true, but it should not be considered as correct, as the way they have approached the task does not match the competence under consideration: they add further terms to the sequence, but do not do so by continuing a number pattern.

THE ABILITY TO EXTEND A PATTERN TO ANSWER A PROBLEM

Even though the use of pattern in problem-solving is only at an early stage in primary school, the relating of patterns to situations is an important step, and should not be neglected, either in teaching or in assessment. The two examples in Figures 6.18 and 6.19 show assessments of two variants of this competence, the ability to find a pattern adequate to the demand and the ability to use a pattern description to solve a problem. The problem in Figure 6.18 concerns

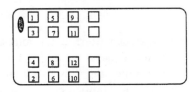

Figure 6.18 *'Bus seat' pattern context*

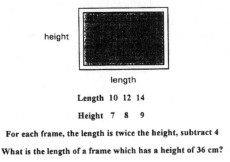

Figure 6.19 *'Picture frame' pattern situation*

the seating on a bus. The problem in Figure 6.19 concerns picture frames. Whenever assessments are placed in 'real' situations (although it should be acknowledged that in pattern work these are often contrived, as truly real situations are usually too complex) the issue that comes through most strongly is that of how the child understands the situation being presented. There are three major dimensions to this: language, context and demand.

Language

Confusing or over-ambiguous language is the *bête noire* of all assessment developers. It often seems that for every possible combination of words there are legions of children perversely determined to misunderstand. The use of the phrase 'window seat' in the bus question in Figure 6.18, for example, may not be understood by every child, but 'next to a window' would confuse others, and 'at the side' might be even worse. All that a question developer is able to do is avoid the obvious traps. For example, if the 'rule' for the picture frame question in Figure 6.19 had been 'The length is 4 less than the height doubled', not only is theuse of the word 'less' problematic, there is a fully ambiguous meaning, as it could mean $2H - 4$ or $2(H - 4)$. What has been used may not be perfect, but it is better.

Contexts

Assessments should be set in contexts with which children have at least a passing familiarity. Normally, it would be inappropriate to offer a pattern question set on a farm to children in some inner-city areas, for example. However, it is not possible to guarantee a common experience for children. It is therefore necessary to rely on a child's ability to generalize from one experience to another. As a result, the context of a bus may not be problematic, even when some of the children answering it have never travelled on a bus.

Again, a question developer can only avoid the more obvious errors. For example, if the context for a set of relationships between two dimensions had been given as the cross-sectional area of different load-bearing supports, many children would not have been able to see the pattern past the context. This would lead to under-performance which would obscure the children's pattern competence.

Demands

Success on any task is not the simple matter of exhibiting one competence. All tasks call on a range of knowledge and skills. There is a problem for assessment when some of the skills required for a task are at a higher level than the competence being assessed, or where it is not reasonable to suppose that the other required skills are automatically available. The most commonly used objections to paper and pencil assessments concern reading demands, where children with the competences being assessed do not succeed because they are unable to read the question. However, there are other kinds of demands within tasks which can also prevent a fair assessment. For example, in the picture frames context, Figure 6.19, if the values used for the frames were accurate measurements, involving decimal fractions, such as 11.4 cm and 18.8 cm, then some children may have been prevented from accessing the pattern aspect.

THE ABILITY TO CALCULATE THE VALUE OF SPECIFIED CASES IN A PATTERN

In situations where there is a variable, it is helpful to assign a variable value to the different instances of the situation, i.e. to designate the first, second and third cases, and so on. Even the simplest patterns can be assigned a variable value on the basis of position. In Chapter 2, an example was given of assigning ordinal values to a repeating pattern of coloured shapes

(Figure 2.7), and asking questions such as 'What colour will shape 100 be?' This principle is often used in simple number patterns, referring, for example, to the first, second and third triangle numbers, as in Figure 6.20, and asking what the hundredth triangle number is. It is

Total	3	6	10
Triangle number	1	2	3

Figure 6.20 *Triangle numbers*

What is the total number of blocks and rods needed to make a 100 storey model?

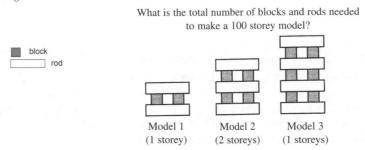

Model 1	Model 2	Model 3
(1 storey)	(2 storeys)	(1 storeys)

Figure 6.21 *'Construction' pattern context*

also applicable to simple situations, such as the 'construction' pattern in Figure 6.21. The ability to calculate the value of a particular case is the first and simplest competence of several concerned with the ability to cope with variables in situations. It is normally the only part to be assessed at primary level. Others, such as the ability to find an expression or rule for the general term, are considered beyond the capacities of all but the most mathematically advanced primary children.

However, the very fact that this is a new and difficult domain brings particular issues, as there is a tendency for assessments to be 'softened', so that they are not 'off-putting'. In particular, the assessments very often ask for particular cases in 'stages'; for example, asking for the tenth, then the twentieth, then the fiftieth (and then perhaps the nth), echoing a common approach in teaching. Again, however, what is best for teaching is not always best for assessment, and the 'staged' questioning leads children to use a step-by-step counting approach, going by way of the fifth, sixth and seventh to the tenth and perhaps the twentieth, but usually then giving up on the fiftieth. In other words, the children are using the competence of continuing a pattern to arrive at the answer, which means that the item is not assessing the competence of calculating a specified term. Asking for the value of the hundredth case, or similar, as the first question is therefore preferable in assessment terms, as the competence, if there, will be more likely to be shown.

It is also vital to pay attention to the level of difficulty of the pattern when assessing this competence. This is because calculating the value of a specified term relies on an intuitive understanding of the relationship between the dependent and independent variables, and this is much more difficult for some patterns than others. For example, the pattern in the constructions in Figure 6.21 is linear, and many primary children are able to calculate the hundredth term by reasoning that for any model there are twice as many of the 'blocks' as the model number (200), and one more of the 'rods' (101), giving a total of 301. They do not fare as well with the value of the fiftieth triangle number, because it is a quadratic relationship, and similar concrete reasoning is less likely to occur (see subsequent chapters).

SUMMARY: THE LIMITS TO ASSESSMENT OF PATTERN

From a review of the preceding discussion, the following conclusions can be drawn:

- a pattern competence is often not a matter of 'whether' or 'if' but of 'to what extent';
- pattern competences are not general, they have to be related to a range of applicability in terms of the numbers and type of patterns involved;
- it is difficult to guarantee that any assessment task requires the pattern competence which is under consideration;
- it is not possible to guarantee that children will answer the assessment question using the competence under consideration;
- there is no unambiguous evidence for any pattern competence;
- any assessment question on pattern might have characteristics that lead to misunderstanding and undeserved failure by the children being assessed, and it is not possible to say for sure whether it has occurred.

In addition, what a child does on a particular occasion may not truly reflect their ability in that area because of any number of factors that are independent of the assessment itself, such as unintended help, distraction, copying, illness and so on.

CONCLUSION: HOW TO APPROACH THE ASSESSMENT OF PATTERN IN THE PRIMARY YEARS

If assessment is to perform its function of supporting the teaching and learning process, it is important to understand the limits of assessment described above, and to allow for it in the actions that are undertaken. This is a matter both of what is done as assessment and what decisions are taken as a result of it.

On the first aspect, it is important to pay attention to the demands of each assessment task, which are partly ensuring that the question fits the competence to be assessed by it, but also working on the language and other demands of the task, so that as far as possible a child with the competence will succeed where one without it will not. Having said that, it is necessary to accept that this is impossible. Any one assessment question will have characteristics that prevent it, and these are unavoidable to a certain extent: language is ambiguous because of the way language works, not because the right words have not yet been found; children will find other ways to answer a question because they act on what they notice, not because the question did not make the task sufficiently clear.

The decisions made as a result of assessment tasks concerning pattern fall into two categories: first, the assessment judgements; second, the decisions about teaching.

Assessment judgements

With the impossibility of a perfect assessment item, the first thing to ensure is that all assessment judgements about pattern are made on the evidence of several different questions. The ambiguities of each separate item have to be accepted, but as long as each is likely to be the source of misunderstanding for only some children, it is reasonable to assume that the overall effect on the total performance is not disastrous for any one child. In other words, some children might misunderstand some pattern questions and others misunderstand others, but overall no particular child misunderstands a significant number more or less than another, so the effect is assumed to 'balance out' in the overall performance. Even then, however, it would be a mistake to treat the assessment judgement as proven. It is much better to treat all assessment judgements as provisional, as working hypotheses, and accept the possibility that further evidence may come to light which changes the judgement.

The second consequence of the limits to pattern assessment on the assessment judgements should be to ensure that the judgement is specific about the competence which is taken to have been demonstrated. Success on an assessment item which is an example of assessment of the ability to continue a pattern does not show that the child has a generalized competence to continue all patterns. The other elements of the assessment item need to be considered to suggest what is the likely scope of the competence manifested in the assessment, e.g. completing linear sequences with whole numbers under 100.

Decisions about teaching

A corollary of taking assessment judgements as provisional is to make all teaching decisions reversible, and that should be kept in mind throughout what follows.

There are two kinds of teaching decisions which are made on the basis of assessment judgements. One is structural, about teaching strategies such as grouping and planning. The other is procedural, about teaching tactics, the detail of what to do and what to say in the classroom situation.

Planning and grouping decisions about the teaching of pattern can be done on the basis of broad assessment judgements concerning pattern competences. Assessments which are done on the basis of a collection of assessment items, each of which assesses a different pattern competence, are appropriate to this purpose – and such an assessment could also form the basis for reporting on children's progress on a summary document like an attainment record, and even a normative comparison of children, to rank order them. This kind of teaching decision can therefore be served by an assessment of prepared items about pattern that are appropriate to the age group. There may even be commercially produced assessments of pattern that would meet this need.

The kind of information which is useful to guide teaching decisions about which pattern tasks to use with a particular group of children at a particular time, or how to approach the teaching of a pattern topic, is not given by broad summary assessments. The assessment judgements which are required are those that relate directly to the work to be done, and even if one of the items in the broad assessment is relevant, it is a mistake to act on the evidence of one item.

There is therefore no alternative to teachers making their own assessments to provide the information that is needed to inform the teaching decision. This demands that the teaching programme has specific intentions and traceable characteristics which can be seen in terms of specific pattern competences, including not only the form of ability to be developed, but a notion of the type of pattern to be included and the size of the numbers to be used. These assessments will therefore be similar in many ways to the teaching materials, except that they will be less exploratory and divergent, and more focused on specifics, with set tasks. It is therefore feasible to adapt some of the teaching materials to serve assessment ends, which should ensure that the information provided is helpful.

However, assessment of pattern has value only if the teaching of pattern is contingent. If the teacher will do the same thing whatever the result of assessment, there is no point in the assessment. For assessment to have its greatest value, therefore, the teacher should be clear about the effects of an assessment judgement before the assessment is done. A definite set of conditional relationships should exist for each competence to be assessed. On each one, if the children are judged to have the competence beyond a given level, then teaching will follow one path, but if not then it will happen in a different way. If these relationships are not there, a great deal of time can be spent making assessment judgements to no purpose. Equally, if the limits to assessment which were described earlier are ignored, then a great deal of time can be spent doing assessment activities which do not lead to a usable assessment judgement.

The assessment of pattern has a great deal to offer to the teaching and learning of number pattern in the primary years, but this benefit will not be an automatic outcome of administering some pattern assessment items. It requires diligence and attention to detail, but most importantly an approach to teaching which will be affected by assessment results.

Chapter 7

Pattern and the Approach to Algebra

Anthony Orton and Jean Orton

PATTERN AS A ROUTE INTO ALGEBRA

Most children and adults have always seemed to find algebra intellectually unpalatable. Algebra is a 'branch of mathematics which remains a mystery to many adults' (HMI, 1979, p. 129). There may be several identifiable reasons for this, yet these reasons are probably also inextricably linked together. The quality and quantity of learning which ensue from experiences presented in any way are dependent on two interrelated factors, namely the level of conceptual difficulty of the subject matter, and the motivation and attitude of the student. The degree of abstractness of what is to be learned appears to be a strong determinant of conceptual difficulty, at least in mathematics, and the intrinsic interest and meaningfulness of the material presented both affect willingness to learn. Thus, algebra loses out on all counts. Many children just cannot seem to make sense of using letters for numbers. The demands of taking this step away from the relative concreteness of numbers and towards a greater degree of abstraction seem to be too much for them to handle intellectually, and, what is more, there is no incentive to work hard at mastering what is perceived as bearing no relationship to the world of day-to-day experiences. As Cockcroft (1982, p. 60) put it, 'algebra is a source of considerable confusion and negative attitudes among pupils'. The critical question is therefore whether new routes into algebra can be found which lead to an improvement in this unhappy situation.

Mason *et al.* (1985b) have described four different roots of algebra, and have at the same time suggested these four as routes into algebra. One of these roots was described as 'expressing generality'. During the past ten years or more, the use of number patterns has become a popular route into expressing generality within school mathematics curricula. Thus, for example, presented with the number pattern 1, 4, 7, 10, ... , children nowadays might be expected first to continue the pattern for a few more terms, then to predict the twentieth or fiftieth number, then to describe the pattern in words and finally to predict what the nth number will be, where n is any number. Younger and weaker children might succeed only on the first step, but many others might find all but the last step within their capabilities. Both teaching experience and research data have confirmed the difficulty of this final step. Thus, as an approach to algebra, it is reasonable to ask to what extent children are able to perceive, understand and generalize a wide variety of patterns of numbers. Just how successful is this new route?

CHILDREN'S COMPETENCE WITH NUMBER PATTERNS

One of the earliest sources of information about pupils' capabilities in extending and understanding number patterns comes from the Assessment of Performance Unit's (APU's) Monitoring in Mathematics project throughout the period from 1978 to 1982. In APU (undated, p. 416) we find the statement that

> Finding terms in number patterns gets progressively more difficult the further the terms are from those given in the question,
>
> More pupils can continue a pattern than can explain it,
>
> Number pattern rules are described by a large proportion of pupils in relation to differences between terms,
>
> Generally, oral explanations of rules ... are given by more pupils than can write an explanation.

Pupils were not expected to produce a formula for the general, or *n*th, term.
The four number patterns reported on by the APU were:

(1) 1, 2, 4, 8, ... , ... ,   (2) 1, 3, 6, 10, ... , ... ,
(3) 1, 4, 9, 16, ... , ... ,   (4) 1, 1, 2, 3, 5, ... , ...

For the fifteen-year-old pupils, this was the order of difficulty, but the eleven-year-olds as a group had greater success on the second than on the first. The expected responses, and corresponding facilities, are shown in Table 7.1. In sequence (1), many more eleven-year-olds (23 per cent) than 15-year-olds (11 per cent) chose 10, 12 or 8 as the next number, presumably by

Table 7.1 *Facility levels for the four APU questions*

	Expected response	Age 11 (% correct)	Age 15 (% correct)
1	16, 32	48	82
2	15, 21	60	77
3	25, 36	41	64
4	8, 13	14	37

focusing their attention on only some rather than all the given numbers and using differencing. In sequences (2) and (3) there was little evidence of common errors, but in (4), which was much more obscure than the other patterns, 7 was quite common, followed either by 9 or by 10. Further, as the sequences became more demanding, more pupils generalized from only some of the data; thus, 46 per cent of the eleven-year-olds and 31 per cent of the fifteen-year-olds did this for the Fibonacci sequence.

The questions which arise from these relatively early APU studies perhaps start with what the pupils were expected to do to continue the sequences. How were the pupils expected to work out what was required in each case? In sequence (1), the pupils were presumably expected to notice that it was based on doubling, and thus a quick and correct solution depended on accurate perception and not on any particular method, whether taught or otherwise. But clearly some pupils, particularly younger ones, did not see the underlying structure of the sequence, and embarked on the use of the method of differencing, which then appears to have led them astray. Why did these pupils try to use differencing? Is that what they had been taught to do? Is differencing the fallback method for many pupils? Is differencing the only method available to some pupils? In the second and third sequences, however, differencing can be helpful, and it is perhaps not surprising that the younger pupils achieved considerable success here. It is also significant that more fifteen-year-olds than eleven-year-olds described the pattern of (3) in terms of squaring or multiplying by itself, although the predominant method used even by the older pupils was still based on the pattern of differences, namely the odd numbers 3, 5, 7, ... In other words, is there a suggestion that many older pupils are much less dependent on differencing than are younger pupils? On the final sequence, differencing is once again of little use, and success rates were comparatively low. In fact, the majority of pupils who answered correctly were able to state fairly clearly that you add the previous two numbers. Most other pupils were not able to provide coherent responses.

METHODS USED BY CHILDREN IN LINEAR PATTERNS

The issue of methods used by pupils in dealing with number patterns is an important one, especially if this is one of the major routes to algebra. There is no chance of pupils being able to generalize correctly and in any acceptable algebraic form if they cannot adopt appropriate methods. Differencing is clearly popular with children, and this suggests that a relatively simple form of number sequence is the linear type, because the difference is constant, as in the sequence 1, 4, 7, 10, ..., quoted earlier, which has common difference 3. Stacey (1989) has described the findings of research studies with pupils aged nine to thirteen years which were based entirely on linear generalizing problems. Some of the problems used were set within pictorial contexts, which means they are more rightly the subject of Chapter 8 of this book, but the methods used by pupils were not affected by whether there was a pictorial context or not. The three tasks gave rise, respectively, to the general terms $3n + 2$, $4n - 1$ and $6n - 2$. The first research study involved only primary school pupils (aged nine to eleven), and analysis revealed four methods, described by Stacey as counting method, difference method, whole-object method and linear method. The counting method only applied when based on pictures, and is self-explanatory. The difference method was based on identifying the common difference and then multiplying it by the term number; thus, the twentieth term of the sequence 1, 4, 7, 10, ... would be 3×20. In other words, Stacey's difference method comprised more than simply using differences to extend the sequence one term at a time. We have adopted the term difference product for this method, as being rather more descriptive of what the pupils actually did. The whole-object method involved the assumption that, for example, the twentieth term would be 4 times the fifth term; that is, 4×13 in this example. Naturally, this method works when the rule is of direct proportion, but it does not work otherwise. For this, and because the pupils are clearly looking for a quick method, we have adopted the term short-cut. The linear method was the one in which it was acknowledged that both multiplication and addition were involved, and use of this method should have always led to the correct answer. There were many examples of pupils mixing methods, perhaps by starting off correctly, but then switching to the difference product or short-cut method to complete the task more quickly.

In the second research study, it was anticipated that the secondary school pupils (aged eleven to thirteen) would fare somewhat better, because it was believed that exposure to certain secondary school topics would provide helpful experiences. However, the same four methods were evident. Counting was more likely to be abbreviated by using successive addition, but it was still assumed to be the same basic method. One interesting feature was the changing of methods between 'near generalizing' tasks (e.g. twentieth term) and 'far generalizing' tasks (e.g. hundredth term). 'Nearly one in seven of those who used a linear method for the near generalization swapped to a whole-object [short-cut] method for the far generalization' (Stacey, 1989, p. 155). Not only was mixing evident within tasks, it was evident between tasks and within students. A mix of short-cut and difference product methods was not common, but it did occur. Many pupils were also observed to move from a correct linear model to a direct proportion model for harder parts of the question. Of course, although it might seem that these secondary pupils had learned little from their more recent mathematical studies, it is all too easy for anyone to fall back on familiar methods which they have used at an earlier stage and which they have always believed were appropriate. Another explanation of the incorrect and inappropriate features of methods is that pupils had difficulty holding all the data about a particular problem in their minds, and in the later steps overlooked certain information. In short, the methods commonly used were the same in all age groups, although the proportions of pupils of different ages using them varied. Constant differences were usually recognized, and were often used accurately by the secondary pupils.

USING DIFFERENCES

The use of differences is clearly a popular approach to linear number patterns, which have already been described as being relatively simple, though no evidence has yet been provided for that statement. Linear sequences produce constant first differences, and can be built up using that property, thus:

```
1      4      7      10      13      16
    3      3      3      3       3
```

and therefore the next number is $16 + 3 = 19$. Quadratic sequences, such as the square numbers, are more complicated, and differencing does not produce constants until the second differences:

```
1      4      9      16      25      36
    3      5      7      9       11
       2      2      2      2       2
```

However, children do often recognize the first differences as the odd numbers, a pattern with which they should have become very familiar throughout the years of schooling, and this appears to help them to extend the sequence of square numbers without them necessarily being conscious of the constancy of the second differences. Another very familiar quadratic pattern in school mathematics is the triangle numbers:

```
1      3      6      10      15      21
    2      3      4      5       6
       1      1      1      1       1
```

Again, this differencing process does help children to extend the number sequence, although it may be that the regularity of the first differences is what enables continuation, and not the constant second difference. This sequence, though common in school mathematics, because it arises from a variety of different topics, is not obviously a quadratic pattern – that is, a pattern involving squares of numbers – which makes the search for the general term more difficult. These two forms, linear and quadratic, are particularly important in school mathematics, but the APU questions discussed earlier hint at the wider range of different kinds of number patterns which exist. Thus, another question concerns which kinds are valuable in the particular route into algebra that involves expressing generality.

Finding more terms in a sequence is, in fact, usually only the first step in the approach to algebra. The critical question is whether the children can find a rule for the general term, and a little thought about what the rules are in the three examples of linear and quadratic patterns analysed above should begin to raise questions in the minds of teachers about relative complexity. Mathematicians have a sophisticated, though not necessarily either short or easy, method at their disposal for dealing with number patterns. If constant differences first appear in the first difference row, then the rule is linear, of the form $N = an + b$. Then, for the linear example above, substitution of $(1, 1)$ and $(2, 4)$ for (n, N) produces two simultaneous equations which can be solved for a and b. If it is the second differences where constants appear, the rule is quadratic and of the form $N = an^2 + bn + c$. Thus, for the triangle numbers, substitution of $(1, 1)$, $(2, 3)$, and $(3, 6)$ for (n, N) produces three simultaneous equations which can be solved for a, b and c. If it is the third differences, then the rule is cubic, and of the form $N = an^3 + bn^2 + cn + d$, and substitution can again be used to produce four equations from which a, b, c and d may be determined, and this is where the procedure is beginning to become quite difficult. And so on for higher powers. When, if ever, should children be provided with this information? Given that the procedure is not simple, particularly for other than linear patterns, is the rule of any value? And if we wish children to have even just some understanding of all that we attempt to teach, providing a rule might be considered unacceptable anyway, particularly since it is unneccessary for linear patterns. Subsequent studies in mathematics, including perhaps a graphical approach to calculus, should help to justify what to younger children would seem to be fact, to be learned by rote, so perhaps the 'rule' should not be introduced until it emerges as a consequence of rather more advanced work.

Linear patterns are the ones most commonly used in the approach to algebra within the eleven to thirteen age range. Quadratic patterns are usually thought to be less appropriate because the systematic study of the quadratic function has not yet taken place, but square numbers and other patterns involving squares of numbers have been encountered over a number of years. Thus, quadratic patterns are not entirely inappropriate. The difficulty raised by focusing exclusively on linear patterns is that they can be so easily extended by differencing, and thus the method of differencing is encouraged and the procedure reinforced. The pattern which is identified by differencing is what is often described as recursive, and does not lead naturally to an algebraic formula (see Tall, 1992), an issue to which we return below. The examples from APU quoted above do not include any linear patterns, but do include the two quadratic patterns described above. Thus, the existence of a variety of number patterns also introduces questions such as the relative difficulty of different sorts of sequences, and whether competence in solving number pattern problems applies uniformly across all kinds of pattern.

A STUDY OF CHILDREN'S PATTERNING

A major study of children's patterning has been carried out by the authors (Orton and Orton, 1996), in which over 1000 pupils completed a written test, and 30 of these pupils were also interviewed about their written responses. (The interviews incorporated additional tasks based on matchstick patterns, the outcomes of which are discussed in Chapter 8.) This project was preceded by a pilot study involving over 300 pupils, which enabled improvement to the test and to the procedures, but which also produced valuable evidence confirming and extending the work of Stacey (1989). In the main study, five different kinds of sequences were used, namely strings, cycles, tables, linear and quadratic. Here, the term 'strings' refers to linear patterns based on simple number sequences, whereas 'linear' refers to the same kinds of sequences but set within tasks where there is an obvious functional relationship. The strings were included partly to provide some simple tasks at the beginning of a fairly lengthy test, but also to see what they would reveal about children's patterning abilities. Tabular number patterns were of two forms: 'cycles', in which the data incorporated a cyclic property, and 'tables', where no cyclic property was present. The 'quadratic' patterns were like the square and triangle numbers described above. These five different kinds enabled comparisons to be made in terms of the ability to complete or continue number patterns, but also provided a great deal of information about each type individually. Words such as 'pattern', 'sequence' and 'algebra' were not used in the test, and the language was kept as elementary as possible throughout.

There were five strings, shown in Figure 7.1 as questions 1 to 5. The reader will easily see that these five are, respectively, linear, linear, quadratic, doubling and ... something rather

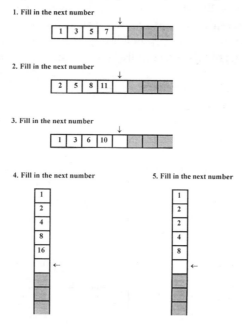

Figure 7.1 *The five 'strings'*

unusual which caused real problems for the children. This last sequence was devised on the basis of two starting numbers, 1 and 2, and then subsequent numbers were calculated as the product of the previous two, analogous to the Fibonacci sequence but using multiplication instead of addition. The facilities (percentages correct) for the five strings are shown in Table 7.2, where the two columns for sequence 5 represent the percentages answering 32 and 8, respectively. Clearly, 32 was the expected answer, but so many children gave 8, a reasonable answer which can be justified by classifying the sequence as involving repetition, that it was thought important that the summary of results should not ignore the data concerning this alternative answer. These results reveal that the order of difficulty was as expected, that the

Table 7.2 *Facility levels for the five strings questions*

			Question number			
Age	1	2	3	4	5(32)	5(8)
10–11	98.6	97.3	70.1	59.9	6.8	36.1
11–12	98.6	97.1	83.1	72.1	10.6	40.8
12–13	99.3	98.2	92.8	86.1	21.3	35.3

pupils did find the quadratic question more difficult than the two linear, which were answered extremely well, and that the doubling question was really quite difficult for the younger pupils (cf. the APU results presented earlier). The data concerning question 5 clearly indicate that the older the pupils were, the more they were beginning to appreciate that the pattern was about multiplication. The most interesting feature of the wide variety of alternative responses to question 5 was that the most common other response was 12, which seems to have been based on repeating the previous difference. Many other incorrect responses were clearly based on trying to understand the pattern of differences. This preoccupation with differences was also revealed by the interviews, which exposed pupils who were unsuccessfully attempting to use differences in question 4, as well as question 5.

The three questions – 6 (numbers), 7 (shapes) and 15 (letters) – referred to collectively as cycles were isomorphic; that is, structurally all the same (see Figure 7.2). Although the main

6. Fill in the missing numbers

1	2	3	4
2	3		1
3	4	1	
	1	2	

7. Fill in the missing shapes

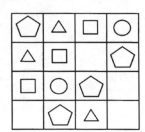

15. Fill in the missing letters

a	b	c	d
b	c		a
c	d	a	
	a	b	

Figure 7.2 *The .*

purpose of all the que.. .ons was to investigate levels of difficulty and methods used, one additional intention here was to try to ascertain whether the performance of the children varied according to whether numbers, shapes or letters were used. In fact, question 7 was the only one involving shapes in the entire test, and was included solely for comparison purposes. Question 15 was also deliberately well separated from the other two, to make it more difficult for pupils to perceive the identical structure. It was thought that it might prove to be substantially more difficult than either of the other two. In all three questions, the children were asked to fill in four missing elements, referred to in the analysis as (i), (ii), (iii) and (iv), relating respectively to the spaces taken in sequence left to right across the rows and down the columns, in the normal manner of reading. Facility levels are shown in Tables 7.3 to 7.5, from which it is clear that there was not much difference in difficulty level between the three patterns, and that overall the pupils coped very competently. The order of difficulty was generally as expected. Question 15, involving letters, was found to be the most difficult, with the

Table 7.3 *Facilities for the four parts of question 6*

		Question number		
Age	6(i)	6(ii)	6(iii)	6(iv)
10–11	97.9	95.2	92.5	91.2
11–12	97.3	96.6	95.0	91.8
12–13	98.9	99.1	96.6	94.4

exception that question 7(iv) produced slightly aberrant results, though the question was not found to be as difficult as had been anticipated. The interviews exposed several different pupil

Table 7.4 *Facilities for the four parts of question 7*

		Question number		
Age	7(i)	7(ii)	7(iii)	7(iv)
10–11	99.3	97.3	88.4	86.4
11–12	96.8	94.6	87.6	82.2
12–13	98.7	97.3	91.7	86.1

strategies being employed, however, with 'making sure there's one of each in each row' the most common. Some pupils argued that 'it can't be a square below a square' and similar, while others noticed the cyclic effect, 'like all in succession' and 'before 1 is 4'. Diagonal lines of the same element were noticed by a few, and the order of the elements in the diagonal lines was sometimes used.

Table 7.5 *Facilities for the four parts of question 15*

		Question number		
Age	15(i)	15(ii)	15(iii)	15(iv)
10–11	93.1	91.7	81.9	85.4
11–12	93.4	93.7	85.7	85.0
12–13	93.8	94.9	90.8	89.1

There were three questions which were collectively referred to as tables, and these are shown in Figure 7.3 as questions 12, 13 and 14. It was thought that all three would provide novel tests of patterning ability. Question 12 was based on multiplication modulo 10

12. Fill in the missing numbers

	2	4	6	8
2	4	8	2	6
4	8		4	2
6	2	4	6	
8		2	8	4

13. Fill in the missing numbers

	1	2	3	4
1	0	1	2	3
2	0	2	4	6
3	0		6	
4		4		12

14. Fill in the missing numbers

31	29	27	
9		5	23
11	1	3	21
13		17	19

Figure 7.3 *The three 'tables'*

operating on the set {2, 4, 6, 8}, a system which possesses the closure property, but this time the pattern is not cyclic. Question 13 was also based on multiplication, this time operating on the set {1, 2, 3, 4} and involving products of the form a × (b − 1). Question 14 was a spiral array of odd numbers from 1 to 31. The facility levels are shown in Tables 7.6 to 7.8, and these reveal that the three tables questions were found to be more difficult than the cycles.

Table 7.6 *Facilities for the three parts of question 12*

	Question number		
Age	12a	12b	12c
10–11	76.4	81.9	79.2
11–12	80.6	86.2	82.9
12–13	83.3	86.5	83.9

Table 7.7 *Facilities for the four parts of question 13*

	Question number			
Age	13a	13b	13c	13d
10–11	72.2	62.5	76.4	68.8
11–12	72.3	66.7	76.7	69.1
12–13	78.3	74.0	79.7	76.0

Table 7.8 *Facilities for the three parts of question 14*

	Question number		
Age	14a	14b	14c
10–11	68.1	36.8	60.4
11–12	63.9	27.9	54.8
12–13	71.6	37.6	64.7

Interviews revealed that many pupils answered question 12 by filling in the missing number in each row. Others thought of it as a multiplication table, and several pupils thus included the tens digit. A few pupils explained that 'you work it out like a times table but only use one number', but no one mentioned modular arithmetic (no longer taught?). Multiplication tables were also perceived in question 13, and pupils generally tackled the question by focusing on the number patterns in the columns, or perhaps in the rows. No one explained it as a combination table involving a product, or a subtraction and a product. Question 14 was found to be more difficult than the other two questions, and many pupils omitted parts, particularly the number in the second row. Pupils again focused on rows or columns, and interviews revealed that they generally did not see the spiral of odd numbers. The drop in performance level between the youngest and the middle age groups is interesting, but the oldest group show that the lost ground has been reclaimed.

Overall, the data from the strings, cycles and tables strongly hint at a number of fixations, such as the use of differencing as the standard approach, and focusing on rows and columns to the exclusion of other possible sources of pattern.

The two items based on linear functions, questions 16 and 17 on the test paper, each included a number of questions based on a problem situation. The items are shown here as Tasks 7A and 7B, and the facility levels are shown in Tables 7.9 and 7.10. Question 16 was intended to be relatively easy, and facilities were high except for the last part of the question, where, for example, only a quarter of the twelve- to thirteen-year-old pupils gave anywhere near acceptable answers involving n. Some children gave numerical answers, the most common being £18 from taking n as 9, and £28 from giving n the value 14, because

---

Task 7A

A bicycle hire firm charges £2 per hour to hire bicycles.

How much would it cost to hire a bicycle for (a) 4 hours, (b) 7 hours?

How much would it cost to hire a bicycle for 20 hours?

How much would it cost to hire a bicycle for 100 hours?

How can you work out the cost from the number of hours?

How many pounds would it cost to hire the bicycle for n hours?

'it's the fourteenth letter of the alphabet'. Interviews revealed some pupils who could manage an oral explanation but who did not feel able to write anything down. Written responses

---

Task 7B

Bobby has just got a new job selling encyclopaedias. His basic wage is £16 per week but he gets a bonus of £5 on top of this for every set of encyclopaedias that he sells.

In the first week he did not sell any encyclopaedias.
How much was he paid?

In the second week he sold 2 sets of encyclopaedias.
How much was he paid?

In the third week he sold 6 sets of encyclopaedias.
How much was he paid?

How much would Bobby be paid if he sold 20 sets in a week?

How much would Bobby be paid if he sold 100 sets in a week?

How can you work out the wage from the number of sets?

How many pounds would Bobby be paid if he sold n sets?

---

showed that more than 60 per cent of pupils were able to mention doubling or multiplication by 2. A few pupils used the answer for 20 hours to obtain the answer for 100 hours.

Table 7.9 *Facilities for the four parts of question 16 (task 7A)*

	Question 16 answers			
Age	First few	20th	100th	nth
10–11	95.2	89.0	74.5	1.4
11–12	95.7	89.1	79.2	10.4
12–13	97.7	94.1	87.8	25.6

Question 17 was, as expected, rather more difficult. The responses for 20 and 100 sets, somewhat intriguingly, yielded higher facilities for the ten- to eleven-year-olds than for the eleven- to twelve-year-olds, but these differences were not statistically significant. The facilities for the twelve- to thirteen-year-old year group were, however, significantly higher than for the other two groups, for all parts of the question, and there were significant increases in performance over the years for supplying an adequate answer for n sets. Individual interviews revealed the common use of short-cut methods like working out the wage for 20 sets by multiplying the wage for 4 sets by 5, or the wage for 100 sets by multiplying the wage for 20 sets by 5. Interviews also showed that pupils sometimes used several different methods within the same question; for example, using the 1, 6, 1, 6 pattern in the units digit and the double

Table 7.10 *Facilities for the four parts of question 17 (task 7B)*

	Question 17 answers			
Age	First few	20th	100th	nth
10–11	68.3	56.8	47.5	0.7
11–12	69.3	52.3	41.7	7.0
12–13	79.6	69.9	62.1	19.4

number pattern in the tens digit, but then switching to continued addition of 5 to obtain the wage for 20 sets, and then a short-cut method to obtain an answer for 100 sets.

The three items concerning quadratic patterns, questions 9, 10 and 11, were all based on this triangular array of numbers:

```
                             1
                          2  3  4
                       5  6  7  8  9
                   10 11 12 13 14 15 16
                17 18 19 20 21 22 23 24 25
             26 27 28 29 30 31 32 33 34 35 36
          37 38 39 40 41 42 43 44 45 46 47 48 49
```

It was thought that this array would provide not only a novel approach, but also a rich source of number patterns, which it does, but the pilot experiment persuaded us to reduce the number of tasks because the pupils were not finding them easy. In fact, after the pilot testing it was thought that pupils might be handicapped by not understanding the structure of the number triangle, and how it was derived. Therefore, in the main study, it was decided that pupils should be asked to construct a similar number triangle themselves, with top row 4, second row 5, 6, 7 and so on. However, rather than helping to avoid misunderstandings, this tactic introduced new problems. Having acquired the facility to complete a number triangle similar to the one here, some children, it seemed, had become conditioned into adding more and more rows to the pattern. Certainly, the number of pupils using this tactic in questions 9, 10 and 11 was much greater than the pilot results would have suggested. Thus, as so often in education, an attempt to provide assistance had, for some children at least, introduced an unexpected and unwelcome effect.

Questions 9, 10 and 11 were based, respectively, on the diagonal line of numbers 1, 4, 9, 16, 25, 36, 49, the column of numbers 2, 6, 12, 20, 30, 42 and the diagonal line 1, 2, 5, 10, 17, 26, 37. Each of the three questions was of the form represented here by Task 7C, and the facilities for questions 9, 10 and 11 are shown in Tables 7.11 to 7.13.

Task 7C

Write down three things you notice about the list of numbers.

If there were more rows of numbers in the triangle what number would come next in the list?

What would be the 20th number in the list?

What would be the 100th number in the list?

Can you see a simple rule for working it out?

If so, what is this rule?

What would be the nth number in the list?

Table 7.11 *Facilities for the four parts of question 9*

	Question 9 answers			
Age	Next	20th	100th	nth
10–11	46.9	4.1	4.1	0.0
11–12	45.7	16.2	12.4	4.1
12–13	64.4	28.2	21.3	15.4

Table 7.12 *Facilities for the four parts of question 10*

	Question 10 answers			
Age	Next	20th	100th	nth
10–11	45.9	3.4	0.7	0.0
11–12	52.0	3.8	1.8	0.7
12–13	61.3	14.0	8.8	7.2

Table 7.13 *Facilities for the four parts of question 11*

	Question 11 answers			
Age	Next	20th	100th	nth
10–11	45.5	0.0	0.0	0.0
11–12	36.6	0.5	0.2	0.2
12–13	45.9	2.3	0.9	2.5

In general, these quadratic questions proved very difficult for the children. About one-half of them managed to give the next number in each sequence, but the many arithmetical errors reduced the facilities for the twentieth and hundredth numbers, and few could cope with the nth term. More than half of all the pupils omitted the question about a simple rule for the first sequence, and this rose to about 80 per cent for the third sequence. Where the facilities for the ten to eleven age group were higher than for the eleven to twelve age group, they were again not statistically significant. The written responses to what was noticed in each pattern showed that many children focused on the differences between successive terms, or described what was noticed in terms of addition. It is perhaps not unreasonable to conclude that this approach of asking pupils to find more terms in the sequences was not a productive way of attempting to elicit the general term.

In relation to what the pupils actually noticed, the alternate pattern of odd and even numbers in the first sequence was widely recognized. Many pupils who wrote 'square numbers' for the first sequence, or who wrote '$1 \times 1, 2 \times 2, 3 \times 3, ...$' did not use this in the calculation of the twentieth and hundredth terms. The individual interviews confirmed that many mixed methods were used. For example: addition of the next odd number followed by a short-cut method; working out the tenth as 10×10 and then using a short-cut; using successive addition of odd numbers for the twentieth and then a rule like 'add a zero' for the hundredth. Rules were sometimes given and then not used. Idiosyncratic responses included using the pattern of the units digit (1, 4, 9, 6, 5, 6, 9, 4), and describing each number in relation to doubling the one before ($9 = 4 + 4 + 1, 16 = 9 + 9 - 2$). Some pupils could not remember how they had obtained their written responses.

For the second sequence, about half of the pupils mentioned that the numbers in the list were all even. Very few pupils, and none in the youngest year group, interpreted the numbers as $1 \times 2, 2 \times 3, 3 \times 4, ...$, so it is not surprising that the facility for giving the nth term is low. One girl who had put 'rectangle numbers' on the written paper could not remember what she meant when she was later interviewed. Short-cut methods were mentioned by some pupils, though they were not written down. It is clear that such erroneous methods are not confined to linear patterns. Considering the relative simplicity of the product rule for the sequence $1 \times 2, 2 \times 3, 3 \times 4, ...$, it was considered surprising that most of the children could make so little sense of the pattern expressed in the form 2, 6, 12, ...

The third sequence was certainly found to be more difficult than the other two. Few pupils, and certainly none of those interviewed, noticed any relationship between the numbers in the list and the square numbers. There were frequent mentions of addition and of differences in what pupils noticed, though about 30 per cent of the pupils did not attempt to answer this part. Most children again seemed well able to focus on sums and differences, and on the way terms increase or decrease, but it seems it is a big step for pupils to relate each term to its position in numerical order, or to a number outside the sequence itself. Considering that this sequence is so little removed from the basic square numbers, the results were considered very disappointing.

STAGES AND LEVELS

Several attempts were made to investigate stages in the development of the children's patterning abilities. An earlier study (discussed in more detail in the next chapter) had revealed that the capabilities of adults answering quadratic pattern questions in an examination situation could be classified in stages. The four questions which made up the item in that earlier study involved stating the next, tenth, fiftieth and *n*th term in a sequence based on dot patterns. If a student was able to answer a particular question he or she was always able to answer all the previous questions, and thus the stages of development were:

Stage 0: no progress.
Stage 1: next term provided.
Stage 2: next and tenth terms provided.
Stage 3: next, tenth and fiftieth terms provided.
Stage 4: next, tenth, fiftieth and *n*th terms provided.

This was a deceptively simple classification which proved difficult to apply to the work with children, involving as it did both linear and quadratic patterns. One reason was that the adults were only required to state answers under examination conditions, while the children were encouraged to elaborate, particularly in the quadratic items. Thus, in analysing the children's responses, a wide variety of statements had to be interpreted and classified. Another reason was that it was not always the case that a correct hundredth term had followed a correct twentieth term. It was difficult to know what to do with pupils who provided a creditable response to the *n*th term but who had not provided a correct twentieth or hundredth term or both. Particular difficulties arose at stage 4; for example, pupils who gave the correct *n*th term but omitted any written explanation and made an error on the hundredth term. In fact, it was decided that the classification of responses concerning stage 4 warranted several substages, e.g.

Stage 4a: a correct verbal statement.
Stage 4b: a creditable attempt at an algebraic expression.
Stage 4c: a correct algebraic representation, but not necessarily the simplest.

These classifications, and the data in Tables 7.14 and 7.15, nevertheless do provide some information about the stages that pupils had reached on the two linear questions. Progression through the three years is self-evident. The percentages for stage 4c indicate that a small but growing number of pupils is able to present an adequate algebraic representation. And the percentages of pupils within stage 4 reveal quite rapid and continuous progress in the ability to describe verbally or algebraically or both in question 16, and significant progress between Years 7 and 8 in question 17. The evidence we have suggests that a verbal description is often available to pupils when an algebraic statement is not. If pupils are to be moved on from the verbal description, whole-class discussion may be the most appropriate route.

Table 7.14 *Stages reached by pupils on question 16 (task 7A)*

Age	Stage							
	4c	4b	4a	4	3	2	1	0
10–11	1.4	0.0	54.5	55.9	23.4	11.7	6.2	2.8
11–12	8.5	1.9	57.0	67.4	16.1	8.7	5.9	1.9
12–13	21.6	4.0	53.8	79.4	11.7	4.0	3.8	1.2

Attempts to use a similar procedure with the quadratic questions proved less satisfactory, because so few pupils were able to progress beyond stage 1 in questions 10 and 11. Thus, a different procedure was adopted in which pupils' responses to what was noticed were placed at one of four levels:

Table 7.15 *Stages reached by pupils on question 17 (task 7B)*

Age	4c	4b	4a	4	3	2	1	0
				Stage				
10–11	0.7	0.0	23.0	23.7	23.7	14.4	21.6	16.5
11–12	5.0	2.0	21.6	28.6	17.6	8.8	27.1	17.8
12–13	14.4	4.8	26.3	45.5	21.0	7.8	17.4	8.3

Level 0: no progress at all.

Level 1: pupil noticed some properties of the numbers, with perhaps partial patterns described.

Level 2: pupil noticed a pattern but this was not described so as to allow the next number(s) to be derived.

Level 3: pupil knew how to derive the next number(s) using patterns extrapolated from the differences.

Level 4: pupil showed clear evidence of understanding the relationship, though an algebraic formula might not be articulated.

Thus, for question 9, 'some numbers are odd' and '16 and 36 are in the four times table' would be at level 1; 'odd even odd even ...' and 'differences are odd' would be at level 2; 'add 3, 5, 7, 9, 11, 13 and so on' and 'keep adding the next odd number' would be at level 3; and 'times the row number by itself' and '$1 \times 1, 2 \times 2, 3 \times 3, ...$' would be at level 4.

In the pilot test paper, pupils had been asked 'What can you say about the numbers that are in the list?', and many had confined their response to one observation. In order to obtain more information about what was actually noticed, the wording for the main study test was changed to 'Write down three things you notice about the numbers in the list'. This produced a wider range of observations, but then it was necesary for pupils to select which of their observations to use in the calculation of further terms. Individual interviews revealed the dangers of us wrongly assuming which method pupils were using to work out the next term. For example, some pupils noticed that the differences increased by 2 but used a counting on procedure based on an extension of the triangle to work out the next term. Others mentioned (in question 9) 'It goes up by 3, 5, 7, ...' but then focused on a different pattern (16, 36, 56, ...) and gave 56 as the next term. In fact, 8 per cent of all pupils answered 56. Individual interviews confirmed that some pupils who mentioned, for question 9 or 11, that the differences go up by consecutive odd numbers were not aware that this pattern would continue for further numbers in the sequence. For this reason, it was decided that level 3 should not be awarded to pupils who had spotted the difference pattern unless they were also able to give the next term correctly or had given sufficient evidence of the application of their difference method. It was recognized that there was a risk of allocating only level 2 to some pupils who had applied the difference method but made numerical errors, and that there was also a risk of allocating level 3 to pupils who had observed the difference pattern, not realizing that it could be extended, but had used some other method to achieve the correct answer.

Some responses to the questions revealed improvement – that is, a progression of levels through the three questions – although this could have been because of better use of language and not necessarily the development of understanding. There was also some indication of other pupils becoming tired of writing down observations. Certainly, for one reason or another, the number who left the observation section blank increased from 10 per cent in

Table 7.16 *Levels reached by pupils on question 9*

			Level			
Age	4 and 3	4	3	2	1	0
10–11	30.6	6.8	23.8	25.9	31.3	12.2
11–12	38.5	20.3	18.2	21.6	28.2	11.7
12–13	53.7	29.1	24.6	24.8	13.9	7.6

Table 7.17 *Levels reached by pupils on question 10*

			Level			
Age	4 and 3	4	3	2	1	0
10–11	24.7	0.7	24.0	40.4	20.5	14.4
11–12	37.6	5.4	32.2	35.8	14.9	11.7
12–13	47.1	13.1	34.2	31.9	7.9	12.9

Table 7.18 *Levels reached by pupils on question 11*

			Level			
Age	4 and 3	4	3	2	1	0
10–11	25.5	0.0	25.5	24.1	18.6	31.7
11–12	25.7	0.7	25.0	24.5	20.0	29.8
12–13	35.0	2.7	32.3	22.3	11.6	31.1

question 9 to 30 per cent in question 11. Using this classification system, Tables 7.16, 7.17 and 7.18 were obtained for the quadratic questions. The data here suggest that many pupils achieved some success with question 9, though it is startling that the numbers of pupils who did not recognize the square numbers were so high. Combining the facilities for levels 3 and 4 gives a good indication of how well pupils could cope with interpreting the number patterns, and clear progression through the age groups is evident.

CONCLUSIONS AND ISSUES

On the basis of the research studies by the APU (undated), by Stacey (1989), by Orton and Orton (1996) and by others who have conducted similar experiments and produced similar results (see Chapter 8), it is possible to begin to evaluate the approach to algebra through generalizing from number patterns. Clearly, the route through number patterns does not remove all difficulties concerning beginning algebra. This should not surprise us, given the long history of innovations in education which often solve some, but rarely solve all, of our problems, and which may of course at the same time reveal new problems. Nor should it disappoint us too much, as long as we can continue to make some progress towards improving the innovation, and through it our pupils' understanding and knowledge in mathematics. In any case, this route is only one of several possible routes, all of which should be considered when introducing algebra. What cannot be determined through the studies described in this chapter is whether number patterns present a more meaningful, and in that sense therefore a better, approach for some or all pupils than other methods of introducing algebra. The number pattern approach remains a justifiable route, as long as we accept its limitations and difficulties and can learn to circumvent the problems it introduces. In fact, the knowledge we now have of pupils' difficulties with the number pattern approach ought to enable us to make considerable improvements to it. Alongside both this new approach and more traditional approaches, however, we have also to reckon with the claims of the various computer-oriented approaches which are now available to teachers (see Sutherland, 1990, and Tall, 1992, for example). No approach can be ignored without conclusive evidence of harmful effects, if we are to get nearer to solving the problems of teaching algebra.

In relation to relative difficulty, we have clear evidence that pupils are more successful with linear patterns than with quadratic, and we can place a variety of pattern questions in order of difficulty. The widespread use of differencing by pupils, particularly the younger ones, stands out from all the studies of the number pattern approach. Given that this method leads to a recursive understanding of number patterns, which then does not necessarily lead the pupils to the general term in a recognizably algebraic form, we need to reconsider what tactics we encourage in the classroom. First, a number pattern does not automatically have to lead to differencing, but we may be encouraging differencing by some of the tasks we set. Second, there is nothing wrong with differencing as a mathematical activity, which ought to lead pupils to a greater understanding of the number pattern in question. However, if it is the general term we are seeking, we perhaps need to discourage differencing at that stage, and replace it with encouragement to look at all the properties of the particular number sequence under consideration. There is some evidence that older pupils are more ready to do this, which in a way might only be revealing that older pupils are more able to cope with this approach to algebra, and this reinforces the view held by many that we attempt to begin algebra too soon for many pupils. Differencing also appears to lead, all too readily, to two particular abuses, namely the use of difference product and short-cut methods. When children reveal these methods, they need to be challenged, which can often be done by drawing attention to the source of the original number sequence (see Chapter 8).

In short, the data reveal that, as children mature, so their performance in the various aspects of the kinds of tasks described here improves. The individual interviewing, in particular, has revealed a number of levels at which generalizing is taking place. Some pupils were able to use a generalized method for finding the terms of a given sequence, but their generalizing ability did not yet enable extension to subsequent sequences. Other pupils revealed a more advanced level of generalizing ability, which allowed them to proceed beyond one sequence. As regards the general term, some pupils were able only to provide more numerical answers, others were able to sum up the relationship using words and some were able to convert this into a recognizable algebraic form. Four major obstacles along the road to successful generalization are also clear. First, in common with much mathematics, arithmetical incompetence sometimes prevents progress. Second, the fixation with a recursive approach can seriously obstruct progress towards the universal rule. Third, a considerable number of students are tempted into inappropriate methods, such as difference product and short-cut. Finally, we can never ignore the fact that idiosyncratic methods are adopted by individual pupils in unpredictable ways.

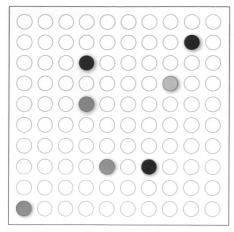

Fig.1.1 Jonathan's pegboard pattern

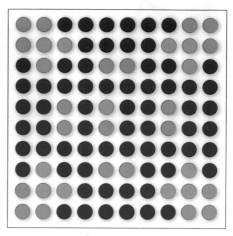

Fig.1.2 Angela's pegboard pattern

Fig.1.12 Tom's bead sequence

Fig.1.13 'Doing all different colours'

Fig.1.14 A 'chaining' bead pattern

Fig.1.15 'Chaining' with equivalent groups

Fig.1.16 A two colour alternating pattern with beads

Fig.1.17 An 'alternated similarity groups' tile pattern

Fig.1.18 A repeating difference series, using beads

Fig.1.19 A two unit difference series, in tiles

Fig.14.31a Quiver from Bhutan

Fig.14.31b Welsh wool blanket

Fig.14.31c Bangladeshi embroidery

Fig.14.33 Detail of beadwork girdle from South Africa

Chapter 8

Pictorial and Practical Contexts and the Perception of Pattern

Jean Orton, Anthony Orton and Tom Roper

ISSUES CONCERNING PICTORIAL AND PRACTICAL CONTEXTS

There are many ways of setting pattern questions within contexts which may be described as pictorial or practical. Such contexts include dot patterns (Figure 8.1), tiling patterns (Figure 8.3) and matchstick patterns (Figure 8.10, on p. 129), as some of the most obvious basic kinds, but for convenience are also taken here to include investigations and problems which lead to pattern spotting and generalization (Task 8.5, on p. 135, illustrates such an investigation). One purpose of setting pattern tasks within pictorial and practical contexts is presumably to try to provide an alternative format to lists of numbers for those who could possibly find support for their thinking from a more geometrical or contextual approach. Thus, it might be assumed that, for some pupils, a pictorial or practical context adds meaning to the task, possibly enlivens it and perhaps even simplifies it. Krutetskii (1976) has, after all, long since drawn attention to the existence of pupils whose preference is for geometric approaches, and yet others whose preference is for analytic (verbal) approaches, though it is likely that the majority of children benefit from a mixture of approaches.

Another purpose of pictorial and practical settings for pattern tasks might be that concrete and pictorial tasks are often thought to be, in a sense, more elementary than purely symbolic tasks. In support of this view, we have the suggestion made by Bruner (1966) that the sequence of stages in learning new ideas is often from the practical (enactive) to the pictorial (iconic) to the symbolic. A contrary view within the context of simple pattern tasks could be that lists of numbers are concrete enough anyway, to children in the middle years of schooling, and setting them within contexts creates additional complications. Yet another purpose of pictorial and practical settings might be just to vary the format, and perhaps even to try to introduce a more realistic or real-life dimension, or perhaps to create more of a problem to be solved. In such cases, however, we may have to accept that, although some pupils could benefit, others might find that the real-life or problem context is more complicated than just presenting lists of numbers. Under what circumstances and conditions different contexts simplify or complicate this approach to generalization through pattern tasks is an important and still largely unresolved question. Teachers would be greatly assisted by knowing much more about when and how to use particular kinds of pattern tasks and, if possible, with whom.

In an analysis of the particular route to algebra described as expressing generality, Mason *et al.* (1985b) stated the view that the first stage for the learner was always 'seeing', and that this referred to 'grasping mentally a pattern or relationship' (p. 8). Thus, in the number pattern 2, 5, 8, 11, 14, ... , we can conjecture that 'seeing' involves appreciating that there is a constant difference 3, and realizing that subsequent terms may therefore be arrived at by adding 3s. In the dot pattern in Figure 8.1, 'seeing' could be based on the pictures, or on the

Figure 8.1 *Dot pattern – triangle numbers*

equivalent number pattern, or on both. The immediate conversion of the pictures into a number pattern has been a common school approach to such tasks in recent years, in which case 'seeing' might be thought to include the extra dimension, or stage, of translation from pictures to numbers. On the one hand, we therefore need to know whether this pictorial presentation introduces a complication and generates the possibility of errors and misunderstandings not found when children deal directly with number patterns. On the other hand, we need to know whether a more pictorial or practical presentation can lead to alternative methods of solution which are simpler than using a number sequence. Is there any evidence that children can stumble over converting a sequence of simple shapes into a pattern of numbers? If there is, then perhaps pictorial and practical approaches are not always as beneficial as might be assumed. Is there any evidence, however, that greater insight can sometimes be obtained from the pictures themselves, and that children can then solve problems without recourse to pattern spotting from numbers?

In converting pictures to numbers – for example, in the task in Figure 8.1 – the first issue which teachers need to be aware of is that different children might use different approaches. One method is to count the dots for each shape presented in the task, thus immediately converting the shapes into a number sequence. A second method is to look at how many more dots each new shape requires, in this case by regarding each new shape as the previous one with an extra line of dots, and then use the number of dots in the extra line to provide the 'differences' in the sequence. Then, successive terms in the number sequence are obtained by adding successive differences. A third method is based on 'seeing' the shapes, and perhaps extending the sequence either in the mind or by drawing, before conversion to numbers, which might then be effected by multiplication or some other arithmetic operation. This last method would be more obviously appropriate if the dots formed rectangular shapes rather than the triangular ones here. Task 8.1, used by Lee and Wheeler (1987), not only revealed these three strategies, including the use of multiplication, but also revealed evolution in the perception of pattern. In this task, the presentation drew deliberate attention to the L-shaped 'borders' which provided the differences in the pattern of numbers. Generally, a 'borders' perception of the task 'eventually gave way to a "boxes" perception' (p. 101). There was, in fact, a distinct suspicion that a 'borders' perception of the problem was likely to get in the way of progress on the task. Admittedly, there is only very limited evidence from this particular source, yet it is important to note that what might be provided as a hint in a task could prove to be an obstruction for a significant number of pupils. In any case, the example from Lee and Wheeler may for some pupils be better solved not by using differences from a number pattern, but by focusing on the rectangular arrays of dots, of dimensions $1 \times 2, 2 \times 3, 3 \times 4,$

Task 8.1

Figure 8.2 shows a set of overlapping rectangles.

The first contains 2 dots.
The second contains 6 dots.
The third contains 12 dots.
The fourth contains 20 dots.

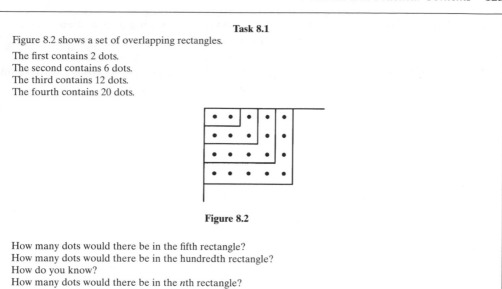

Figure 8.2

How many dots would there be in the fifth rectangle?
How many dots would there be in the hundredth rectangle?
How do you know?
How many dots would there be in the *n*th rectangle?
How do you know?

$4 \times 5, \ldots$, and therefore $n \times (n + 1)$. We shall return to the difficulty of the particular task in Figure 8.1 in the next section of this chapter, which concerns some work with adults.

The possible complexities of 'seeing' shapes are discussed by Warren (1992) in the context of a flower bed pattern, in which hexagonal flower beds in a line were to be surrounded by paving slabs of the same shape (Figure 8.3). Warren suggests that component parts (the various flower beds) need to be identified first, and then generalities need to be identified; for

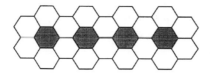

Figure 8.3 *Hexagonal paving slabs*

example, that each new flower bed requires four more paving slabs, that if there is only one flower bed there are six paving slabs and that this is two more than the four added on for each new bed. These generalities then need to be converted into a formula. Thus, not only does completion of the task require an ability to manipulate symbols, it requires 'sound visual skills' and 'an array of specific thinking skills' (p. 253). Ursini (1991), on the basis of an experiment using much simpler shapes, suggested that children need to realize that there are two representations of the same situation (visual, and analytic or verbal), need to be able to switch from one to the other, need to grasp the pattern which underlies the growth in both forms and need to realize that both rules are the same rule. The suggestion from both Warren and Ursini is that such an analysis confirms just how complex pattern questions like the flower bed task really are. Many other issues follow on from this. One important point is, first, whether visual thinking is given sufficient emphasis in school mathematics, and, second, whether enough attention is devoted to working with both systems in parallel, so that children become accustomed to moving from one to the other. Presmeg (1986) has claimed that both teachers and the curriculum tend to present visual reasoning as a first step, or as an accessory. This claim is supported by the approach to pictorial pattern questions in which the first step is to get as quickly as possible to the equivalent number sequence.

The danger of ignoring the pictures, and rushing into pattern spotting from a list of numbers, is clearly revealed in an example reported in Mason *et al.* (1985b) (see Task 8.2). The pattern spotting approach suggested in some of the literature would involve collecting and tabulating data concerning length (L), breadth (B) and number of border squares (N), and then studying the table of numbers (some possible values are shown in Table 8.1) to determine relationships between L, B and N. The children here, however, eventually appear

---

Task 8.2

Figure 8.4 shows a rectangle 2 squares wide and 3 squares long.

Figure 8.4

I want to put a border one square thick all the way round. How many squares will I need?

Investigate how many squares will be needed for other rectangles.

---

to have produced three different ways of arriving at the solution $2L + 2B + 4$, which were in essence (a) $L + B + L + B + 4$ (corners); (b) $2(L + 2) + 2(B + 2) - 4$ (because of counting corners twice); and (c) $(L + 2)(B + 2) - LB$ (based on subtracting an inside rectangle from a larger rectangle). What transpired before these solutions were obtained is not clear.

Table 8.1 *Length, breadth and number of paving slabs*

L	B	N
1	1	8
2	1	10
3	1	12
4	2	16
4	3	18
4	4	20
6	4	24
7	4	26
8	2	24

There is no information concerning level of teacher support or amount and nature of discussion between pupils, and nor are the ability levels of the children available, but the solutions are impressive. None of these approaches depends on collecting and tabulating large quantities of data and then trying to use the numbers to generate the relationship independently from the context. The collection of some data might well have been very valuable for sparking off ideas, but the crucial insights surely came from relating these data to the original context.

A variation on this task was used by Pegg and Redden (see Pegg, 1992). Approximately 700 pupils in the age range eleven to thirteen years were asked to write, in words, a rule for the number of tiles around the perimeter of a square swimming pool, and then to rewrite the

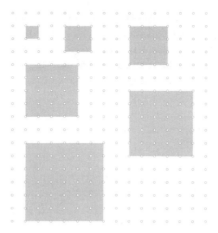

Figure 8.5 *Tiling around square swimming pools*

rule 'using algebraic symbols' (see Figure 8.5). The responses were of five types, and their diversity suggests that the pupils covered a wide range of levels of mathematical competence. The first group used drawing or counting or both, or perhaps even just said that you had to go round the pool to see how many tiles were needed. A second group moved on from counting, and perhaps used tabulation to summarize the data they had collected relating pool length to number of tiles, but were not able to use letters as variables. A third group generalized the process, but only in terms of a relationship between one pool and the next, such as adding four tiles to the previous pool, perhaps expressed as $T = S + 4$. This is, of course, the recursive approach discussed in detail in the previous chapter. A fourth group focused on the perimeter of the pool in producing responses similar to the previous group, but there was also little use of drawing or counting. The pupils in the final group were able to relate the length of side of the squares to the number of tiles, and most pupils were able to write a correct algebraic expression, such as $T = 4L + 4$. There is the clear suggestion of a developmental sequence in this work, and indeed the five types are described by Pegg in relation to the SOLO taxonomy. The step from the fourth to the fifth groups appears to be large, and it is clearly a critical one.

FROM DOT PATTERN TO RULE: INSIGHTS FROM TESTING ADULTS

Mature adults wishing to train as teachers in England have for some years needed to provide evidence of satisfactory attainment in mathematics, whatever age range and subjects they expected to teach. A legitimate qualification in mathematics could be obtained via a specific examination provided by the training institution to which candidates were applying. One question each year in the paper provided by the University of Leeds involved generalizing from a pattern of dots. The nature of these questions was naturally constrained by the format of a written examination, so data were obtained only from test scripts; nevertheless, valuable insights have been gained. These adults were selected for teacher training on the basis of their other qualifications, and thus were all academically very able overall, and some, in fact, proved to have considerable mathematical talent. The standard idea in each question over the three-year period used here was to provide a sequence of configurations of dots (see Figure

8.6), and the candidates were asked to predict the number of dots for the fifth, tenth, fiftieth and nth picture in the sequence. In all cases the rule was quadratic, that is, it involved a term in n^2. The numbers of candidates involved in each year, and the numbers of candidates who were successful on the overall examination paper each year were both very similar, and a total of 123 adults were involved in the three years together.

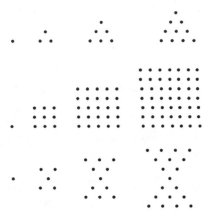

Figure 8.6 *Dot patterns used in adults' examinations*

Several general outcomes are of significance and need to be stated here. First, success on the fifth, tenth and even fiftieth numbers did not automatically lead to an acceptable expression for the general term. Given that the major objective of posing pattern tasks in this sequential way (fifth, tenth, fiftieth, nth) is to try to prompt the nth term, this was very revealing, and concurs with other results from research with children. In fact, somewhat conversely, there were examples of candidates who were able to find the general formula after the tenth term and who were then able to use it to calculate the fiftieth term, particularly with the third task. This raises the question of what this sequential guidance suggested to the candidates, and not surprisingly it appeared to suggest listing and tabulating numbers, and using differences. The use of differencing was indeed always the first approach, for all candidates, in all three years, and many candidates even persevered with using differences to try to obtain the fiftieth term, which is of course very difficult, and so not surprisingly they were often unsuccessful. Differencing does indicate a recursive understanding of the pattern, but as with children (see Chapter 7), this was not an adequate kind of understanding, and was possibly even misleading when it came to finding the nth term. It was, in fact, basically only those candidates who were prepared to reject differencing and look for other methods who made progress beyond the tenth term.

The second outcome was that success rates in finding the general term increased throughout the three years, from 0.0 to 20.5 to 33.3 per cent. The reason for the very poor showing in the first year requires separate consideration later. Looking at the other two tasks, it should be relatively clear that the second one involves squares, and that the pattern of numbers is of alternate square numbers, 1, 9, 25, 49, ... , or alternatively that it consists just of the squares of odd numbers. Many candidates did seem to appreciate this, but not all of these were able to use it to find a formula for the general term. Many other candidates, however, proceeded to use differencing in a kind of automatic way, and were again largely unsuccessful. Thus, it seems that the picture could be used here to guide the search for a rule, though it was not possible from the data to determine the extent to which students did make such direct use of the pictures. The third task does not at first sight depend on square numbers, yet was answered correctly by a large proportion of the candidates. Differencing was again very common with those candidates who only reached the tenth or fiftieth term. The candidates who successfully obtained the general term generally commenced by differencing, but quickly gave it up as a bad job, and went in search of a better method for finding not only the nth term but the fiftieth as well. Consequently, if they found the nth term at this stage they were then able to use it to fill in the fiftieth term. Usually, they hit on using the squares of the shape numbers as a consequence of trying out ideas, and for many of them it was the first idea they tried out. It is not clear why more of this group of candidates were prepared to look for other methods than in previous years, though they did have access to the examination papers from the previous years. Certainly, the pictures do not really provide direct guidance in this situation.

The task set in the first year was based on the very familiar pattern of triangle numbers. Children meet this number sequence frequently in the course of their mathematical education, and thus it is highly probable that the adults concerned here had previously encountered the sequence in both dot pattern and numerical form. The evidence of attempts to solve this task reveals that the only method pursued was differencing. It is possible that some candidates looked for other methods, but if they did, they certainly did not record any. A few candidates came close through the differencing approach, but were unable to convert their discoveries into a correct formula. It was very clear that differencing alone is not likely to lead to success on this task, and that the pattern, though very familiar even to children, is probably much less suitable for use in the context of generalizing from patterns than those based more obviously on square numbers. In other words, the given configurations of dots do not provide any direct help. The numbers and their differences do not provide any direct help either, and squaring the shape number yields a new pattern which is too remote from the original pattern for any connection to be appreciated. So, all in all, it should not be surprising that this is such a difficult pattern from which to generalize! A further comment is perhaps relevant. The triangle numbers are related to the simple rule of growth $1 + 2 + 3 + 4 + 5 + ...$, which is met very frequently, and which clearly highlights the differences. The dot patterns in the other two years were not based on any such well known rule of growth, so perhaps some candidates approached these tasks with a more open mind. If this rule of growth is pictured using staircases built from squares, or using right-angled triangle dot patterns, the rule can be appreciated much more readily than from either the given dot patterns or the number sequence. Figure 8.7 illustrates how $2 \times (1 + 2 + 3 + 4 + 5) = 5 \times 6$, and hence the required formula is $\frac{1}{2} \times n \times (n + 1)$. Without being taught this approach, however, it seems unlikely that pupils will discover it for themselves.

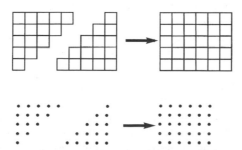

Figure 8.7 *Staircases and right-angled dot patterns for generalizing triangle numbers*

Other comparisons with the outcomes from studies with children are worth a brief mention. First, some candidates misread 'fiftieth' as 'fifteenth', and this has certainly been noted with pupils. This may indicate a reading difficulty, but it could just as easily be either because of assuming the simpler sequence 5, 10, 15, or because of wishful thinking, since fifteen is much easier to deal with than fifty. It certainly suggests that in setting such questions, words which can easily be confused should be avoided. Second, a number of candidates who were able to express the general term could only do so in words, or could not express it in the most succinct algebraic form. Again, work with children has revealed that the ability to express a result in words may often be present when the symbolic algebraic form is not. Just a very few candidates interpreted the request to find the nth term as a request to find the ninth term, which is a phenomenon often revealed when working with children.

In summary, it was clear that these mature adults, like many children, are first likely to base their attempts on differences, can usually handle the recursive pattern based on the differences very competently, but then have great difficulty in dropping this approach and seeking a better approach which will lead them more successfully towards the general rule. This obstacle, noted so frequently with children, is seemingly just as evident with adults. Most of all, it was clear that additional maturity does not lead to the elimination of the kinds of difficulties which children encounter.

USING MATCHSTICK PATTERNS TO INVESTIGATE GENERALIZING

Matchsticks provide another popular form of support in both teaching and researching the use of patterning leading to generalization and algebra. Stacey (1989) included a matchstick ladder question based on Figure 8.8 in two group tests, the first with pupils aged nine to

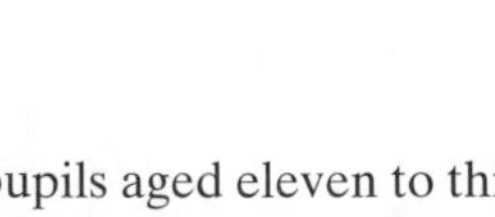

Figure 8.8 *Matchstick ladder question*

$$\triangle \qquad \triangle\triangledown\diagup \qquad \triangle\triangledown\triangle$$

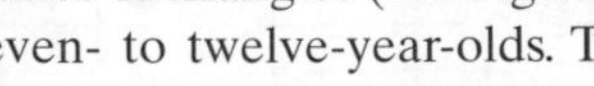

Figure 8.9 *Matchstick triangles*

eleven years, and the second with pupils aged eleven to thirteen years. Some discussion of the results has already been included in Chapter 7, and there are no additional comments relating to context which need to be made. Pegg and Redden (1990) reported on a study which used matchsticks in the shape of lines of triangles (see Figure 8.9) as the first activity in a new curriculum topic devised for eleven- to twelve-year-olds. This was clearly a commendable early attempt to research the effect and value of curriculum change, but several important comments and questions are relevant. First, it seems that the matchstick task, and possibly other picture-based tasks, were used before questions based only on numbers, as if tasks based on such iconic representations of concrete situations are easier than a more symbolic approach, and should therefore come before symbols alone. Second, 'all pupils achieved success with little or no assistance from the teacher' (p. 387), but the implication is that some pupils did require some help. It is not clear how many pupils needed help, or what form this help took, or indeed what the pupils were able to do and not do before and after help was provided. One particularly interesting feature of the topic was that, having worked with patterns based on concrete representations and then numbers, pupils were challenged to construct concrete representations from number patterns such as 4, 7, 10, ... , and 1, 4, 9, ... This is a good idea for an extension task, but it is not clear how successful pupils were on it, though we read that it 'proved a challenging one that the more capable students found interesting' (p. 388). The topic then moved on to devote considerable attention to language activities, that is, to describing patterns and developing rules, as the next stage.

Our own work with pupils of all levels of mathematical competence in the age range nine to thirteen has also included matchstick tasks (Orton, 1997) in which the pupils were encouraged to build the shapes themselves. Thirty pupils were interviewed as they constructed additional shapes in the sequences begun by the interviewer and shown in Figure 8.10. It was clear

Figure 8.10 *Matchstick tasks*

from the interviews that different pupils 'saw' the sequences in several different ways. Looking at responses to 'steps', there was clearly a group of pupils who saw the next shape as requiring an extra match along each of four lines. Some of these described the additions in terms of one extra on the base, one extra up the side, and one extra for each of the rise and tread of the new step, though they did not necessarily use such clear language to express their interpretation. Another group saw the extra step at the top requiring two sides and a top (i.e. three matches), and then seeing that a fourth match would also be needed at the bottom, perhaps by starting with a complete square and sliding the bottom match down to the level of the base. A more unusual interpretation was to see the shape as 'sort of half a square', in which matches around the perimeter of a square are pushed down or to the right to form a staircase (see Figure 8.11), and thus the shapes were equivalent to squares. Numerically, some

Figure 8.11 *'Steps', seen as 'half a square'*

pupils saw each new step as requiring the addition of another four matches, and some quickly saw the products $2 \times 4, 3 \times 4, 4 \times 4$. For the 'sheep-pens', the most common visualization was a variation on the addition of three matches at the end, two at the top and bottom and one at the side. Some pupils saw this as the addition of a square and the removal of a match from the side. An unusual interpretation from Nicola (based on four squares) was to say it was 12 (4 + 4 + 4), 'because it's four across the top, four across the bottom and four in the middle'. This interpretation incorporates an error of counting, although the pupil did subsequently realize that there was one extra in the middle, yet the method unfortunately did not seem to help her to build the next shape in the sequence.

Although most pupils did succeed in building the fourth shape without much difficulty, there were some problems introduced by the practical nature of these tasks. The most difficult task in this respect was undoubtedly 'steps'. Catherine was one of several who at first built the fourth shape incorrectly, in her case placing only three matches across the base, but she then realized the number pattern had been broken when she counted the matches. After some delay in which she rethought her numbers, she was then able to correct the shape by referring to the number pattern. Rachel kept 'losing her place' in making shapes, and generally had a great deal of difficulty with manipulating the matches. She also had difficulty in counting, in particular in remembering where she had started each time. Sarah had similar counting difficulties, but recognized a 'going up in fours' pattern from the numbers, and was then able to ignore the matchsticks. Emma was able to 'see' the 3, 5, 7, ... , pattern in 'containers', but then got into all kinds of difficulties, as this excerpt shows:

Emma:	*3 in the first, 5 in the next, 7, ... all you have to do is add 2 on.*
	Next is 9, ... next is 11.
Interviewer:	So how many for number 20? Number 1 is 3, number 2 is 5, number 3 is 7, number 4 is 9, number 5 is 11 (pointing at a systematic written record of these results). How many for number 20?
Emma:	*... 23. There's 3 at number 1, and then if you just had one (indicating the bottom match in each shape) and you added up all the ones up to 20 you'd get 20. And then if you added 3 you'd get 23.*

It is at such times that the interviewer is always tempted to put on the hat of teacher, in order to try to help the child. In this case, however, Emma was allowed to continue with her own way of reasoning, and thus some time later we have:

I:	So what would it be for number 100?
E:	*... 2003 ... I've got 23. If I added on 100 × 23s, I'd get 2003.*

And subsequently, for the 'sheep-pens':

E:	*You add on another pen each time. It's 4, 7, ... I've already worked out the pattern. You always add on 3 ...*
I:	So what will the next be?
E:	*10, ... then 13, ... then 16.*
I:	And for the twentieth?
E:	*24 ... It's the same method as last time. [20 for those along the bottom and add on 4 for the first.]*
I:	And for the hundredth?
E:	*2004 ... It's the same method as I used before, ... 100 times 24, add on 24 [!].*

It is not uncommon for 'habituation' to take hold in children's reasoning, so perhaps it is not surprising that Emma tried to repeat her method. The point at issue, however, is that the matches did not help her once she had deduced the first few numbers of each pattern, though perhaps it is the case that she did not allow herself to use them to advantage.

A different difficulty was apparent confusion between shape number and number of matches. Amy, for example, had no difficulty in building the next sheep-pen, and she correctly counted 4 and 7 for the first two. She then deduced that the number pattern was one of going up in threes, so she gave 10, 13 and 16:

I:	So for the twentieth?
A:	*It will be 60 ... it's the same method as before (goes up in*
	threes hence multiply by 3).
I:	Are you sure about your answer?
A:	*... Yes.*
I:	So what would it be for the hundredth?
A:	*No, that's too hard ... It will be 40 ... you have to add on 40, ...*
	add on 40 to 60 to make 100. [40 is the difference between the
	previous answer for the number of matches and the shape number 100.]

Sarah, similarly, went through a period of confusion between shape number and number of matches in 'sheep-pens', but she was one who worked her way through that particular difficulty to a correct interpretation. However, she subsequently introduced the following method:

I:	What is the answer for 20 pens?
S:	*... 68.*
I:	Can you tell me how you worked that out?
S:	*Well, there's ten pens here.*

I counted how many sticks in all of these and then timesed it by 2 [i.e. (4 + 7 + 10 + 13) × 2 = 68].

I:	So if I asked you for 100 pens?
S:	*Oh, no!*
I:	Would you have a method for that?
S:	*There are 34 matchsticks (for 10 pens), ... so times it by 10, ...*
	that gives, ... I don't know.

It should be clear already that strange methods did appear; in fact there were many examples of this phenomenon. Jeremy, for example, obtained his answer for 20 pens by using the fact that the first shape was a square of 4 matches, but the second was only 3 matches, so the answer for 20 pens was $4 \times 10 + 3 \times 10$. His generalization of this was $4 \times n + 3 \times n = 7n^2$ ('it's lucky really, because we've been doing this in school recently'!), which takes us into a different well known kind of error. In the same way he obtained $5n^2$ for 'containers', and was not at all concerned to discover that his 'formulae' did not seem to work for the smaller numbers of shapes. Andrew, when asked how many matches for n steps, gave the answer 3, and his construction then clearly revealed his logic ($|\diagdown|$). And, having obtained the answer 20 for his tenth container, he justified this to his own satisfaction by saying there would be one at the bottom, 10 up one side and 9 up the other side. Pupils automatically used differencing in their first attempts at 'seeing' the patterns of numbers, and this usually constrained their thinking about rules. There were many examples of the use of the difference product and short-cut methods described in the previous chapter. There were also many examples of changing methods from difference product to short-cut to own unique reasoning, of algebraic-type expressions without any understanding and of arithmetic confusion Occasionally, the matchsticks were used to good effect. Laura's short-cut method for 20 containers produced the answer 44, from 11 (for 5 containers) × 4, but she was then able to picture 20 + 20 + 1 matches in her mind, and in this way she corrected her answer to 41. Gill explained the rule for sheep-pens by building a line of three open pens (9 matches), and then stated that a complete square of 4 matches would be needed at the end, which was one extra match. Unfortunately, she was then unable to transfer this reasoning to containers. Daniel was one who was able to continue to build correct containers, and thus obtain a correct answer for the twentieth shape.

The main focus of this analysis is on the use of concrete support for pupils, but it would be remiss of us not to report the very considerable success of some pupils in terms of generalizing from their work. Lindsay and Amy were both able to come up with statements of the form $n \times 3 + 1$ and $n \times 2 + 1$. Claire wrote her versions rather differently, as $n4$, $n3 + 1$ and $n2 + 1$. Paul's response to 'containers' revealed that he had learned from his recent school work:

P:	*3, 5, 7, 9, ... gives 11, ... up by 2.*
I:	So what would the twentieth be?
P:	*44, ... just multiply by 4.*
I:	And for the hundredth?
P:	*It will be 11 times 20, ... or 44 times 5.*
I:	And for any number, *n*?
P:	*(Long pause) ... It will be* n *multiplied by 2 and add 1. I've just remembered doing something like this before. I know what you mean now ... what you were asking for.*

At this point Paul was taken back to 'steps', for which he quickly offered $4n$, and 'sheep-pens', though this took rather longer to produce the rule. He showed no desire to go back to his answers for the twentieth and hundredth numbers, which were incorrect in all three tasks. In other words, the generalizations were deduced from the first few terms in each sequence.

Several children showed evidence of being able to generalize with numbers. Katie, working on 'containers', was also able to see alternative numerical forms from her consideration of the twentieth term:

K:	*It's 2 times 20, then ... hang on, ... 2 times 19 add 3, ... add 4, ... hang on, ... mm, ...*
I:	Keep going.
K:	*Yes, 19 times 2, ... 19 times 2 add 3.*
I:	Can you explain how you got that?
K:	*Because if you forget about that (pointing at the bottom three matches forming a sort of U-shape) for the moment, and then you add, ... you always add 2, and there's 19 of them, ... and then you add that (pointing again at the initial U-shape). It could be 20 times 2, and then it would just be add 1.*
I:	Now do you think you could get the hundredth?
K:	*99 times 2 add 3, ... or 100 times 2 add 3, ... sorry, add 1.*

Laura, having worked out the twentieth term in 'sheep-pens' as '19 × 3 and then plus the 4', and the hundredth as '99 × 3 + 4', was asked about the *n*th:

I: And if we want any number? I'm not going to tell you what the number is, I'm going to call it *n*. What would it be for *n* pens?

L: *Whatever the number was, ... you times it by 3, a number less, and then add 4.*

For 'containers', she first used the short-cut method for the twentieth, but then corrected herself by visualizing the shape as 20 + 20 + 1. She then gave the hundredth as 100 up each side plus one at the bottom, so 201, and generalized as 'You'd times whatever the number was by 2 and plus 1'. Several other children produced similar arguments and statements of rules.

On the basis of the evidence available, the case for using matches as concrete support remains unproved. Some children could clearly manage without the matches. Others did make some use of the matches, though perhaps they were simply something concrete to picture in the mind. Other pupils chose not to use the matches once they had deduced the common difference, and in many of these cases they then moved on to incorrect deductions. Some children were slowed down by the matches, and occasionally found them a handicap, because they couldn't handle them, or couldn't count them. In other words, as is often the case in education, this particular concrete support was of use some of the time to some of the pupils. It is still the case, however, that matches and other simple concrete apparatus provide variety and context, both of which might be important in broadening the experiences of learners. Thus, it would be helpful to know about the relative difficulties of matchstick questions, so that simpler ones can be set first, and harder ones reserved until later, and perhaps only for certain pupils. A number of examples of additional matchstick questions are shown in Figure 8.12. Younger and weaker pupils might benefit from beginning with an example like 'tents',

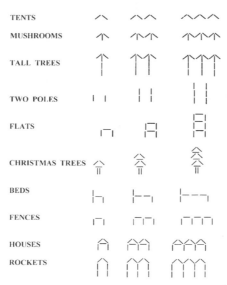

Figure 8.12 *Additional matchstick questions*

where the numbers are small and the pattern is one of doubling. Other shapes revealing direct proportion include 'mushrooms' and 'tall trees'. Such patterns provide good opportunities for pupils to see the relationship as a multiplicative one, relating the number of matches to the shape number. The identification of patterns which are not based on multiplication alone, like 'containers' and 'sheep-pens', might be assisted through comparison with patterns like 'two poles' and 'flats'. An example where the different kind of structure, $3n + 2$, can be clearly seen is 'Christmas trees'. Another example of a similar nature is 'beds'. It might be helpful to use such examples to guide children into deciding whether any part of the shapes remains the same in all shapes, and then to look at how the remainder of the shapes change. Pupils might then be ready to move on to 'fences', 'houses' and 'rockets', as well as the 'ladders' in Figure 8.8. More advanced work could include suggesting that pupils invent a rule and then try to make matchstick representations in some attractive sequence of shapes. Experience with a large number of patterns should provide the opportunity for common strategies to be adopted and general methods discovered. Informing pupils that 'if they go up in 3s it must be $3n +$ or $-$ something' may often not be appropriate guidance, not only because it deprives pupils of making their own discoveries, but also because it is unlikely to help pupils whose generalizing ability is weak.

INVESTIGATIONS AND PROBLEMS

Investigating and problem-solving are two of the styles of teaching and learning from the list of six recommended in the Cockcroft Report (1982). The difference between these two styles, and their distinguishing characteristics, has been discussed in many other books (see, for example, Orton and Frobisher, 1996), and does not concern us here. Both styles can be used to provide extended work for pupils and, when they do, both are frequently assumed to depend on pattern spotting, with the hope or expectation that a rule will be found. In this way, some would claim that such tasks are yet another way of leading up to algebra through generalizing. A long-standing example is 'diagonals' (see Task 8.3). Here, the collection of data, and the use of pattern spotting, often lead students fairly quickly to the conjecture that the number of squares crossed by the diagonal (D) is the length (L) plus the breadth (B) minus 1; that is, $D = L + B - 1$. This rule seems to work most of the time, but it does not always work, for example with a 9×6 rectangle, and thus the real problem then

---

Task 8.3

On squared paper draw a rectangle 5 squares by 4 squares.
Now draw a diagonal of this rectangle.

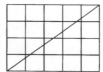

Figure 8.13

How many squares does this diagonal pass through?
Investigate for other rectangles.
Can you forecast the number of squares passed through if you know the length and width of the rectangle?

---

begins with this realization. Many pupils and older students find great difficulty in getting any further. In fact, some produce a collection of rules which apply to different categories of rectangles. The systematic collection of further data, coupled with a modicum of insight, can lead students to one single rule which always works, but our experience is that even mature students with high qualifications in mathematics can fail to find this all-embracing formula. Often, the ultimate insight does not depend on amassing data, but depends on studying the characteristics and properties of categories of rectangles, and then deducing why the characteristics of the various categories make a difference to the rule.

Another example of a widely used task is usually referred to as Pick's theorem (Task 8.4). Here again, it is common to find pupils tabulating data under the three headings A (area), P (number of dots on the perimeter) and I (number of dots in the interior), and this approach is often encouraged. Once a pattern has been deduced, it is possible to express the relationship between A, P and I in the form of an identity, and thus an algebraic statement is once again the outcome. The task is, for most students, even more difficult than 'diagonals', for the establishing of the rule from such a table of values requires the use of the data in an even more obscure way than in 'diagonals'. One approach which ought to be successful here is to hold one variable constant while collecting data and studying relationships between other variables, then repeating with a different constant variable, but mathematics specialists are often not accustomed to using this 'experimental' method, and therefore sometimes make little progress. This method might be more familiar to students from other subject disciplines, whereas mathematicians might be more accustomed to being challenged to prove the rule once it has been conjectured.

Task 8.4

Using a rectangular lattice of dots, draw shapes by connecting dots. Figure 8.14 shows several such shapes.

Figure 8.14

Find a relationship between the area of a shape, the number of lattice points on its perimeter, and the number of lattice points contained within the shape.

The pack of problems (Shell Centre, 1984), devised at least in part to encourage work on investigations and problem-solving in secondary schools, actively encouraged the pattern spotting approach to problem-solving; for example, 'skeleton tower' (Task 8.5). It was as if there is only one way to solve such tasks, and that way is based on pattern spotting. Hewitt (1992) is one who has criticized the over-dependence of investigative approaches to mathematics on pattern spotting, and for a number of reasons. The danger is that pupils will come to see mathematical problem-solving as being ultimately dependent on making sense of a pattern, and thus, as Hewitt has said, the original problem is forgotten, and the task becomes purely one of juggling with numbers. Although both 'diagonals' and 'Pick's theorem' can be solved from the numbers, in both cases the solver benefits from constant reference to the nature of the original context. In some cases, a problem is best solved by not focusing on the numbers; for example, the swimming pool tasks discussed in this chapter. Almost nothing is known about the value of the contribution of tasks such as 'diagonals' and 'Pick's theorem' to the development of a feel for the algebraic representation of a relationship, through the use of pattern or otherwise. Here is an area of study which needs to be tackled. More will

---

Task 8.5

Figure 8.15 shows a picture of a tower made from cubes, and with height 6 cubes.

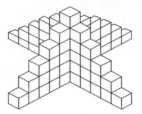

Figure 8.15

1. How many cubes would be needed to build this tower?
2. How many cubes would be needed to build a tower like it but 10 cubes high?
3. How would you calculate the number of cubes needed for a tower n cubes high?

---

be said about such approaches to investigations and problem-solving in later chapters.

If it is agreed that students should be encouraged to investigate mathematical situations as part of their curriculum, then all the above tasks, and many others, have some value. The use of such tasks does, however, raise a number of questions and issues to which we have no definite answers. Some involve the place and value of such tasks, and do not concern us here, but others are related to the issue of the perception of pattern. There does not appear to be a body of research concerning the advantages and disadvantages of the use of such problems and the relationship with pattern spotting and generalizing. Our studies lead us to suggest that placing a pattern in a context, or deriving a pattern from a context, must not automatically be assumed to help the pupil or student to extend, generalize or prove the pattern. Subsidiary to this message are the following points: (a) that some contexts are more difficult than others; (b) that there may be graduations of difficulty in both pattern and context; (c) that the relationship of the pattern and the context to prior knowledge is likely to produce significant individual differences in the responses; and (d) that the relationship between the context and the pattern and how this relationship is perceived by pupils may both be problematic.

Chapter 9

Children's Understanding of Graphic Relations

Christopher S. Burke and Anthony Orton

NUMBER PATTERNS, SYMBOLS AND GRAPHICS

The identification and analysis of number patterns such as those described in earlier chapters are likely to be greatly assisted by the spatial arrangements of the numbers. It would very likely cause great consternation to many children if a sequence of numbers was not evenly spaced in printed text, and was presented, for example, as the Fibonacci sequence here:

1, 1,   2, 3, 5,   8,   13, ...

Not only are children accustomed to regularity of spacing in number sequences, but any exercise in pattern spotting might be much more difficult without uniform spaces; indeed, it could be impossible. Any triangular array of numbers, such as the one used to generate number patterns in the study described in Chapter 7, depends absolutely on being uniformly spaced. Without strict observance of uniformity of spacing, the patterns of numbers which pupils were intended to identify would not be clear, and the whole point of the exercise would be lost.

Another very common triangular number pattern for which regular spacing is assumed is Pascal's triangle:

```
                1
            1       1
          1     2       1
        1     3     3       1
      1     4     6     4       1
    1     5    10     10     5      1
```

Here, it is essential that the numbers are spaced in this careful way in order that sequences of numbers are revealed in at least four different directions (across, down and two oblique directions), and the structures of their respective underlying patterns are accessible to the pupils' thinking. Not only that, but the derivation of numbers in any new row of Pascal's triangle depends on summing numbers in the previous row, and this procedure might well be obscured without uniform spacing. Whenever a number line is drawn, when axes are prepared in readiness for drawing a graph, when a thermometer or other scale is represented on paper, in all of these cases and in many more, regular spacing must be used. The manner in which symbols are arranged, connected and separated is part of the graphic dimension of that subject, and it should be clear that children need to understand all such graphical considerations. Thus, the theme of this chapter is children's interpretation and understanding of graphic arrangements and relationships.

At first sight, there may seem to be many ways in which symbols can be arranged, connected and separated graphically in identifiable and understandable patterns or arrays, so as to draw attention to particular relationships. Even in the writing of the number 13 427 it should be clear not only that the position of each digit affects its value, but also that the space between the 3 and the 4 has special significance. The use of indices reminds us of the distinction between two digits written in two different ways, 32 and 3^2, another example of the effect of different positioning. Sometimes, however, it is necessary to dissociate symbols or elements which are in close proximity; that is, to indicate that they are distinct entities as in (x, y) rather than joined or associated as in (xy). In (x, y) a comma is used as the disjunctive or separator, but other devices can be employed, such as the straight lines separating labels and sets of values in the table which represents the mapping $x \rightarrow f(x)$:

x	0	1	2	3	4	5
$f(x)$	1	2	5	10	17	26

Other examples in which lines are used as disjunctives are the tables of values from Chapter 7, such as the table for multiplication (mod 10) on the set $\{2, 4, 6, 8\}$:

	2	4	6	8
2	4	8	6	2
4	8	6	4	2
6	2	4	6	8
8	6	2	8	4

Here, we can also see how the patterns contained within the table would be obscured without the regular spacing in two perpendicular directions.

Disjunctives of considerable variety are used in mathematics. Perversely, they can also help the association of elements by demarcating them from the rest of their surroundings. In the expression $x (y + z)$ the parentheses indicate that y and z should be considered, at least in the first instance, as distinct from x. The Venn diagram in Figure 9.1 is another example of

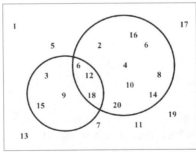

Figure 9.1 *A Venn diagram to illustrate the use of boundary lines*

the use of boundary lines to separate, and hence literally to delineate. Lines, of course, are not just a means to dissociate, but can also be used to link elements together. Thus, in the mapping diagram shown below, lines connect numbers together:

$$1 \longrightarrow 2$$
$$2 \longrightarrow 5$$
$$3 \longrightarrow 10$$

Arrows, or at least line segments, are also used in flow diagrams to indicate relationships and directions. Matrix multiplication is a particularly complicated arrangement, in which positions and lines carry very specific meanings:

$$\begin{bmatrix} 1 & 2 \\ 1 & 3 \end{bmatrix} \begin{bmatrix} 2 & 1 \\ 5 & 3 \end{bmatrix} = \begin{bmatrix} 12 & 7 \\ 17 & 10 \end{bmatrix}$$

The examples given constitute just a few of the many ways in which information and knowledge may be recorded and conveyed in a structured or patterned format in mathematics. At least two important questions emerge from all these examples: first, how many distinctly different graphical arrangements or relationships are there; second, how do children interpret and comprehend these various forms?

GRAPHIC RELATIONS IN MATHEMATICS

From the previous section, it should be clear that these issues are important, because whenever knowledge is communicated visually it is done by means of symbols, signs, diagrams and pictures. Not only are these 'graphics' used to denote physical and mental entities, they are also used to convey information about the relations between them. Thus, graphics can be thought of as the repository of all visually codified knowledge, and graphic space as consisting of elements and the relations which bind them together. These relations include degree of proximity as indicated by spacing, devices like commas and brackets which are used as separators and, correspondingly, devices like network or tree diagram lines which are used as associators. Clearly, the study of mathematics as a whole, and not just number patterns, requires the comprehension of graphic elements and relations, and this might not be as straightforward a matter as teachers might hope. Mathematics incorporates a massive collection of graphic elements, as illustrated by the selection in the box. Many of these elements are compound, in that they consist of a combination of other, simpler, elements and therefore involve a relationship between elements. In fact, compound elements are the norm in the

2	$r!$	a^0	a_{ij}	^nC_r	ln
=	$\bar{a}$	%	$\pm$	f^{-1}	$\Leftrightarrow$
Σ	$\sqrt{5}$	σ_x	$\forall x$	$\sin\theta$	$\int x^2 dx$
$y=f(x)$	(x, y)	$[a, b]$	$(\sin\theta, \cos\theta)$	$a < b$	$\begin{bmatrix} a & b \\ c & d \end{bmatrix}$

hierarchy of psychological processing. Students of mathematics have to be able to decode graphic elements and relations in their everyday pursuit of knowledge, including their interpretation of patterns. It is therefore important that teachers have some knowledge of both the complexities involved and the capabilities of the pupils.

Plunkett (1979) seems to have been the first to attempt a proper analysis of the graphic relations contained in the diagrams used in mathematics. He realized that all mathematical diagrams are constructed from only a small set of graphic relations, and he posited four basic ones, all of which are spatial in nature:

- 'is inside', such as in the Venn diagram in Figure 9.1;
- 'is connected to', as used in a mapping diagram;
- 'is next to (linearly)', as used in any number sequence;
- 'is next to (two-dimensionally)', as used in any table, such as that for multiplication (mod 10).

This simple set has much appeal. However, Plunkett had to elaborate the 'is next to' relation in three different ways. The first of these was 'is opposite to', as used in tabulation, but it is suggested here that this is not necessary if the inverse of association, namely dissociation, is accepted. The second elaboration was 'continuity', but this can be interpreted as an iteration of 'is next to' or 'is connected to'. The third was 'circle', but this is just a set of 'is next to' relations arranged in a special way.

It seems to us that Plunkett's categories are not the simplest possible; that is, they are not a true set of primitives. Beyond the three elaborations of 'is next to', if we adopt only the most primitive graphic relations, then the two-dimensional 'is next to' is unnecessary, because the one-dimensional version is sufficient. Another, but less obvious, deletion is 'is inside', because this can be incorporated within the simpler relation of disjunction, described fully later.

It is also relevant to enquire whether Plunkett's list is deficient in any way: in other words, was anything overlooked? Watson (1981) subsequently proposed seven relations, namely 'is near to', 'is larger than', 'is connected to', 'is next to (one-dimensional)', 'is next to (two-dimensional)', 'is opposite to (one-directional)' and 'is opposite to (two-directional)'. It seems to us, however, that the two relations 'is near to' and 'is next to' are identical, that 'is opposite to' is redundant, as suggested earlier, and that one- and two-dimensional variants are never necessary to the identification of basic relations. At first sight, the 'is larger than' relation seems worth including. Yet the 'is near/next to' relation can be considered as a continuous variable, and therefore can be used to incorporate information of a metrical nature. Thus, it could be claimed that Watson's list does not add anything new to our classification.

The Plunkett and Watson models were both based entirely on an analysis of a wide range of existing graphic relations. We consider it a weakness that, in the search for the real primitives, they did not take into account that an entity can exist in two possible states with respect to another entity – it can be either related or unrelated. Graphics must convey not only when objects need to be associated, but also the inverse, when they need to be dissociated. Thus, to us, the most basic system should consist of a set of inverse pairs of graphic relations. We suggest that the real primitives are near/far proximity and conjunction/disjunction. The latter pair counteract the former: conjunction links elements which are distant from one another, thus overcoming their far proximity, and disjunction separates elements which are close together, thus cancelling their near proximity. There are three types of conjunction/disjunction. First, there is that achieved using lines, commas, brackets and the like, which we have called 'formal', since an additional formal element is involved. Second, there is that achieved by using the same colour or different colours, referred to here as 'chromatic' conjunction/disjunction. Third, there is that in which the same shape or different shapes are used, called 'morphological' conjunction/disjunction). All the graphic relations are illustrated and summarized in Figure 9.2.

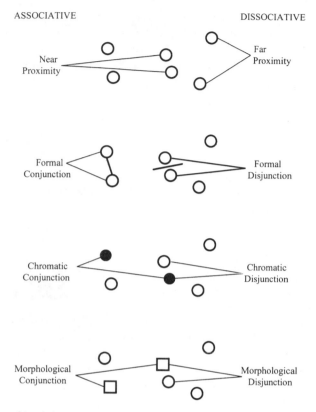

Figure 9.2 *The basic graphic relations*

ANALYSIS OF A GRAPHIC

To illustrate our claim that all graphics can be analysed using the four pairs of graphic relations near and far proximity, formal conjunction and disjunction, chromatic conjunction and disjunction, and morphological conjunction and disjunction, we use the elementary mapping diagram in Figure 9.3. It should be clear that even with such a simple diagram a formidable

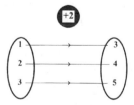

Figure 9.3 *The mapping diagram for analysis using the basic graphic relations*

collection of associations is involved in the analysis, as shown in Figure 9.4. Repetition is avoided by selecting only representative sections of the mapping diagram. This example serves to illustrate how complex the processing of these graphic relations is, even in a seemingly elementary case.

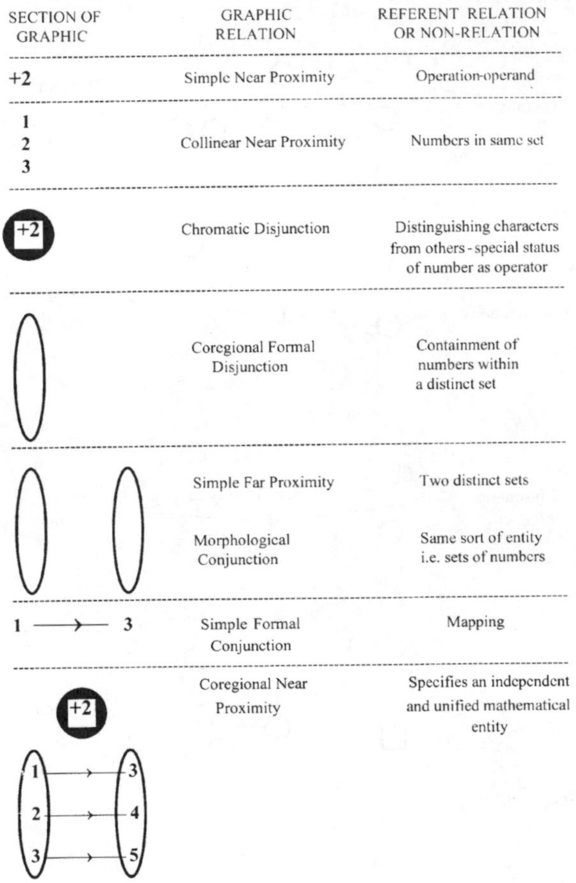

Figure 9.4 *The mapping diagram analysis*

CHILDREN'S REACTIONS TO GRAPHIC RELATIONS

In order to test whether children readily ascribe significance to the graphic relations of near/far proximity and formal conjunction/disjunction, a small experiment was conducted (Burke, 1989). The subjects were a convenience sample of fifteen boys and fifteen girls in the age range eleven to thirteen years. The experiment consisted of presenting a succession of seventeen white cards bearing various arrangements of graphic elements and inviting the children to interpret these in terms of friendship. The order of presentation was varied randomly so as to counteract learning effects. Friendship was chosen as a suitable referent relation because it was a familiar concept. Each graphic element on the cards represented a 'person', and the children were simply asked which of these persons were friendly with each other. The responses were recorded and subsequently analysed for evidence as to how the relations between graphics had influenced the interpretations. Clearly, this is a relatively simplistic way of obtaining relevant data, but it seemed appropriate for a first attempt.

The graphics themselves were designed with great care to fulfil the following conditions:

1. The elements had to be very simple, discrete and as homogeneous as possible. However, they also had to be easily identifiable in the taped conversations with the pupils.
2. The crucial distances between graphics had to be both visually easy to distinguish and unambiguously quantifiable.
3. Because the subjects were children, the graphics had to be 'user-friendly'.
4. The graphics could not have inherent characteristics which suggested *a priori* groupings or order. Thus, they had to be as neutral as possible with regard to any conventional or obvious classifications.
5. They had to be small enough for several to fit into a format which left wide margins in order to avoid visual influences by the edges of the card.

Seven sample sheets serve here to illustrate the outcomes, between them indicating the range of findings. Each sheet consists of a diagram showing the arrangement of graphic elements with letters indicating the actual colours (B, blue; G, green; N, brown; R, red; Y, yellow); a table giving the objective data on the proximities between graphic elements as multiples of the size of the graphic elements; a table giving the percentage of the sample of children who did decide that the graphic relation between each pair of elements signified a friendship relationship; and a graph representing the relationship between the proximity data and the significations contained in the two tables. Comments on the results are also included.

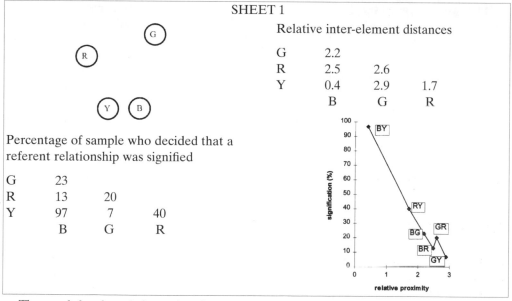

SHEET 1

Relative inter-element distances

G	2.2		
R	2.5	2.6	
Y	0.4	2.9	1.7
	B	G	R

Percentage of sample who decided that a referent relationship was signified

G	23		
R	13	20	
Y	97	7	40
	B	G	R

The graph for sheet 1 shows that the percentage of the sample thinking that friendship was signified steadily decreased as the inter-element distance increased. This is a strong indication that children in this age range can interpret near/far proximity with considerable success. The discrepancy for the GR relation is only small and could be accounted for in several ways. First, having compounded B and Y, subjects could have associated the remaining two single elements. Second, an interpretative bias towards horizontality, reinforced by that of BY, could have been operative. Third, the BR relation could have been comparatively weakened by the intervening offset Y element, thus making it less powerful than the GR, despite its nearer proximity (other evidence suggests this is a common syndrome, which we have called the offset intervention effect).

SHEET 7

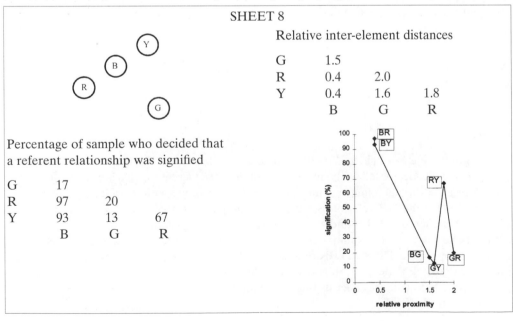

Relative inter-element distances

G	1.8			
N	1.0	1.0		
R	1.0	1.0	1.8	
Y	3.2	0.4	2.1	2.1
	B	G	N	R

Percentage of sample who decided that a referent relationship was signified

G	20			
N	53	47		
R	53	53	47	
Y	13	93	10	7
	B	G	N	R

What we have called simple (to distinguish it from 'collinear' or 'coregional', which involve more than two elements) near proximity, in the form of GY, is dominant in sheet 7. The coregional near proximity of GBNR seems to have equally associated all referents except that the 'vertical' GN is slightly smaller. RY and NY seem to have smaller significations than might be expected, perhaps because of offset intervention. There is a striking difference in the significations of the equally proximate BG and NR, where the former has probably been relatively weakened by GY. BY seems to have a slightly higher signification than expected, presumably because of what it is convenient to refer to as the collinear near/far proximity of BGY. In this sheet, the results are not particularly easy to explain.

SHEET 8

Relative inter-element distances

G	1.5		
R	0.4	2.0	
Y	0.4	1.6	1.8
	B	G	R

Percentage of sample who decided that a referent relationship was signified

G	17		
R	97	20	
Y	93	13	67
	B	G	R

The high significations for BR and BY on sheet 8 were predictable. The striking level of RY's signification demonstrates that subjects did appreciate the transitive nature of collinear near proximity when it was not distorted by a stronger simple near proximity involving one of the elements. The relations of element G to each of the others have comparable significations, which do not vary much according to the inter-element distances. This could have been because R, B and Y were regarded as a compound with a single relationship to G. However, there seems to be a slight orientation effect, with signification being stronger when the proximity axis runs closer to the 'horizontal', so GR is stronger than GY.

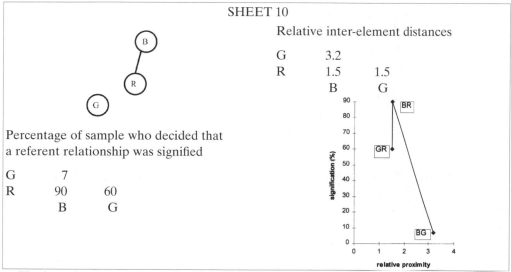

SHEET 10

Relative inter-element distances

G	3.2	
R	1.5	1.5
	B	G

Percentage of sample who decided that a referent relationship was signified

G	7	
R	90	60
	B	G

The introduction of simple (involving only two elements) formal conjunction in sheet 10 had a dramatic effect on the interpretation of BR, which has the same inter-element distance as GR but 50 per cent greater signification. Obviously, subjects mainly understood the significance of the conjunctive line associating BR. The other two proximity relations had levels of signification broadly similar to those in sheet 1.

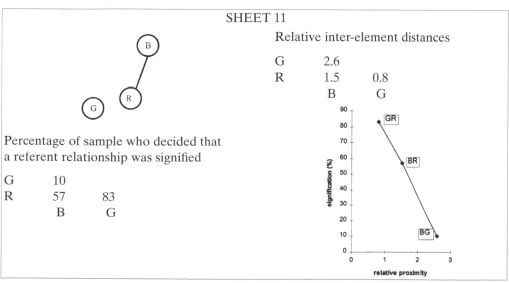

SHEET 11

Relative inter-element distances

G	2.6	
R	1.5	0.8
	B	G

Percentage of sample who decided that a referent relationship was signified

G	10	
R	57	83
	B	G

The strength of BR's signification in sheet 11 is only a little better than would be expected without being conjoined. GR has about half the inter-element distance of BR, but has already become a much more dominant relation. It seems that simple near proximity has a very powerful effect on the children's decoding, and quickly overtakes the signification of simple formal conjunction.

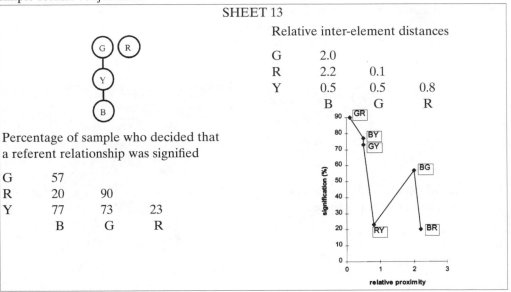

SHEET 13

Relative inter-element distances

G	2.0		
R	2.2	0.1	
Y	0.5	0.5	0.8
	B	G	R

Percentage of sample who decided that a referent relationship was signified

G	57		
R	20	90	
Y	77	73	23
	B	G	R

The very high position of BG in sheet 13 shows that over half of the sample understood the transitive nature of collinear formal conjunction, even when one of the elements is involved in the near proximity relation GR. This contrasts sharply with cases of collinear near proximity on other sheets, whose transitivity was seriously weakened by intersecting simple near proximity. The low value for RY must be at least partly due to offset intervention, but this could be exacerbated by the presence of the nearby conjunction.

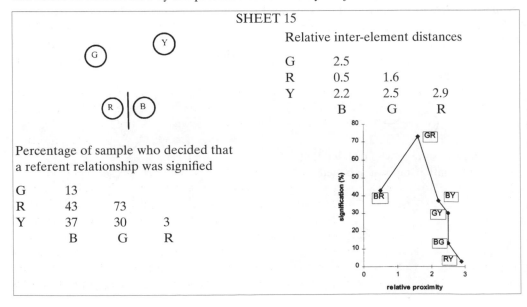

SHEET 15

Relative inter-element distances

G	2.5		
R	0.5	1.6	
Y	2.2	2.5	2.9
	B	G	R

Percentage of sample who decided that a referent relationship was signified

G	13		
R	43	73	
Y	37	30	3
	B	G	R

The introduction of simple formal disjunction in sheet 15 seemed to produce two distinct effects. First, most children did take account of it in their decoding, because the signification dropped enormously, so it successfully counteracted the small inter-element distance. Second, it markedly enhanced the signification of most of the other graphic relations. The exceptions to this were BG and RY, which were slightly depressed, either by the offset intervention effect or by the disjunction itself.

Discussion

Overall, the experimental results show several trends which are too consistent to be ignored. First, it is clear that children in the eleven to thirteen age range can decode simple near and far proximity with a considerable measure of success. In all the sheets containing only simple proximity (for example, sheet 1) there was a gradual falling off of signification as the inter-element distance increased. Where there were anomalies they mainly fell into the distinct pattern labelled the offset intervention effect. This is peculiar in its working, as can be seen in Figure 9.5. The effect of element B on AC's signification is comparatively neutral when B

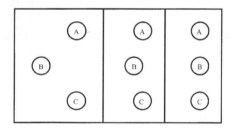

Figure 9.5 *The effects of offset intervention*

is relatively remote, but is more noticeable as B moves in to take up the offset intervention position. When B is situated along the AC axis, however, the signification of AC increases again, presumably due to collinear near proximity. In sheets 1 to 9, all of which featured only proximity, this effect occurred ten times, and only in two cases did it not seem to affect the signification. In all the other eight cases, weakening due to the offset intervention effect was clearly evident.

The orientation of the inter-element axis seemed to have little or no effect on near proximity's signification (sheet 1). However, there did seem to be some effect as the inter-element distance grew. Thus, for larger gaps, the signification was stronger when the axis was across the card, and weaker as it moved towards the perpendicular ('vertical') direction (sheet 8).

Formal conjunction does seem to have considerable power, especially in sheet 10, where 90 per cent of the sample decoded it successfully, but also in sheet 13. However, its effect waned surprisingly quickly when the inter-element distance of the proximity relation became less than that of the conjunction (sheet 11). Formal disjunction, even when the disjoined elements are very close, appeared to have the expected effect on many children. Sheets 1 and 15 have very similar arrangements, with BY in the former corresponding to BR in the latter, but the respective significations are 97 per cent and 43 per cent. It also seems that the introduction of formal conjunction or disjunction into a graphic arrangement does not just affect the interpretation of the specific relation, but appears to have complex field effects throughout the graphic space.

It should also be noted that a proportion of the children did not seem to understand the conventions of graphic space. Even the nearest of proximities rarely achieved 100 per cent signification, 10 per cent of the subjects failed to ascribe any significance to the conjunctive element in the most simple case (sheet 10) and 43 per cent of the sample likewise completely ignored the disjunctive element in sheet 15. It is possible to argue that the children concerned had none of the parallel oral and textual cues available in normal learning situations, but the study does at least raise a note of caution about the ability of a significant minority of ten- to thirteen-year-olds to interpret non-verbal graphic patterns in the manner intended.

It should be clear that this small experiment represents a scratching of the surface of the complex issue of how children interpret and understand graphic relations. For one thing, in using apparently dichotomous descriptors like near/far proximity, it suggests that the continuous variation implicit in the idea of proximity is being ignored. Proximity is, of course, an inherently continuous graphic relation, and is able theoretically to represent an infinite number of values in a graphic relationship; for example, in scale drawings. Thus, proximity is frequently metricated in much graphical work in mathematics. On the other hand, formal conjunction and disjunction are intrinsically less likely to lend themselves to continuous situations. They are more Boolean in character. For example, two closely set elements are either separated by a disjunctive or they are not, that is, either there is a referent relationship or there is not. Yet even here some variation is possible, usually by varying the thickness of lines. Chromatic conjunction is particularly valuable in representing continuous variation, through the use of subtle changes in colour. Even morphological conjunction can use different sizes of the same symbol.

In summary, we have tried to do two things in this chapter. First, we have attempted to describe a fundamental syntax of graphic relations with which diagrams are constructed and understood. Second, we have presented an experiment which indicates that children can use this syntax to understand simple diagrams, but interpretations were not universal, and revealed subtle and complicated effects.

Chapter 10

Children's Perception of Pattern in Relation to Shape

Jean Orton

PATTERN AND SHAPE

Pattern features in the display of many classrooms. The study of symmetry provides a golden opportunity for folded cut-out patterns and ink blob designs, and work with tessellations can result in many brightly coloured patterns to decorate the walls. Awareness of symmetry is fundamental to later work on transformation geometry, and tessellations can provide more opportunities for pupils to experience ideas of transformations and area (Orton, 1994a). There is no shortage of patterns for pupils to observe under their feet, on floors or pavements, and in the structure and walls of many buildings. Geometrical patterns abound in everyday life, from man-made clothing to butterflies and birds. Providing a definition of pattern in geometry, however, is not easy. Indeed, Grünbaum and Shephard (1986) claim that they have been unable to find a satisfactory definition, but to Sawyer (1955, p. 12), pattern 'is any kind of regularity that can be recognized by the mind'. A study of pattern and design with fabrics or wallpapers would suggest that the idea of repetition is important. A geometrical pattern seems to need regular repetitions to distinguish it from other designs. The programme 'Patterns' in the BBC TV series MI.10, *Mathematical Investigations*, opens with a sequence of natural and man-made patterns. What they all have in common is that something is repeated in several different places, and the opening words of the programme are 'Designing a pattern means repeating something'. Bidwell (1985), however, refers to all arrangements of three shaded squares on a 3×3 grid as being patterns and Zusne uses the word pattern to refer to 'a configuration consisting of several elements that somehow belong together' (Zusne, in Reed, 1973, p. 4). This use of pattern is more like the idea of a pattern as a model, example or template to be recognized or copied, as with a knitting pattern. Thus it seems that, in relation to geometry, pattern has more than one meaning. In this chapter, the word pattern will not be confined to repeating patterns but will include ideas about shape recognition, congruence and similarity.

SHAPE RECOGNITION

What shapes can a young child recognize in Figures 10.1 and 10.2? Naming shapes is likely to be less successful than identifying the shape when its name is given (Gibbs and Orton, 1994).

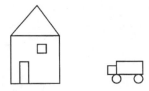

Figure 10.1 *Picture using simple shapes*

Figure 10.2 *Picture using some shapes in non-standard orientations*

However, finding the correct name may be merely a language exercise, testing familiarity with the correct label and masking conceptual understanding. There is no guarantee that a child who correctly names all the shapes in Figure 10.1 will recognize the square feet or the rectangular legs in Figure 10.2. Kerslake (1979) studied children's recognition of shapes drawn in non-standard ways, and her results for recognizing ◆ as a square are shown in Table 10.1.

Table 10.1 *Results for children's recognition of a rotated square*

Age of children	5+	6+	7+
% recognizing ◆ as a square	54	56	80

There can be confusion when one is talking to children about squares and rectangles, because children tend to classify these shapes as different, whereas mathematicians prefer to think of squares as special rectangles. To avoid this difficulty, some books use the word 'oblong' for a non-square rectangle.

The usual illustration of a triangle is ▲, so it is hardly surprising if pupils fail to recognize the arms in Figure 10.2 as triangles. Greenes (in Dickson *et al.*, 1984) reports the words of a nine-year-old when asked whether ▶ is a triangle: 'No. Because it fell over.' Not only have the triangles in Figure 10.2 'fallen over', they are also not equilateral and thus a different shape from the norm. Children who *do* recognize the two triangles may not appreciate, however, that the two triangles are congruent. It is a considerable step from recognition of a shape to analysing its parts (Van Hiele, 1986) or to visualizing the shape in a different position.

A child's knowledge of shape is rooted in experience of 'concrete' objects, according to Piaget (see, for example, Piaget *et al.*, 1960). During the 'sensorimotor' stage (roughly age nought to two years) there is much tactile exploration and coordination with perception, and the infant learns by experience through the development of schemata. Once the child recognizes that an object continues to exist when removed, some form of imagery and 'representational' thinking becomes possible. To Piaget, the image is initially an interiorization of the child's own actions in relation to the object. The child's development of shape progresses through becoming aware of different geometrical properties. Initially, shape and size are not appreciated but there is topological awareness (of junctions, lines and regions), so that a circle and square would be classified in the same way but seen as different from overlapping squares. Then there are projective distinctions as the child becomes aware of objects from different angles, and finally the Euclidean properties of size, distance and direction are grasped. Critics, however, suggest that Piaget's experiments give different results when the conditions are varied, and that the idea of his topological stage is questionable. Fuson and Murray (in Dickson *et al.*, 1984) studied the ability of two- to seven-year-old children to recognize shapes by touch and to draw them, and found the circle easiest to identify, followed by the square, then the triangle and lastly the rhombus. Shape copying was also studied by Noelting (in Dickson *et al.*, 1984), who found a similar development. Graham *et al.* (in Vernon, 1970) also showed that there is a gradual improvement of copying with age, though sudden jumps had been suggested by Piaget and Inhelder (in Vernon, 1970). Children learn to copy a geometric shape much later than they learn to discriminate between shapes, perhaps because copying involves division into parts and relating the parts to the whole.

Van Hiele (1986) has suggested that there are levels of spatial development and at level 1 children are not aware of the relationship between parts of a shape. Figures are only distinguished by their individual shape as a whole. It is only at level 2 that a child will recognize, for example, that a rectangle has four right angles and its opposite sides are of equal length.

SYMMETRY

Children have many early experiences of symmetry, from their own bodies and clothing to the natural world of flowers, leaves and insects, but whether these experiences heighten their awareness of symmetry in other contexts has not been proved. The National Curriculum (DfE/WO, 1995) expects children to recognize reflective symmetry of 2-D and 3-D shapes and the rotational symmetries of 2-D shapes at Key Stage 2. Using mirrors and tracing paper, what symmetries are pupils likely to find in the shapes shown in Figure 10.3?

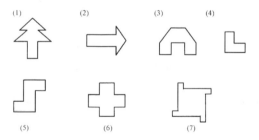

Figure 10.3 *Symmetrical shapes*

Some studies have suggested an order of difficulty for symmetrical patterns. Paraskevopoulos (1968) used dot patterns with children aged six to twelve (see Figure 10.4). The children were shown a set of four patterns, asked to try to remember them, and then given blank grids to try to fill in the dots. They found that double symmetry was the easiest to remember, that 'vertical' symmetry followed at age seven but that 'horizontal' symmetry was not decoded until age eleven. Similar results were obtained by Chipman and Mendelson (1979). Children aged six, eight, ten and twelve and college students were shown pairs of patterns (see Figure 10.5) and asked to select the simpler pattern. The amount of contour in the

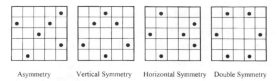

Asymmetry   Vertical Symmetry   Horizontal Symmetry   Double Symmetry

Figure 10.4 *Examples of dot patterns*

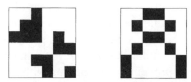

Figure 10.5 *Patterns similar to those used by Chipman and Mendelson*

pattern had no apparent relation with received complexity, but sensitivity to visual structure was again seen to increase with age:

> Sensitivity to double symmetry and vertical symmetry appeared quite early while sensitivity to horizontal symmetry, diagonal symmetry and checkerboard organization appeared considerably later. Sensitivity to rotational organization was not fully evident even in the oldest subjects. (Chipman and Mendelson, 1979, p. 375)

These studies would suggest that at Key Stage 2 the symmetry in shapes (1), (3) and (6) in Figure 10.3 would be easily spotted, the symmetry in shapes (2) and (4) would be harder to recognize and the rotational symmetry of shapes (5) and (7) might be missed. Cross-cultural studies of pattern perception (Bentley, in Deregowski, 1980) revealed the same sequence of pattern difficulty among pupils from Scotland (aged twelve years) and pupils from Western Kenya (average age eighteen years), namely:

- median (vertical) and transverse (horizontal) symmetry;
- diagonal symmetry;
- skew (rotational) symmetry;
- random arrangements.

At these ages no difference was found between vertical and horizontal symmetry. Vertical symmetry is so common and so easily recognized that there could be the danger that pupils expect to find such symmetry even when it is absent. To test whether pupils have a tendency to impose reflective symmetry on a shape where none exists, pupils aged nine to fifteen were asked by the author to copy the shapes shown in Figure 10.6. It would have been interesting to have had more data from a younger age group, but nevertheless the results suggested that the tendency to impose symmetry does seem to decrease with age.

TRANSFORMATIONS

Consider the activity in Figure 10.7. Does the order of difficulty for transformations correspond with the order for recognition of symmetry? Piaget suggested that the order in which children learn transformations is: translations, reflections and then rotations. Perham (in Dickson *et al.*, 1984) distinguished between horizontal, vertical and oblique transformations,

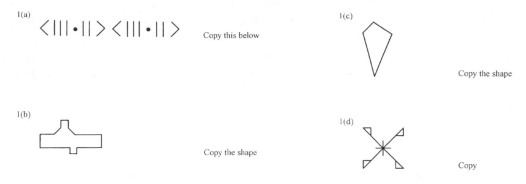

Figure 10.6 *Shape copying question*

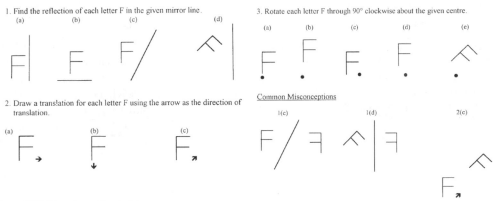

Figure 10.7 *Transformation tasks*

and found that the last caused repeated difficulty even after instruction, and Shultz (in Dickson *et al.*, 1984) found similar results, noting that if children (aged six and eight) *did* attempt an oblique translation, the image was often given in the direction of the translation (cf. the common misconception for 2(c) in Figure 10.7), and with reflection and rotations the tendency was to turn the image so that it faced the direction of reflection or turn (cf. the common misconception for 1(d)).

The first APU survey (APU, 1980) showed that only 14 per cent of eleven-year-olds could find the reflection of a shape in an oblique mirror line (cf. 1(c)), and Küchemann (1980) found that many fourteen-year-olds ignored the slope of an oblique mirror line and reflected horizontally or vertically (cf. the common misconception for 1(c)). His work suggested that children were operating at different stages. At the global stage, the object would be considered as a whole and reflected as a single object, while a fully analytic approach was to reduce the objects to points and reflect these before drawing in the lines. Some children, at a semi-analytic stage, reflected part of the object and then drew in the rest. The CSMS results (Hart, 1981) which Küchemann discussed also showed that fourteen-year-olds had difficulty with rotating a shape if the centre of rotation was not on the object (cf. 3(b) to 3(e)), and only 17 per cent could successfully indicate the image when the object (a flag) was obliquely orientated (cf. 3(e)). Research by Bell (1989) has shown two prevalent misconceptions:

- that horizontal and vertical objects always have horizontal or vertical images (cf. the common misconception for 1(c));

- that a line which divides a shape into two parts of equal area must be a line of symmetry (e.g. the diagonal of a rectangle).

Perham (in Dickson *et al.*, 1984) found that the ability to select an image from several alternatives preceded the ability to construct the image. This may explain some of the reflection and rotation results obtained by Thomas (in Dickson *et al.*, 1984) with children aged nine, twelve, fifteen and seventeen years. Subjects were required to imagine the results of reflecting or rotating a cardboard square with a letter of the alphabet printed on it and to choose from four given images. Her main findings were:

1. Rotating a figure which already has rotational symmetry – S and N – was very difficult for pupils of all ages to visualize.
2. Horizontal reflection with the non-symmetric J was difficult.
3. The youngest group (nine years old) scored much lower on all transformations.
4. There were no striking differences between direction of turning on the rotation tasks, nor between horizontal and vertical on the reflection tasks (Dickson *et al.*, 1984, p. 66).

Most textbooks approach the idea of reflection through mirror activities or the use of folding paper, and rotation tasks are initially explored with the help of tracing paper and a pin. In the absence of such concrete support how do pupils imagine the result of reflecting or rotating an object, shape or drawing? Is there such a thing as a mental image? Those who support the idea of a mental image refer to a close relationship between imagery and perception. The same cognitive processes are said to be involved, although the stimulus input that would give rise to perception is absent (Neisser, in Eysenck, 1984). Critics (for example, Pylyshyn, in Eysenck, 1984) pour scorn on the idea of a 'mental photograph' and believe that all knowledge can be represented in the form of propositions. Clements (1982) gives a good summary of theories supporting and opposing visual images, and Cooper (1990) provides more recent evidence in support of mental representation of 3-D objects. The recognition of congruent shapes in different orientations would seem to involve some form of mental transformation, but is the image that is transformed pictorial or propositional? In recognizing two different rotations of a triangle as congruent, does a pupil's mental activity use a set of propositions (expressing the properties of each triangle) or has one triangle been mentally rotated to match the other? It is possible that the answer to these questions depends on the pupil. Krutetskii (1976) has suggested that there might be three different types of mathematical mind:

- the analytic, where thinking is verbal or logical;
- the geometric, where thinking is visual or pictorial;
- the harmonic, which combines the characteristics of the other types.

This also suggests that analytic thinkers do not use mental images. Research by Presmeg (1995) explores the use made of visual images by high school students of mathematics in three different countries, and presents a frequency distribution of visuality scores. Solano and Presmeg (1995) refer to visualization in terms of the relationship between images rather than mental manipulation.

RESEARCH AT LEEDS

Research using a pattern recognition test was conducted by the author at Leeds with nearly 300 pupils aged nine plus (Year 5) to fifteen plus (Year 11). Additional information was

6(a)

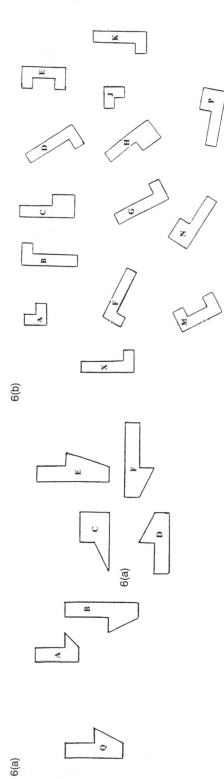

6(a)

Which of the shapes could be cut out and placed on top of shape Q?

6(c)

Which shapes could be cut out and placed on top of shape Y?

6(b)

Which shapes could be cut out and placed on top of shape X?

6(d)

Which triangles could be cut out and placed on top of shape W?

Figure 10.8 *Mental manipulation question*

Table 10.2 *Results for mental manipulation (question 6, Figure 10.8)*

Age	Year	6(a)	6(b)	6(c)	6(d)
9/10	Y5M	61.4	63.2	52.3	45.8
9/10	Y5F	44.4	55.6	50.4	51.9
9/10	Y5A	53.8	59.8	51.4	48.5
11/12	Y7M	68.1	57.5	53.8	52.5
11/12	Y7F	56.4	70.3	62.3	54.7
11/12	Y7A	62.8	63.3	57.6	53.5
13/14	Y9M	84.3	77.7	73.4	64.7
13/14	Y9F	62.2	54.6	51.7	53.6
13/14	Y9A	75.0	67.9	64.3	60.0
15/16	Y11M	66.7	54.1	53.4	51.9
15/16	Y11F	91.3	53.0	47.2	52.2
15/16	Y11A	78.0	53.6	50.6	52.0

obtained from individual interviews conducted with twelve of the pupils. Some of the questions which explored the mental manipulation, or otherwise, of 2-D shapes are shown in Figure 10.8.

Performance with 6(a) was variable. Table 10.2 shows a slight suggestion of improvement with age in the percentages for all (A) but with boys (M) giving more correct responses than girls (F) at the lower levels. The most common wrong response was F. Question 6(a) involved only rotation, and there was some confusion as to whether reflection was allowed in 6(b), (c) and (d). Some pupils asked 'Are you allowed to turn them over?' A few either assumed that you couldn't and discounted B, D and K in 6(b), or were unable to match the shapes. Another complication was the assumption that only *one* shape was required for the answer. Pupils who assumed that reflection was not allowed would be expected to omit E, F, H and K in 6(c) and G and M in 6(d), but in fact only one pupil consistently left out all reflections and no other shapes, suggesting the influence of other factors too. Shape G in 6(b) (which required only a slight rotation to be in the same orientation as the given shape) was very rarely missed out, whereas the more complex shape B in 6(c) was missed out despite being in the same orientation as Y, and likewise shape E was missed out in 6(d). Scores for

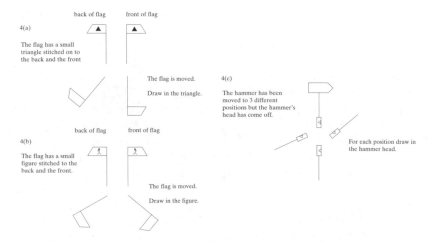

Figure 10.9 *Transformation question to explore frames of reference*

6(c) and 6(d) were generally lower than for 6(a) and 6(b), perhaps because of the added complexity in the shapes but, with some pupils assuming that only one shape was required, the scores were perhaps not as meaningful as had been hoped. During individual interviews an attempt was made to time the pupils as they wrote down their answers to these questions, and there was some evidence that the length of time decreased with age.

Question 4 (Figure 10.9) was designed to explore the possible influence of a frame of reference when transforming a shape. It was not easy to analyse. The drawings of the backs of the flags allowed ambiguity of interpretation with the transformed flags. For example, in (a) one transformed flag is either a reflection of the front of the flag in a horizontal axis or a rotation of the back of the flag, and the other could be either a reflection of the back of the flag in a diagonal axis or a rotation of the front of the flag. Individual interviews revealed that some pupils completed 4(a) and 4(b) using the outline of the flags as a frame of reference and filled in the triangles and figures in relation to the top and bottom of the flag, perhaps without any mental transformation being involved. Indeed, many of the pupils physically moved the answer paper round to align the flagpoles with the 'vertical' of the desktop. Table 10.3 shows the percentage of the total marks available scored by pupils in each part of the question at the different age levels.

Table 10.3 *Results for exploring frames of reference (question 4, Figure 10.9)*

Age	Year	4(a)	4(b)	4(c)
9/10	Y5M	85.2	55.7	54.6
9/10	Y5F	54.2	33.3	36.1
9/10	Y5A	71.3	45.6	46.3
11/12	Y7M	94.7	78.7	72.3
11/12	Y7F	79.5	66.7	53.0
11/12	Y7A	87.8	73.3	63.6
13/14	Y9M	91.2	85.3	76.5
13/14	Y9F	94.6	87.8	72.1
13/14	Y9A	92.6	86.4	74.6
15/16	Y11M	87.0	94.4	75.3
15/16	Y11F	91.3	84.8	76.8
15/16	Y11A	89.0	90.0	76.0

Question 4(a) was generally found to be easier than 4(b), where the asymmetrical figure required more consideration of direction, and caused difficulty especially with younger pupils. Older pupils seemed to make more errors with 4(c) than with the other parts. No frame of reference was available in this part and the orientation of the handle was often ignored and all the transformations taken as rotations. It had been anticipated that the horizontal reflection would be found easier than rotation but this was not found to be so in either 4(c) or in 4(a). It was not surprising, however, that a frame of reference simplified the question. Küchemann (1980) has reported on the effect of the presence of a grid on the facility of both reflection and rotation items (see Figure 10.10) and Bryant (1974), in discussing young children's difficulty in distinguishing between | and /, claims that the difficulty is removed when children can use a perceptual framework like the side of a page. The presence of a frame of reference seems to remove the demand for visualization and enables pupils to transform a shape by applying certain rules. There are, however, instances of inappropriate use of a frame of reference. Piaget and Inhelder (in Dickson *et al.*, 1984), for example, reveal the misconceptions of young children about the level of water in a bottle when the bottle is

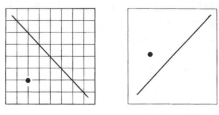

Facility of 86%   Facility of 61%

Figure 10.10 *Reflection task with and without a grid*

tilted. It is only at ages five to seven years that children are able to free the water level from the frame of reference of the bottle.

Among the hardest questions on the pattern recognition test were two which involved the recognition of rotation (shown in Figure 10.11). D was the most common response to question 7. Perhaps some pupils thought the question involved shape matching and matched the

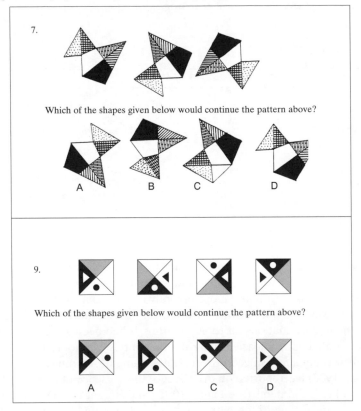

Figure 10.11 *Questions using rotation*

first shape with D. One ten-year-old pupil, when interviewed, explained it differently: 'because that's where it starts again. The three shapes form the pattern and then it starts again, so D'. That sort of reasoning would give the correct answer for the wrong reason in question 9, but in fact performance with 9 was generally lower than with 7, and wrong responses were varied. Individual interviews revealed that children were very good at seeing a different pattern from the one intended, as this explanation for the choice of C in question 7 reveals: 'The three shapes are like ducks. It must be C because it's not like a duck. It has an extra line'. It was also clear from the interviews that some children spotted the rotation but still gave a 'wrong' answer.

It had been hoped that question 10 (Figure 10.12) would be a fruitful question for comparing the difficulty of mental transformations. Table 10.4 shows the mean scores for each part of the question at the different age levels. Clearly (a), which involves vertical reflection, was the easiest, and (e), a reflection in a diagonal, was the most difficult. Part (g) was also a reflection in a diagonal, but this was generally found no more difficult than other parts (with the exception of (a)). The difference between (e) and (g) was that in (e) the orientation of the

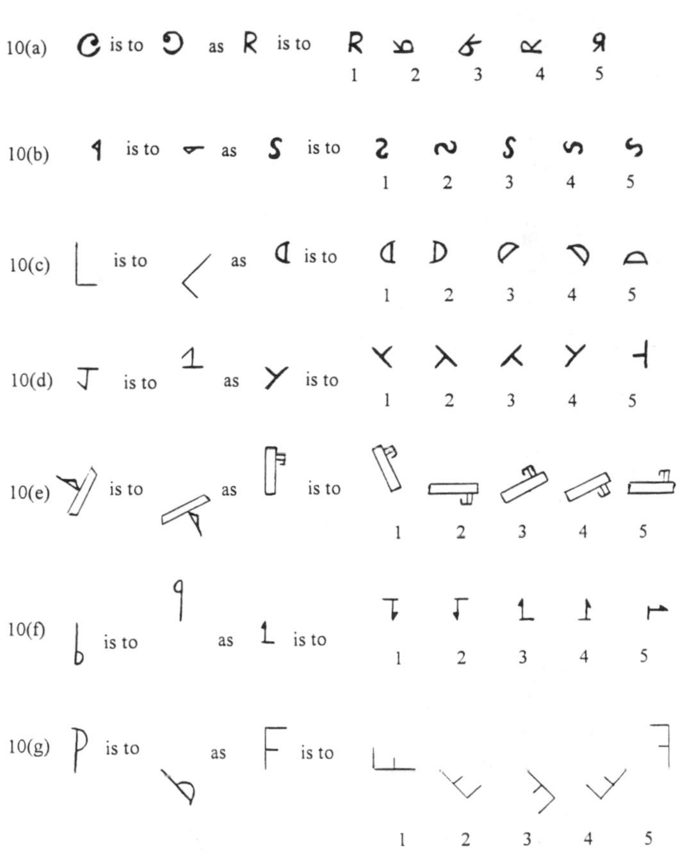

Figure 10.12 *Question to explore mental transformations*

Table 10.4 *Mean scores for question 10, Figure 10.12*

	a Ref.	b Rot. 90°	c Rot. 45°	d Ref. —	e Ref.	f Rot. 180°	g Ref.
Y5	0.70	0.31	0.43	0.40	0.04	0.33	0.48
Y7	0.76	0.52	0.65	0.53	0.07	0.47	0.70
Y9	0.97	0.63	0.86	0.69	0.08	0.69	0.75
Y11	0.96	0.64	0.90	0.58	0.00	0.62	0.72

shape to be transformed was different from the orientation of the model shape. It was no longer possible to use the orientation of a significant line of the transformed model shape in the example as a guide (or frame of reference) in choosing the answer. Table 10.5 shows the frequency of wrong responses, and it can be seen that 3 and 4 were the most popular choices for (e), supporting the hypothesis that the answer was chosen to match the orientation of the transformed model shape.

Table 10.5 *Frequencies of wrong responses for question 10, Figure 10.12*

		10(a)					10(b)		
Answer	1	2	3	4	1	2	3	5	
No. of responses	15	3	3	4	21	76	18	4	
		10(c)					10(d)		
Answer	1	2	4	5	1	3	4	5	
No. of responses	11	28	20	3	25	58	20	3	
		10(e)					10(f)		
Answer	1	2	3	4	2	3	4	5	
No. of responses	22	26	93	114	67	18	27	3	
		10(g)							
Answer	1	3	4	5					
No. of responses	13	32	10	15					

Parts (c), (f) and (g) all have a vertical line of the transformed shape matching the orientation of a line in the original shape, enabling the correct answer to be selected partly using this line as a frame of reference. It is possible that some pupils used this method without any mental transformation. The method would give 3 as a clear answer for (c), would give 2 or 3 for (g), but would only eliminate 5 for (f). Certainly, the popular choice of the wrong answer 3 for (g) would support this, and it could help to explain why (c), a rotation question, was not found as difficult as expected, and why (f) was found more difficult. Pupils' explanations during individual interviews give added support, for example: 'That one's swapped around to that position so F will swap around too.'

It had been expected that (d), a reflection in the horizontal, might be an easy question, but this was not the case, confirming Thomas's result 2, quoted on page 154. The most popular wrong answer was 3, suggesting recognition that reflection in the horizontal was required but inaccuracy in the mental transformation. The relative complexity of the shape might well have had some effect too. Part (b), a rotation, was not expected to be easy. It is possible that pupils imagined a vertical line through the S to compare with the example ('standing upright, moving on to its side', as one pupil explained it) or that rotation was recognized but inaccurately performed. The most common error 2 would be expected in both cases.

Pupil explanations revealed that reflection in a diagonal line was not generally recognized. The transformation was seen as a combination of turning over and rotating: 'Gone round and then over'; 'Move round and then flip over'; 'Turn and then tilt'; 'Reflection in what would be the *x*-axis and then gone anti-clockwise a bit'. From that point of view, (e) becomes an unreasonable question. The size of rotation is considered important and none of the options show the correct angle of rotation. It is not clear whether the pupils' explanation indicates a transformation carried out in the mind.

Individual interviews revealed variation not only in understanding but also in mastery of mathematical language. One of the extra questions given at the interviews is shown in Figure

10.13. Pupils were asked how each line related to the first. Here are some of the responses: 'You fold over'; 'A straightforward reflection'; 'You put a mirror along there'; 'That's a symmetry of the first line'; 'Swing it round'; 'Turn around 180°'. Pupils differed most in their

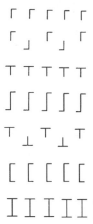

Are these lines of shapes related to each other?
If so, how?

Figure 10.13 *Extra question used during individual interviews*

explanation of the third line. Many saw these shapes as completely unrelated to the top line. Some saw them as the same shape with a bit added on. Very few suggested 'Turned over a vertical axis', although line 6 was clearly identified as involving a turn about a horizontal axis. Perhaps the fact that the shape and the image would share the same vertical line caused confusion, just as embedded shapes sharing contours are less easily distinguishable (cf. Table 10.7). Some pupils explained line 4 as a double reflection (horizontal first) rather than a rotation, perhaps confirming the relative ease of recognizing reflective symmetry (see also Orton (1993)).

PATTERN DEVELOPMENT

Mean scores were calculated for the ten questions in the pattern recognition test for each age group. Questions 5 and 6 were similar questions and taken together. Mean totals were also computed (see Table 10.6). The mean totals show some clearly increasing values with age, and

Table 10.6 *Mean scores for the complete pattern recognition test*

Q.	1	2	3	4	5 + 6	7	8	9	10	Total
Y5	4.53	1.56	1.56	3.73	14.04	0.30	0.59	0.30	2.68	29.25
Y7	4.66	1.71	1.70	5.13	14.68	0.56	0.60	0.44	3.70	33.12
Y9	4.83	1.91	1.92	5.82	16.56	0.68	0.70	0.55	4.63	37.58
Y11	4.84	1.82	1.94	5.86	13.46	0.64	0.58	0.56	4.42	34.12

these increases are significant except between Years 9 and 11, where the large number of less able girls in this sample appear to have affected the results.

Analysis of pupils' responses suggests three developmental stages in terms of the items of the pattern recognition test. Their content includes:

Stage 1: copying a shape; detection of embedded pictures; simple completion of pattern; matching picture shapes; recognition of reflection in a 'vertical' axis; simple rotation and reflection completion tasks with a frame of reference.

Stage 2: matching of embedded shapes; matching of simple geometric shapes in different orientations; more complex rotation and reflection tasks with a frame of reference.

Stage 3: matching of more complex shapes in different orientations; more complex completion of pattern tasks including rotation; recognition of most reflection and rotation.

Further descriptions of levels of understanding have been provided by Küchemann (1980) in relation to reflection and rotation tasks. The Van Hiele levels are more general, and extend beyond the visual first level of shape recognition and the descriptive second level of properties and rules to a third theoretical level, where definitions and relationships are worked out and proof becomes possible, and then to two further levels of deductive reasoning and abstract thought. Failure to take account of the levels of thinking of our pupils and to provide appropriate teaching material may create problems. Nasser *et al.* (1996) discuss the difficulties of Brazilian school children working with textbooks which require them to provide proofs for the congruence of triangles (SAS, SSS, ASA) when their thinking is still at the first two levels and consequently not advanced enough to reason deductively. At a lower level, teachers may assume that ◩ may be helpful in illustrating the meaning of one-quarter, but if pupils are unable to see the four triangles as congruent shapes their concept of one-quarter will not be very meaningful.

PATTERN AND ABILITY

It might seem reasonable to assume that pupils' general ability will be a good indicator of their ability to perceive pattern, but is there any evidence? The research at Leeds explored this possible relationship by correlating the pattern recognition totals with scores of general ability based on the AH4 test (Heim, 1970). The relationship did not seem to be a simple one. There was more correlation in the lower half of the ability range than the upper and, although correlation was evident over the whole ability range, the results suggest that it might not be detected in a setted class.

THEORIES ABOUT PATTERN RECOGNITION

These reflect many different perspectives, all of which are discussed briefly here.

Template Matching

Template matching ideas have been used in many studies. A pattern is thought to be recognized by comparing it with templates in the human memory. The templates are presumably internal representations of what has been noticed in the past, and the theory could suggest the need for a hypothetical template for each pattern. It seems more acceptable to consider that what we store is not a template for each individual pattern but instead is a smaller number of prototypes, where each prototype represents the central tendency or most typical member of a set of stimuli (Donahoe and Wessels, 1980). Any stimulus (shape or pattern) is thus seen as a member of a set represented by the prototype, and the essential characteristics of a prototype are given by a set of rules or a schema. A schema for the prototype of a triangle might be 'A shape with three straight sides', but the abstraction involved in forming a prototype might suggest that prototypes are not used by young children! Rosch (in Roth and Frisby, 1986) suggests an adaptation of the prototype model. Her proposal is that a prototype can be seen as a list of features.

Feature Analysis

Feature analysis considers features such as size, length or orientation to be extracted from the stimulus and compared to lists of defining features in the memory. This approach is more flexible than that of template matching. Instead of a unique match between stimulus and stored template, a set of features is abstracted from the stimulus and compared with shape representations in memory. Failure to recognize a pattern could be due to:

- poor feature extraction from the stimulus;
- inability to match the extracted features with representation in memory;
- inaccurate representations in memory;
- a faulty decision about final categorization.

Thus pupils failing to recognize an isosceles triangle might:

- have missed the feature that one side was a different length from the others;
- have an inaccurate representation for isosceles triangle in memory;
- be unable to match the external features with their representation of isosceles triangles;
- have made the wrong decision about the categorization of the triangle.

Feature models are attractive because they seem to have physiological support. Hubel and Weisel (in Wilding, 1982) experimented with the visual cortex of a cat and found that certain cells only responded to specific visual stimuli, such as a line of particular length or orientation, while other cells responded to angles of a particular size. It is tempting to conclude that these cells are functioning as detectors for specific visual features, but other evidence from the study of frogs suggests a more complex process. However, Marg *et al.* (in Wilding, 1982) are reported to have found indirect evidence that there are probably units in the human cortex responsive to straight lines and curves.

Symmetry of the Brain

Study of the brain has influenced much theory of pattern recognition. The confusion of young children between shapes like b and d which are mirror images has been attributed to the symmetry of the nervous system and the fact that the two cerebral hemispheres are mirror images (Orton, in Bryant, 1974). Perception of an object was thought to involve the same pattern of firing in the two hemispheres, except that the two patterns are mirror images. Hence children would confuse left–right reflections, as both would produce the same pattern of excitation.

This confusion would eventually be overcome when the two hemispheres took on specialized functions. Corballis and Beale (1983, p. 83) consider left–right confusion to be 'a problem of labeling not of perception'. They generally support Orton's ideas describing symmetrical changes, but in memory, not the visual system as Orton hypothesized.

Connectionist Model

Neurophysiology has influenced many theoretical ideas. Current understanding of neurons has led to the connectionist model of pattern recognition. Activity in the nervous system is 'represented as the set of simultaneous individual neuron activities in a group of neurons. Neuron "activity" is considered to be related to a continuous variable, the average firing frequency' (Anderson *et al.*, 1977, p. 415). Individual cells have their own properties and, although cells near to each other may show similar response properties if studied in detail, each can be seen to behave differently: 'The fundamental premise of connectionism is that individual neurons do not transmit large amounts of symbolic information. Instead they compute by being appropriately connected to large numbers of similar units' (Feldman and Ballard, 1982, p. 208). It is possible to model such an interconnected system using the techniques of linear algebra (see Anderson *et al.*, 1977) and most accounts of connectionist models are very mathematical. There would seem to be the possibility of the model explaining the sudden realization of a pattern or the experience of 'illumination' (Hadamard, 1954), although no accounts have yet been found.

A major assumption of connectionist models is that visual processing involves parallel processing or the taking in of much visual information at the same time. However, the influence of computers, which for so long have been sequential, has caused most information-processing models to be given in sequential (or step-by-step) terms. The human brain may indeed be massively parallel, but it might be easier to understand some aspects of a complex process using a serial model.

Kosslyn's Theory of Imagery

The language of computers seems to have infiltrated many psychological models; for example, Kosslyn's computational theory (Kosslyn, 1981). In this theory, the image of an object or pattern is thought to have two components, the 'deep representation of the information in long-term memory', and the 'surface representation' (that is generated from the deep representation) in 'quasi-pictorial' form in the 'visual buffer' (Eysenck, 1984, p. 184). Several processes are involved when a surface image is formed; for example, FIND, which searches the visual buffer for a particular part when putting together multiple encodings to form a single image, and PUT, which forms the image in the correct location. Other processes, like SCAN and ZOOM, are used when the image is inspected.

It seems likely that there will never be one satisfactory theory of pattern recognition, but each may add something to our search for the understanding of intricate human processes.

THE ISSUE OF WHOLE OR PARTS

Consider the shape shown in Figure 10.14. What do children perceive? The outline? Two overlapping triangles? A rhombus and four small triangles? Two overlapping parallelograms?

According to the Gestalt theory of learning (see, for example, Resnick and Ford, 1984), the basic process of perception is the identification of a shape or form by its outline; it is the contour of a shape which distinguishes it from its background. This is referred to as the 'figure–ground' experience. The Gestalt psychologists have emphasized that perception is

Figure 10.14 *What is seen? Whole or parts?*

more than the combination of separate elements of sensory data. 'Gestalt', roughly translated from the German, means 'shape', 'form' or 'whole', and the theory encompasses the view that whole configurations are perceived first and then separate elements.

The feature analysis theory emphasizes the features or parts of a shape but ignores the relation between the parts. Reed (1973) suggested a formal system of structural descriptions for geometric figures, such as Figure 10.14. His experimental work shows how some pattern parts – for example, the rhombus – were found to be easier to identify than others – for example, the parallelograms. Reed's hypothesis was that people store the presented patterns as parts together with rules for linking them up (see Roth and Frisby, 1986). Ghent (1956) worked with children (aged four to thirteen years), showing them drawings of overlapping figures, and concluded that 'young children have difficulty in perceiving a given boundary as simultaneously belonging to more than one form' (p. 585). She suggested that this could be due to a 'narrow perceptual span'. The author used the task shown in Figure 10.15 with pupils aged nine to fifteen years and obtained the results shown in Table 10.7, which suggest a definite progression in identification of the correct shape.

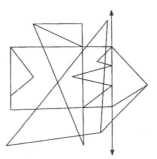

Shade in the triangle which could be placed on top
of the triangle Z, if you cut it out.

Figure 10.15 *Question to explore identification of embedded shape*

Table 10.7 *Results for identification of an embedded shape, Figure 10.15*

Age group	9–10	11–12	13–14	15–16
% correct	61	73	95	92

Vitz and Todd (1971) have suggested a model for the perception of geometric figures in terms of a hierarchy of perceptual elements: lines, angles and areas. Perceptual organization is said to involve a sampling process beginning with lines and, after all lines have been exhausted, moving to the next hierarchical level, which is angles. It is assumed that the probability of sampling an element is proportional to the magnitude of the element.

Hierarchical structure is also basic to Palmer's theory of perceptual representation (Palmer, 1977). It is an attractive theory, as it combines the Gestalt psychologists' holistic ideas with the structuralists' emphasis on the relation between parts. Perceptual representation is seen to involve 'highly organized data structures containing many embedded levels of detail' (p. 442). A whole pattern has global properties as well as component parts with specific perceptual relationships between them. Each part also has global properties and a further set of component parts. The highest structural unit for $\not\!\!\!\nearrow$, for example, would represent the figure as a whole with global properties like symmetry, closedness and compactness. At the next lower level could be structural units for the triangles and perhaps the Γ and the $\nearrow\!\!\!\nwarrow$ shapes. Each would be associated with global properties, and relationships between parts would also be encoded. At the next lower level could be angle size, orientation and position, and lower still might be structural units for lines with global properties of length. Kolinsky *et al.* (1987) used some of Palmer's figures with pre-school children, primary school children and unschooled adults, and found that the ability to find more deeply embedded segments was not present in the pre-school children and the unschooled adults. They concluded that 'the processes of post-perceptual analysis necessary to find a part in a figure are neither built-in nor the consequences of mere cognitive growth, but depend on the instruction or experience usually found in school' (p. 399). This suggests that primary school pattern activities and discussion of what is perceived in a pattern are likely to contribute to pupils' future pattern recognition.

CONCLUSION

There seems to be a clear body of pattern recognition 'knowledge' established by ages nine to ten years (stage 1, above) of which teachers should take advantage. Individual interviews have shown that pupils often recognize pattern but lack the vocabulary to explain fully what they perceive. There are many opportunities for the creation and copying of pattern in art, design, logo activities, etc., and the casual introduction of new vocabulary and ideas could help future understanding. Describing different orientations and ideas of rotation would seem particularly appropriate.

Wells (1988, p. 94) discusses the drawing and analysis of tessellations: 'It is a curious and mysterious feature of our brains, that they often take a long time to work out, in so many words and images, what they can see as an underlying pattern in no time at all.' Drawing a tessellation reveals the need for a deeper understanding requiring words and images. The creation of Islamic patterns starting with squared paper has proved an exciting and enriching activity for some children (see Delaney and Dichmont, 1979; Antonouris and Sparrow, 1989), and the discussion of such patterns could be very fruitful. Further ideas for creating tessellations are given in Mottershead (1978), and Orton (1994b) elaborates on other classroom mathematics which tessellations might inspire. African textiles are a rich source of pattern (Picton and Mack, 1989) and are becoming more accessible in a multicultural society. Cheap wrapping paper and wallpaper samples are also a good source of patterns for analysis.

Identifying and joining corresponding points produces a skeleton for the pattern and can lead to more discussion of shape and the relationship between shapes; and comparison of different patterns may lead to an awareness of structure and isomorphism. The important interchange between the conception of the whole and discrimination between parts has been emphasized in this chapter, and giving opportunity for parts/whole analysis and synthesis is obviously vital.

Another activity would be for pupils to study a pattern and write down in words some rules for continuing the pattern. These could be compared with the rules from other pupils in a group, and discussion would lead to extension of vocabulary and deeper understanding of the relationship between parts. Rules, in the form of transformations, for creating patterns with pattern blocks are given by Mottershead (1985), and the suggested activities appear simple and motivating and would give familiarity with the nature and language of transformations.

Several pupil difficulties and misunderstandings have been mentioned in this chapter. Readers can no doubt add more examples from their own classroom experience. Bell (1989) recommends 'conflict' lessons which allow such misunderstandings to be exposed and thoroughly discussed as an effective way of eradicating the errors. Teachers need to pose a known difficult problem which pupils first think about on their own, then writing down their response before going into small groups to discuss and possibly amend their conclusion. This ensures that wrong ideas are expressed and challenged in an unthreatening atmosphere. Finally, whole-class discussion allows a wider range of ideas to be faced in a critical way, and the ultimate conclusion drawn.

The opportunities for exploration and testing of hypotheses using computer dynamic geometry packages could also help to dispel pupils' misconceptions. The Geometer's Sketchpad, for example, allows the investigation of translation, reflection and rotation in a very straightforward and motivating way. An interesting area for further research would be to investigate to what extent such a dynamic geometry package could further pupils' understanding of pattern in geometry.

Chapter 11

Pattern and Randomness

Tom Roper

INTRODUCTION

The antithesis of pattern is random behaviour, yet, in order to achieve some control over random behaviour, we attempt to impose a pattern upon it. If random trials are taking place with a fixed probability of success at each trial, then we model the behaviour by the binomial distribution and extend this to such events as testing whether or not individuals can detect a difference in the taste of similar products. The distribution of various physical attributes throughout the population is modelled by the normal distribution. Clothing retailers stock sizes according to this distribution, and thereby hope to satisfy the majority of their customers without carrying stock that they will not be able to sell. The combination of distributions, analysed mathematically, enables us to enter lifts with confidence, knowing that the advertised limits are well within the calculated safety limits.

Yet where our own personal interaction with random events is concerned, the mathematics of the situation may very well take second place. The nature of the pattern which we might seek to impose could be very different according to the situation in which that random behaviour is occurring. At a very simple level, the overwhelming majority of people would be prepared to admit that the chance of a coin coming down heads or tails is 50:50. However, many of the same people, when faced with the toss of a specific coin, will have a favourite call and will nearly always make that call. When playing games which require a six on dice to start, the players often feel that getting that six is either very difficult or very easy.

The mathematical model which is imposed on the situation is not always the one which we choose to accept, sometimes leading to contradictions that we find hard to explain to ourselves or to our pupils. This clash between the mathematical and the intuitive models was brought to the author's attention in introducing classes of pupils who were towards the end of Year 10 (fifteen-year-old pupils) to what A level mathematics might be like. A game was offered to one of the pupils in which the author and that pupil would take turns to toss a 10 p coin, and the first player to get a head would win the coin. Having selected a volunteer, the question was posed to the pupil and to the class: 'Do you want to go first or second?'

The debate which always ensued never failed to astonish and intrigue. Some of the pupils would argue that since the coin had an equal chance of coming down heads or tails it did not matter who went first. Others would argue that you had to go first to have the best chance of winning the coin, but could not provide any reason why you had to go first – you just did.

Others seemed to want to have a foot in both camps; that is, it does not matter who goes first because there is an equal chance of the coin coming down heads or tails, but if you go first, you get your half chance first.

The debate was always lively, and never reached a conclusion where all the class could agree on one view. Pupils would change sides and then change back again as they heard the arguments of others or as they tried to put the arguments themselves for their own, current, point of view. The difficulty appeared to lie in the fact that the mathematical and intuitive model for one toss of the coin did not extend to a sequence of tosses in the game situation. Either the lack of knowledge to go beyond one toss of the coin or the strength of the model for one toss of the coin usually meant that the majority of the pupils agreed that it did not matter who went first.

The mathematical resolution of this particular situation is easily achieved. The chance of the first player is 1/2, the chance of the second player is then half of a half chance, as the pupils would frequently express it, or 1/4. Building up the probabilities at each go for the two players, Table 11.1 is rapidly established. Once the randomness of the behaviour of the coin had

Table 11.1 *Probabilities of winning on each toss of the coin*

Number of turns for each player	Probability of first player winning	Probability of second player winning
1	1/2	1/4
2	1/8	1/16
3	1/32	1/64
4	1/128	1/256

been tied down into another pattern, the obvious conclusion could be made: the chance of the first player is double that of the second player, 2/3 to 1/3. Adding up the geometric series then provided an introduction to some A level mathematics. While the mathematics is convincing to a person prepared to be convinced by it, chance, ignorance about probabilistic thinking and personal belief make a powerful cocktail. On more than one occasion a child was heard to mutter as they left the room, 'I still think it doesn't matter who goes first'.

Several authors have called for the teaching of probability and statistics in a systematic and organized way, deploring the ignorance of statistical and probabilistic thinking. Paulos (1988, p. 3) defines 'innumeracy' as 'an inability to deal comfortably with the fundamental notions of number and chance' and writes passionately of the need for people in general to come to terms with probability: 'Probability, like logic, is not just for mathematicians anymore. It permeates our lives' (p. 134). The Schools Council Project on Statistical Education (POSE), in its submission to the Cockcroft Committee, argued along very similar lines: 'statistics is not just a set of techniques, it is an attitude of mind in approaching data. In particular it acknowledges the fact of uncertainty and variability in data and data collection. It enables people to make decisions in the face of this uncertainty' (quoted in Cockcroft, 1982, paragraph 775).

The arguments have been accepted within the National Curriculum of England and Wales. One-fifth of the curriculum in mathematics is given over to probability and statistics, under the title of 'data handling'. But while the original intention was to start with ideas concerning chance at an early age, in the five to eleven age range, such ideas have, with successive revisions of the National Curriculum, found themselves being reserved for older pupils (DfE/WO, 1995). Teachers have found the ideas difficult to put over to younger pupils, and perhaps have found the ideas difficult to understand themselves. Personal interest and experience do not always evoke the mathematical pattern. The pattern of a string of heads tends to convince one that a tail is due soon, rather than that at the next toss of the coin the odds are still 50:50, the same as at every other toss. Similarly, despite the fact that the odds of physical damage to an infant from something such as a vaccination are so small as to be almost non-existent in the case of a normal child, personal interest can often produce an emotive response which goes against the mathematics: the next case could be my child. How, then, do we intuitively impose pattern upon random behaviour and how do we interpret the random behaviour which we observe?

LEARNING PROBABILITY

Fischbein (1975) analyses a number of probability learning experiments carried out by various researchers on children ranging from around age three years up to sixteen and seventeen years old. In these experiments, the subject has to 'learn' the relative frequencies of two competing stimuli and on the basis of this learning predict which stimulus will occur next. Typically, the subject has in view two lights and must predict which light will come on next. After the prediction is made, one of the lights comes on at random but in line with predetermined relative frequencies. The subject continues to make predictions, all the time 'learning' from the previous exposures of the lights. In effect, the subject is experiencing random behaviour governed by an underlying pattern of relative frequencies, and is being asked to identify that pattern. How well the subject has learned, or has identified, the relative frequencies is measured by how well the predictions made by the subject mirror the relative frequencies in question.

In presenting his conclusions from these experiments, Fischbein observes that the tendency for the predictions to match the underlying relative frequencies is present in all ages studied, even in children as young as three years old. Further, as the subjects get older, their predictions come to match the relative frequencies more quickly. Not only that, but by the age of five or six at the latest, children do actually match the underlying relative frequencies.

These results are intriguing, for they would seem to imply that we are all capable of identifying the underlying pattern of some simple random behaviours, provided that we concentrate upon the behaviours and try to learn from previous instances of the pattern. For example, we know that when a coin is tossed, it is equally likely to come down heads or tails; we have learned that particular relative frequency very well. This makes acts such as betting on a head after a string of tails through the reasoning that a head is now more likely to occur, the gambler's fallacy, all the more difficult to understand. It would make more sense to use the pattern of tails to suggest that in this case the coin is biased in some way, that a tail is more likely to occur next and hence bet on tails. Further, such reasoning would agree more closely with the conclusions noted so far.

Fischbein goes on to note some further conclusions. The first is that if a reward is offered for each successful prediction, then the subjects attempt to maximize their reward. In some cases, this means that they select the more frequent stimulus to the complete exclusion of the other; in other cases their predictions are in a higher ratio than the relative frequencies. Such behaviour does stress, however, that the underlying relative frequencies must have been learned in the first place. Two other conclusions are quoted directly:

(4) Between the ages of 7 and 9 there is a tendency toward stereotyped responses, particularly alternating responses. After the age of 11, however, predictions are determined more by patterns extrapolated from antecedent sequences of events ...

(5) Older children increasingly seek more sophisticated strategies based on the conviction that there are rules determining random sequences. (Fischbein, 1975, p. 56)

These conclusions suggest very strongly that the urge to seek for order, for pattern, for a deterministic solution is a compelling one, and one which grows with age. Current suggested methods of introducing and teaching algebra according to the US Standards (National Council of Teachers of Mathematics (NCTM), 1989) and the National Curriculum in Mathematics (DfE/WO, 1995) to some extent overtly rely upon this urge. However, if the conclusions of Fischbein are correct, these methods in algebra may in fact impede the establishment of a sound conceptual and applicable understanding in statistics and probability.

Fischbein argues in similar vein: 'In probabilistic thinking, the problem is still more complex. We have to take into account the tendency toward rationalization of events. This tendency, which becomes stronger with age, is fostered by school and by the whole social environment in which human development takes place' (p. 61).

The gambler's fallacy can be explained in terms of this urge to rationalize. On average, an equal number of heads and tails will result, there has been a long run of tails and so it might be considered reasonable, rational, that there is now a greater chance of obtaining a head since there must at some time be a trend towards evening up the numbers of heads and tails. In effect, the reasoning takes the correct primary intuition of the equality of the relative frequencies and deduces an incorrect secondary conclusion based upon the desire to be able to predict and hence control.

PATTERN AND THE HEURISTICS OF PREDICTION

Representativeness and the perception of randomness

The gambler's fallacy is an example of what has been called 'negative recency', where what has happened in the recent sequence of events is negated to arrive at a prediction of what will happen. An alternative explanation for it can be given in terms of one of the several heuristics which Kahneman and Tversky (1972, 1973; Tversky and Kahneman, 1971, 1973, 1974) claim to have identified in probabilistic thinking and have written about widely. These accounts, together with similar work, are also available in Kahneman *et al.* (1982). The heuristics are representativeness, availability and anchoring. They are discussed below, together with their interpretation in terms of pattern and implications for other work in pattern.

The heuristic of *representativeness* is used when the probability of a sample is estimated according to how well the subject feels that it, the sample, represents the population from which it comes and the process by which it was generated. One characteristic of a representative sample is the degree to which a subject feels that it represents the population from which it is drawn. Kahneman and Tversky (1972, p. 432) give the example: 'All families of six children in a city were surveyed. In 72 families the *exact order* of births of boys and girls was GBGBBG. What is your estimate of the number of families surveyed in which the *exact order* of births was BGBBBB?' Although the two sequences are equally likely from the point of view of the mathematics, the authors argue that because the sequence BGBBBB does not reflect the population property of roughly equally proportions of boys and girls, it is seen as being less representative of the population than the given sequence. Hence it will be judged to occur less frequently. Experimental results which confirm this are quoted: 75 out of 92 subjects judged BGBBBB to be less likely to occur than GBGBBG.

Another characteristic of a representative sample, and a more important one from the point of view of pattern, is the fact that it should reflect the random process by which it has been obtained. In other words, it should appear to be random, which of course prompts the questions: what is randomness, and what are the properties which subjects associate with randomness? Sequences of coin tosses form a good place to start to look at this characteristic of representativeness and the subjective appearance of randomness.

Kahneman and Tversky report that sequences of coin tosses which contain obvious patterns, THTHTHTHTH, or have long runs, HHHHHHTTHT, are rejected as being non-random and are judged to be relatively unlikely. Similarly, when subjects are asked to simulate the generation of random sequences they avoid such patterns and long runs, producing sequences with 'far too many short runs' (*ibid.*, p. 435). Thus, the subjective appearance of randomness in a sequence of coin tosses is one where the sequence is not too regular, but all parts of the sequence are similar to the population in its important property of having approximately equal relative frequencies of heads and tails. Kahneman and Tversky note that for six tosses of a coin, neglecting labels and direction of reading, only HTTHTH might appear to be random. For four tosses, they suggest that there might exist no representative samples. Replacing a sequence of coin tosses by a sample, we have the definition of a representative sample: 'A representative sample, then, is similar to the population in essential characteristics, and reflects randomness as people see it; that is all parts are representative and none is too regular' (*ibid.*, p. 436).

It is perhaps reasonable to suppose that people might therefore look at randomness in terms of pattern. Clearly, for a sample or sequence to appear random there cannot be too much obvious regularity or pattern. However, the essential underlying patterns in the population must be apparent; hence there cannot be too little pattern. Another way of giving expression to this competition between non-pattern and pattern is the idea that chance is somehow 'fair', and that it achieves a balance in the end. In terms of the gambler's fallacy, the long run of tails has to be balanced by the appearance of a head in order to be fair. This search for fairness is an attempt to assert the essential characteristics, or pattern, of the whole population in all parts of the sample, what Kahneman and Tversky (1972) term local representativeness, and have discussed elsewhere in the following terms: 'People's intuitions about random sampling appear to satisfy the law of small numbers, which asserts that the law of large numbers applies to small numbers as well' (Tversky and Kahneman, 1971, p. 106).

Other researchers have looked at how subjects perceive randomness. Much of the work of Kahneman and Tversky is with adults or older adolescents. Green (1982, 1991a, b, c) has researched in some detail the probabilistic and statistical thinking of children in both the primary and secondary sectors, including their perceptions about randomness. In questionnaires presented to groups of school children, several of the questions asked the children to review particular situations and their outcomes, and in effect to distinguish between random and invented data. For example, in question 4 from the test Random Two, Appendix C, page 32 (Green, 1991b) we find:

4. Two children were told to toss a coin 40 times. One did it properly. The other made it up. They put ● for Heads and ○ for Tails.

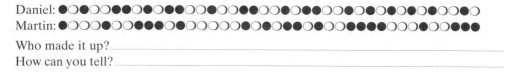

Daniel:
Martin:

Who made it up?
How can you tell?

Where the reasons given are analysed, it is clear that pattern plays an important part in those reasons. In question 4 above, the responses to the question 'How can you tell?' were analysed in terms of three main categories. These were: (a) pattern (the reasoning made use of patterns); (b) count (the reasoning made use of a count of heads and tails); and (c) run (the reasoning took into account ideas to do with the length and/or number of runs of heads or tails). All other reponses, or where the subject did not respond to the question, were classified under other/omit. The resulting analysis is shown in Table 11.2. In this particular example, pattern is used as a means of analysis by approximately 40 per cent of the subjects, the largest category of response.

Table 11.2 *Response categories for question 4*

Age (years)	Response category (%)			
	Pattern	Count	Run	Other/Omit
11–12	40	12	26	22
12–13	38	10	30	22
13–14	38	10	23	29
All	38	11	28	23

Roper and MacNamara (1994) ran a small trial with students undertaking one-year initial teacher training courses in secondary mathematics and primary teaching to see if they were capable of distinguishing between random and invented data. The students were split into four groups. In two of the groups, students were asked to invent data for fifty tosses of a coin and in the other two groups they were asked to generate the data by actually tossing a coin fifty times. One group from each of the pairs of groups was then given training in the form of analysing ten sets of fifty coin tosses in terms of the number of heads and tails in each data set and length of runs. The group which had originally invented the data was given invented data to analyse, and was told they were invented data; the group which had originally tossed the coin was given real data to analyse, and was told that they were real. All the students were then subsequently asked to consider two more given data sets and indicate which, if any, they thought was real and give a reason.

Coding of the reasons given by the students, according to Green's criteria (1991b), revealed that many of those who had analysed invented data selected the wrong set of data and did so on the grounds of pattern. This was not the case for those trained on real data or for those who had had no training at all. Those trained on real data seemed to be more willing to access the mathematical model, and to state that there were no grounds for making a choice between the two since each was equally likely. However, in explaining why he found it impossible to distinguish between the two sets of data, one student wrote: 'There is an equal chance of having T or H, i.e. probability of T is the same as probability of H. By looking at the pattern thrown I would think A is more likely to be invented as it appears more regular'. Roper and MacNamara (1994) felt that there were good grounds in the reasons given by the students for believing that pattern provided a strong framework for reasoning about random

events, even where subjects can apparently access the underlying mathematical model.

A second context through which the conception of randomness has been explored is that of the pattern made by falling raindrops. Piaget and Inhelder (1975) asserted that 'Nothing is more common ... than the form of distribution which drops of rain give when falling fortuitously at the beginning of a small shower ... Will the subjects not have, in this phenomenon familiar to all of them, a special chance of understanding intuitively the law of large numbers?' (pp. 49–50, quoted by Green, 1991a, p. 46).

Green explored this through the test question presented in the box. Options A and B are the same, one raindrop in each square, but with the distribution being somewhat disguised in B by the apparent random placing of the raindrops within their individual squares. A is called the regular pattern, B the semi-random. Option C is the random distribution, and was chosen by 44 per cent of the 504 secondary school age respondents, while 39 per cent chose option B. The almost complete rejection of option A, the very obvious pattern, is encouraging. However the popularity of option B could be interpreted as a compromise between the need for some form of underlying pattern based upon the total population of all the raindrops, which will eventually cover the whole roof, and the need to reflect the randomness of their distribution on falling.

2. The flat roof of a garden shed has 16 square sections. It begins to rain a little. After a while 16 raindrops have landed on the roof.
Here are three pictures showing raindrops on the roof.

Which picture best shows the pattern you expect to see?

A   B   C   None is   Don't
                best   know

☐   ☐   ☐   ☐   ☐

In the presentation of the results for this and a similar question featuring snowflakes, for other groups of both primary and secondary age pupils, there is a remarkable consistency to be seen in the fact that in each case approximately 40 per cent of any group chose option C, with just under this figure choosing option B. A significant trend identified by Green (1991a) as underlying these figures is one which indicates that, as the mathematical ability of the children decreases, they become more likely to select option A or B as opposed to C.

Whether the almost equal selection rates of B and C means that the pupils in question do not or do have a concept of randomness is, as Green (1991a) observes, a matter for debate, and 'depends critically upon the validity of the underlying model' (p. 47). Who can tell what the experiences of the children are in respect of the context in which the question has been posed, that of rain or snow falling on a flat roof? In seeking to explore this aspect further, Green posed a set of questions based on the placing of sixteen counters upon a grid of sixteen squares, which was represented in exactly the same way as the shed roof, through a random process. The subjects had the opportunity to do this process for themselves before they were given the test questions, which were a series of eight grids done by eight different children with the question posed in each case: 'Did ... cheat?'

By comparison with the previous figures, high facility rates were found in identifying regular and random patterns, including one which was exactly the same as option B above. Green feels that these figures 'indicate that young children (7–11 year olds) do have a sound conceptual awareness of randomness' (*ibid.*, p. 49). However, he does point again in his conclusions to the importance of the context in which such questions are posed. Certainly, these results are encouraging, but seem to go against those of other research findings noted above, which indicate that the conception of randomness more generally held is one in line with the heuristic of representativeness.

However, chance is not fair, it has no respect for patterns, it does not balance out the events, it is not self-correcting, indeed it has no 'personal qualities' at all. As Feller (1968, p. 436), quoted in support of the description of how randomness is perceived by Kahneman and Tversky (1972), puts it, 'To the untrained eye randomness appears as regularity or tendency to cluster.' In the light of this, the use of patterns as a means of analysing random data is of little help and must, it seems, inevitably mislead the subject. To overcome this particular heuristic, and the others, various teaching programmes involving real situations, real data and computer simulations have been tried with varying degrees of success, for example Shaughnessy (1977) and Cox and Mouw (1992). These situations and devices are intended to challenge the false logic of reasoning via the heuristics, and to prompt students to look for other, more mathematical, methods of analysing the situations. It is quite challenging to the intuition to see a computer simulation of a coin being tossed a thousand times, and to realize that the absolute difference between the number of heads and tails grows quite rapidly and ends up surprisingly large, while the ratio of the two numbers is approximating more and more closely to 0.5. Fischbein (1975) is right to note that learning probability is about gaining an appreciation or intuition of relative frequency, not absolute frequency.

Pattern, availability and anchoring

The heuristics of *availability* and *anchoring* are much less directly associated with pattern than representativeness is. Nevertheless, all three are linked by Fischbein (1987) as aspects of the concept of immediacy, which is associated with intuitive cognitions, and as such suggest a possible implication for the study of pattern in mathematics. Availability and anchoring will therefore be described briefly here.

The heuristic of availability is used to estimate the frequency or the probability of events, 'by the ease with which instances or associations can be brought to mind' (Tversky and Kahneman, 1973, p. 208). Thus, if asked to estimate which is greater, the number of words which begin with the letter r or the number of words which have r as their third letter, a subject using the heuristic of availability would choose the former because it is easier to bring to mind words which begin with r than those which have r as their third letter. Tversky and Kahneman report on trials which show the majority of subjects choosing the first alternative – yet it does occur with a lesser frequency than the latter alternative.

When subjects use an initial set of values to estimate some final result, perhaps making some adjustments on the way, then the final result could be described as being anchored in the initial values. Typically, according to Tversky and Kahneman (1974, p. 1128), the adjustments are insufficient: 'That is different starting points yield different estimates, which are biased toward the initial values. We call this phenomenon anchoring.' Thus, if two different groups of subjects were asked to estimate the value of the identical products, $8 \times 7 \times 6 \times 5 \times 4 \times 3 \times 2 \times 1$ and $1 \times 2 \times 3 \times 4 \times 5 \times 6 \times 7 \times 8$, in a fixed time of 5 seconds, one would expect the results from each group to be very different, since the starting points for each estimate would presumably be different, and each would be an underestimate. Tversky and

Kahneman report that this was exactly the case. The median estimates were 2,250 and 512 respectively, while the correct answer is 40,320.

Fischbein (1987) notes that in using the heuristic of availability, subjects do not question the basis on which they make their estimates, they take their estimates for granted. He extends this idea:

> 'In other terms, *the important finding here is the influence of availability itself as a mechanism for producing intuitive solutions.* There are no objective data determining the choice in this case, but some subjective factors, the main role of which is to guarantee the immediacy and *the immediate acceptance* of the solution. The need for immediacy seems to be a stronger factor than the need for objective reliability.' (p. 106, author's italics)

Following the Tversky and Kahneman (1974) analysis of anchoring, Fischbein (1987) notes the way in which the subject, in using anchoring, ignores important information in certain circumstances 'for the sake of immediacy', adding: 'Since the selection is automatic the subject not only does not use a part of the information, but he even ignores its importance for the validity of the judgement' (p. 108).

These heuristics have been introduced as the means by which probabilistic judgements are made, but Fischbein (1987) asserts that 'the same phenomena are discernible in all types of intuitive judgements' (p. 110). From many of the sources quoted elsewhere in this volume, it is reasonable to conclude that the most commonly taught method of analysing number patterns is through looking at successive differences. This inevitably means that it will be the most available and hence the one which is intuitively applied irrespective of its suitability. Once it is applied, other information may well be ignored or its importance not recognized, as the calculations based upon differencing proceed apace. The consequences of this have been highlighted in Chapter 12 where, in one example quoted, the pursuit of a constant difference effectively ignores the sequence of square numbers. Tversky and Kahneman (1973, p. 230), in discussing the retrieval of occurrences and construction of scenarios in relation to availability, make the point that

> The production of a compelling scenario is likely to constrain future thinking. There is much evidence to show that, once an uncertain situation has been perceived or interpreted in a particular fashion, it is quite difficult to view it in any other way (see, e.g., Bruner and Potter, 1964). Thus the generation of a specific scenario may inhibit the emergence of other scenarios, particularly those that lead to different outcomes.

Interpretations of the work in other chapters of this current volume could be seen to point to similar conclusions about number patterns and their analysis.

CONCLUSION

Pattern and randomness, while the antithesis of one another, are apparently inextricably linked in the minds of many pupils and adults. The former would often appear to be the means by which random events and samples are analysed, frequently erroneously. There are suggestions that specific approaches to the teaching of probability can help to alleviate these misconceptions, but they are deeply entrenched, many authors reporting evidence of the heuristics in people who are well qualified in statistics. This state of affairs has a parallel in the research into alternative conceptions in mechanics (Roper, 1985).

Further, the emphasis given to patterns in number, patterns in algebra and patterns in geometry in current syllabuses cannot help but persuade the student that patterns exist in randomly occurring events, or that it is legitimate to analyse such events in terms of the perceived patterns. The natural urge to create order out of chaos means that patterns will be sought, but the student needs to be guided towards the underlying structure, the mathematically significant patterns, and not the patterns of arrangement and convenience.

Chapter 12

Pattern and the Assessment of Mathematical Investigations

Tom Roper

INTRODUCTION

Several countries have attempted to introduce or raise the profile of what is seen as the process element of mathematics, namely investigating mathematical situations, problem-solving within mathematics and applications of mathematics to real world problems, within the teaching of mathematics. The United States has attempted to do this through 'The standards' (National Council of Teachers of Mathematics (NCTM), 1989), an approach to the curriculum which is to be taken up voluntarily by teachers of mathematics. The state of Victoria in Australia has introduced a curriculum and assessment system for the sixteen to nineteen age range which gives emphasis to these elements (Blane, 1992; Stephens and Money, 1993). However, only in the National Curriculum for England and Wales has the step been taken of making the process element of mathematics an obligatory part of the curriculum throughout the years of compulsory schooling. This chapter looks at the development of the assessment of the products of one aspect of this part of the curriculum, namely investigations, the central role which pattern spotting has come to assume in their assessment and the effect that this central role has in the classroom.

A BRIEF HISTORY OF USING AND APPLYING MATHEMATICS IN ENGLAND AND WALES

The Cockcroft Report (Cockcroft, 1982) contains the oft quoted paragraph 243 about what mathematics teaching should consist of, at all levels. Two of the recommendations of that paragraph are:

- problem-solving, including the application of mathematics to everyday situations;
- investigational work.

When the report was published, many teachers had little or no idea what mathematical investigations were, what problem-solving was and how the two might be related. Was a mathematical investigation a kind of problem? Was solving mathematical investigations the same as solving problems? The questions seemed to be without clear answers, and therefore progress towards implementation of these particular recommendations in the classroom was always likely to be slow.

The report was not compiled in a vacuum. A great deal of research into problem-solving and the use of mathematical investigations was coming to a head at that time. Shortly after the publication of the report, several volumes and teaching packages designed to help the teacher-educator, the teacher and the pupil to come to grips with these recommended elements of the mathematics curriculum appeared on the market. Examples are *Thinking Mathematically* (Mason *et al.*, 1982 and 1985a), *Thinking Things Through: Problem Solving in Mathematics* (Burton, 1984a) and *Problems with Patterns and Numbers: an O-level Module* (Shell Centre, 1984), the so-called 'Blue Box'. The work of George Polya on the heuristics of problem-solving, well known to a few, was rediscovered by many, and his volume *How to Solve It* appeared in numerous bibliographies and resource lists. The latest version (Polya, 1990) is one of many published since 1945.

The examples quoted are but a few of those published in the wake of the Cockcroft Report. The volumes of guidance and exemplar coursework published by examination boards in later years contain lists of source materials which include the above and many others. Local education authorities (LEAs) published similar lists, often through their mathematics advisers and regular circulations, e.g. Leeds LEA *Maths Mail*, a newsletter for all teachers of mathematics, and the Leeds LEA resource booklet, *Problem Solving Exercises* (Barnes, 1989).

Such a string of publications would of course be commercially unsustainable unless there was some underlying cause which created a market. In 1985, Sir Wilfred Cockcroft was appointed as the Chairman of the newly established Secondary Examinations Council (SEC), charged with the task of reforming the then existing two-tier system of examining at sixteen plus in England and Wales: the General Certificate of Education at ordinary level (GCE O level) and the Certificate of Secondary Education (CSE). The outcome was the General Certificate of Secondary Education (GCSE). Within the framework of this qualification, it was realized that the way to ensure that the kinds of classroom experiences recommended by paragraph 243 of the Cockcroft Report actually took place was to assess the results of these activities. GCSE coursework in mathematics was born, although mathematics teachers were given a three-year period in which to experiment with investigations and problem-solving, and in this period it was not compulsory to submit assessed coursework for consideration alongside the traditional examination.

The first candidates sat GCSE in 1988, but before the three-year experimental period had expired, when the use of coursework was to become compulsory, the National Curriculum was introduced, in 1989. It has since been revised twice, in 1991 and again in 1995. The attainment target 'Using and Applying Mathematics' is a compulsory Programme of Study in the National Curriculum in Mathematics (Department for Education/Welsh Office, 1995) across the whole of the five to sixteen age range, and represents the absorption of the two recommendations of the Cockcroft Report into the statutory curriculum. It is examined at sixteen plus via the GCSE examinations, either through coursework which can count for a percentage of the total score or through specially designed examination papers. The assessment at other key stages is as a component of the overall teacher assessment across the other attainment targets.

Particular forms of coursework tasks are mathematical investigations and practical investigations. These are described below in some detail and are the focus of this particular chapter, because they

- are one of the commonest forms of coursework task used in the GCSE (Wolf, 1989);
- represent a form commonly asked for by some GCSE boards (for example, see Midland Examining Group (MEG), 1996a), as part of the assessed file of work to be submitted by a pupil;
- are used in structured formats on GCSE papers which purport to assess problem-solving and investigations (see, for example, Northern Examinations and Assessment Board (NEAB) 1996);
- are often used by teachers to introduce problem-solving to secondary pupils.

DESCRIPTIONS OF THE PROCESS OF PROBLEM-SOLVING

The process of problem-solving has been described by various authors. The purpose here is to look at two descriptions available to teachers and to contrast them.

The 'Blue Box' (Shell Centre, 1984) is a teaching pack aimed directly at teachers to support what was then an O level module in problem-solving, allowing pupils to attempt a question, similar to those posed in the pack, set within the section of the then Syllabus C JMB GCE papers, where there was a choice of questions to be attempted. It provides several examples of problems to be solved, suggestions as to how this kind of work can be introduced into the classroom, hints and support for pupils in terms of checklists, some examples of pupils' work which have been assessed and departmental activities. Perhaps what is important about all the problems posed is that they begin with some kind of problem statement, from which several simpler cases can be set up, and calculated or counted. The tabulated results are then susceptible to analysis for patterns which can be translated into algebraic statements. Second, the basis of the problems is often a simple game, a puzzle of the kind frequently found in children's puzzle corners in comics and other magazines; for example, how many squares on a chessboard, or a property of the integers.

The nature of the problems often places them within mathematics as opposed to the real world. Where they appear elsewhere they are often referred to – for example by GCSE boards – as investigations within mathematics, and they might be categorized as number-algebra investigations, since they are 'solved' by moving from numbers into algebraic statements via the spotting of patterns.

The Blue Box provided the following list of what it termed 'key strategies':

- try some simple cases;
- find a helpful diagram;
- organize systematically;
- make a table;
- spot patterns;
- use the patterns;
- find a general rule;
- explain why it works;
- check regularly.

These strategies form the basis of the pupils' checklists for those investigations which are used for teaching. Included within the checklists is the suggestion that the rule should be checked, and where the investigation is based upon a game, encouragement to explain the rule in terms of the game is given. Pupils are also encouraged to look for extensions to the investigation. Differencing is highlighted as a tool for deriving patterns in the numerical data collected. All the problems or investigations posed are susceptible to these strategies, and another addition to this list is 'If you get stuck try a different approach' (p. 54). However, just what a 'different approach' might be is not discussed.

Burton's *Thinking Things Through* was written specifically for teachers, and early on makes clear the cyclical nature of the problem-solving process. Thus, on page 22 we have:

The problem solving process is not a linear one: problem ➤ solution, but a cyclical one:

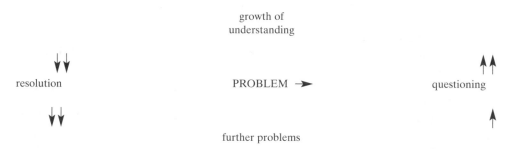

Burton then goes on to describe four phases of activity (entry, attack, review, extension), illustrating how these link to the cyclical process described in the diagram: 'Successful extension leads to the adoption of a new problem and the spiralling process of Entry, Attack, Review and Extension begins again' (p. 25).

Detailed lists of 'organizing questions' and 'procedures' are given for each phase. The 'procedures' have much in common with the Blue Box list of strategies. A third list of 'skills' for handling data, representing a problem, enumerating, finding patterns and testing is provided. While these supports to problem-solving are provided in list form, there is no suggestion that there is any order of precedence within the list. They are to be accessed as required by the many different types of problem which Burton then goes on to provide for teachers to use in the classroom.

Burton's programme has much in common with that of Mason *et al.* (1985a), and within the programme the four phases of Polya's programme can be identified:

- understanding the problem;
- devising a plan;
- carrying out the plan;
- looking back.

'Understanding the problem' can be identified with 'entry', 'devising a plan' with 'attack' and 'looking back' with 'review' and 'extension'. The sub-questions posed by Polya under each of his four phases have their counterparts in the organizing questions, procedures and skills of Burton.

Essentially, the Blue Box shows, and stresses through the pupil checklists, a linear process that is listed down the page in the order in which it is intended the steps should be carried out. A central feature of this process is the compilation of numerical results within which a pattern or patterns can be observed and generalized statements made about them. Nothing in the package indicates any cyclical process. It is aimed at teachers as a teaching tool that is to be used directly in the classroom. Extensions are seen as a continuation of the linear process, and appear to be a relatively minor addition to the process. The only looking back is the checking of results: the calculations or the pattern or the generalization. There is only the one process described and this is heavily dependent upon pattern spotting within the numerical data for resolution of the problem.

Burton's process is clearly intended to be cyclical, the cycling coming from the extension phase of the first cycle. There is no hint of a linear process in either the presentation of examples of pupils' work or the problems and investigations posed. Support is offered for the teacher in terms of what might be the most suitable organizing questions, procedures and skills. Thus there is more than one strategy or programme available, the programme is not solely dependent upon pattern spotting for resolution of the problem in hand. A consequence of this is that a wider variety of problems can be attempted than those provided by the Blue Box. Extensions are offered for each problem so that there is meaning to the idea of pursuing the cycle again. Again this reflects the programmes of Mason *et al.* (1985a) and Polya (1990).

Polya (1990), Burton (1984a), and Mason *et al.* (1985a) were written for the teacher-educator, the teacher and the individual pupil; they are not classroom texts. They require some form of teacher input to make the material in them usable in the classroom. The Blue Box is directed at the classroom and can be 'plugged into' it, with little or no extra input from the teacher. There is no help with assessment from Polya, Burton and Mason *et al.* Indeed, because the three works are aiming at curriculum development, or changing the climate of the classroom, or both, as opposed to the assessment of the pupils' work, one would not expect that assessment would be a major concern. The Blue Box, on the other hand, is linked directly to assessment, in terms not only of enabling the teacher to assess problem-solving in the classroom, but also of helping the teacher to prepare the pupils for an examination question which will directly mimic the problems in the module.

THE ASSESSMENT OF INVESTIGATIONS

The assessment structure suggested by the Blue Box (p. 162) is under four headings:

Evidence of (i)   Understanding the problem,
          (ii) Organizing the attack on the problem,
          (iii) Explaining what has been tried and what has been found,
          (iv) Finding general rules, verbally or algebraically.

The guidance is very clear that pupils should have some idea of what will score marks – 'it is desirable that the children should understand how the marks are awarded' – but mark schemes have to be constructed so they can be used reliably by examiners and 'it may not be obvious when looking at such a scheme that credit is given for the four general points made above'. Nevertheless, the exemplar investigation, 'Skeleton Tower' (see Figure 12.1), fits the number-algebra format described in the previous section and the assessment scheme fits precisely the structure above.

Four points can be followed up from this assessment structure. First, the four headings are to be seen directly or can be identified in all the original headings of GCSE coursework assessment schemes. They can also be identified in the three strands of Using and Applying Mathematics as set out in the National Curriculum in Mathematics (DES/WO, 1991), these three being 'Applications' (subdivided into 'Making decisions' and 'Monitoring decisions'), 'Mathematical communication' and 'Reasoning, logic and proof'. In a handbook

Investigations

Frogs:

In Frogs the question posed is: What is the least number of moves required to interchange the two sets of counters where a move is either sliding into an adjacent empty space or hopping over an adjacent counter of the opposite colour into an empty space immediately beyond the counter which is hopped over?

There are usually equal numbers of counters on each side of the central empty square and the counters only move 'forwards'.

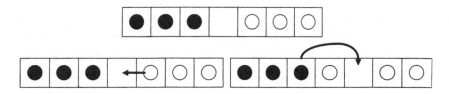

Skeleton Tower:

The objective is to find the law of growth for towers similar to the one shown below.

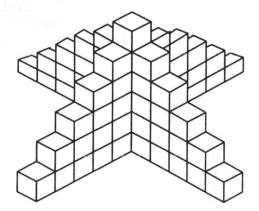

How many squares on a chessboard?:

The objective is to predict the number of squares on a chessboard of given side.

For a chessboard of side 2 squares there are 5 squares, for one of side 3 squares there are 14 squares.

The handshake problem:

If there are five people in a room and each shakes hands once and only once with every other person in the room, how many handshakes are there altogether? What about other numbers of people?

Figure 12.1 *Investigations*

issued by the National Curriculum Council (NCC, 1992), on page 12 it is clear that 'Applications' corresponds to headings (i) and (ii), 'Mathematical communication' to heading (iii) and 'Reasoning, logic and proof' to heading (iv). The strands of Using and Applying Mathematics are still the basis of the latest GCSE assessment structure for coursework. These three are 'Strategy, making and monitoring decisions to solve problems'; 'Communication, communicating mathematically'; 'Reasoning, developing skills of mathematical reasoning'. This would suggest that there has been a common structure to the assessment of investigations for a considerable period of time, and that this structure should now be well understood by teachers. The GCSE examination boards are constantly reinforcing this knowledge, publishing new volumes of exemplar coursework which has been assessed with every change of the National Curriculum.

Second, the recommendation that pupils should know exactly what they are being asked to do and what the criteria are which they have to meet is one that many school mathematics departments have taken on board. It is common to see, in classrooms dedicated to mathematics teaching, the criteria for the assessment of coursework displayed, either directly as published by one of the GCSE examination boards or translated into the language of the pupils. Indeed, one of the published formats of the National Curriculum in Mathematics (DES/WO, 1991) was a poster showing what had to be achieved in the various divisions of the curriculum (using and applying, number, algebra, shape and space and data handling) at each of the then ten levels. It was, in this case, very unusual to see a mathematics classroom which did not have this poster prominently displayed. It is therefore reasonable to conclude that pupils have a very good idea of what is expected of them when they do an investigation, and the procedures which they are expected to follow.

Third, despite the note of warning about the way in which individual mark schemes might not show how credit has been given under the four headings, the scheme for the marking of Skeleton Tower clearly does show this and fits very well with the pupil checklist. Thus, the four headings are now interpreted, respectively, as:

(i) Showing an understanding of the problem by dealing correctly with a single case,
(ii) Showing a systematic attack in the extension to a more difficult case,
(iii) Describing the methods used,
(iv) Formulating a general rule verbally or algebraically. (p. 46)

The Statements of Attainment for Using and Applying Mathematics are in DES/WO (1991). In looking at the exemplar pieces of coursework for GCSE and their assessment schemes, we can see that the interpretation of the Statements of Attainment of Using and Applying Mathematics fits very well with the procedure defined by the Blue Box list of strategies shown above. For example, the interpretation by the University of London Examinations and Assessment Council (ULEAC) (1992), on page 24, in the context of the investigation called 'Frogs' (see Figure 12.1) is:

Level 4 a, b, c
Obtain results
$1 \times 1 \to 3$
$2 \times 2 \to 8$
$3 \times 3 \to 15$
Record results to 3×3.
Explains basic strategy of avoiding an impasse.

Level 5 b, c
Records results to 3×3.
Uses table of results to extrapolate beyond 4×4 to at least 5×5. Recognizes 'odd' numbers.

Level 6 c, b
Full extrapolation – differences.
Answers specific questions such as 10×10 –
50×50 – *only* by extrapolation.
Draw graphs of results to 5×5. Some
justification of graph with explanation.

Level 7 b
From results obtained recognizes the pattern
$n \times n + 2n$ or $(n \times n + n + n)$ or $(n + 1)^2 - 1$
etc.
Expresses result without symbols i.e. $5 \times 5 - 5^2$
$+ 2 \times 5$. Expresses result in symbolic form.

Level 8 a, possible b
Can reverse the problem by saying that 120
moves – 10 counters without merely looking
up in a table.

The procedure laid out in the strategies list of the Blue Box is clearly observable in the interpretation:

Level 4: single, simple cases.
Level 5: organization of the single cases into a table or equivalent form.
Level 6: extrapolation or extension to more difficult cases;.
Levels 5 and 6: pattern spotting of the recursive function that the differences down the table are the odd numbers.
Level 7: spotting of the functional pattern across the table and its statement verbally or algebraically.

Fourth, the Blue Box assessment structure calls for explanations, it does not call for proof. Thus, we see that the assessment structure for Frogs set out above calls for explanations, justifications and extensions but not proof, which appears only at level 10 in the Statements of Attainment. The position of proof as the ultimate step is reinforced in the ULEAC (1992) guidance by the following statement prefacing each exemplar coursework activity:

During the coursework activity you should

- undertake any practical work, describing what you do;
- show any strategies you use;
- record the data/results you obtain;
- note any observations;
- predict and test any conjectures or hypotheses;
- note any exceptions or counter examples;
- record any generalization, explanations or justifications;
- attempt any proof.

Further, within the checklist statements, an extension is sometimes nominated as an activity to be carried out towards the end of the list. For example, in the context of the Frogs investigation, the extension is to reverse the problem; that is, given the number of moves, how many counters were there on each side of the board? This is seen as being at level 8. At level 6 in the Statements of Attainment we have the statement, 'pose their own questions or design a task in a given context'. The emphasis of this interpretation is usually on the words 'given context', and this would mean that the pupil in the case of Frogs might extend the investigation to look at cases where the number of counters on each side of the board was different. Thus the extension is within the same context and demands similar mathematics. Such an interpretation is supported by *Pupils' Work Assessed* (School Examinations and Assessment Council (SEAC), 1993) and a private communication from a Key Stage 3 moderator.

Hence, proof is to be postponed until other avenues have been explored, most notably those of extensions. Such a view has also been encouraged by statements made by the mathematics officers of the School Curriculum and Assessment Authority (SCAA) at the launch of the latest version of the Mathematics National Curriculum (DfE/WO, 1995), and elsewhere, to the effect that a pupil's level in Using and Applying Mathematics should be within one level of the other content-based Attainment Targets. This means, since proof occurs only at level 10, that pupils are being asked to construct proofs with the mathematics available at levels 9 or 10, a very difficult task for even able pupils to pursue.

Current assessment schemes published by the boards now mark each strand out of a maximum of 8. However, the basic structure of the Statements of Attainment is retained, and proof is only required to achieve full marks in the strand 'Reasoning, logic and proof'.

From these four points which emerge from considering the structure and underpinning assumptions of the assessment schemes for investigations, several conclusions can be drawn which are supported by evidence from other sources and have much to say about the effect of current assessment schemes upon the teaching of methods of solution of mathematical investigations which depend upon pattern spotting.

PROCESS BECOMES CONTENT

Given that teachers are well aware of the assessment structure and the interpretation that will be given to that structure in particular types of activity, and that pupils will share in this knowledge, either in their own terms or through their teachers' interpretation of the board's, then one might expect to see an almost uniform approach to the solving of investigations. This is exactly what is seen. Evidence for this conclusion is drawn from a number of sources. For several years, the author set an investigation for the thirteen to sixteen age group as part of a series of mathematical competitions run by the Yorkshire Branch of the Mathematical Association (YBMA) and the School of Mathematics of the University of Leeds, and sponsored by Yorkshire Television. Each year, between twenty and thirty schools submitted the best solutions of their pupils, usually an average of about fifteen per school, and mostly from pupils in the fourteen to fifteen age range. The uniformity of these solutions was remarkable. Each year, in all but a few scripts, exactly the same process was observable, namely simple cases, tabulate, predict the next case based upon some pattern spotting among the numerical data obtained, make a generalization, check the generalization using data already gathered and new data, formulate the generalization in algebra if it had not already been done and seek an extension within the same context. The few remaining scripts showed some variation in this process, often generalizing from the structure and offering a form of proof. It was from these few that the eventual winners of the competition were inevitably drawn.

The author has been involved in running a series of in-service courses on Using and Applying Mathematics and its assessment. One version of the course required teachers to experience and review a set of tasks related to Using and Applying Mathematics, then return to their schools to try out one or more of the tasks, then send the work of their class back to the course organizers, who would prepare it for the second day of the course, which was concerned with the assessment of the tasks. The thirty-five schools represented on the course came from across the North of England. Some twenty schools returned work and, of these, fifteen were all on the same task, a task susceptible to the approach described above. Further, even though the task had clearly been attempted by classes of widely varying abilities as shown by both the age of the pupils and the mathematics used, exactly the same process was evident in all the work.

Exemplar material on investigations published by the GCSE examination boards illustrates the same process, as does the exemplar material published by SEAC for the assessment of Using and Applying Mathematics at Key Stage 3 (SEAC, 1992), 'Octagon loops' and the two collections of pupils' assessed work at Key Stage 3 published by SEAC (1993) and by SCAA (1995). Since the introduction of investigations in the teaching of mathematics, these publications have all added legitimacy to the process described, and have reinforced the necessity to teach it and for pupils to follow it. In effect, a kind of 'long multiplication of investigations' has been established, and what was envisaged by many authors, Burton and Mason *et al.*, for example, as being a flexible problem-solving process has become a rigid prescription, with pattern spotting in numbers as the central plank. Burton forecast just this situation in 1984: 'But even where attempts have been made to introduce an emphasis on process into the curriculum, little impact is visible. The reason is partly that once process is enshrined in texts, it becomes content' (Burton, 1984b, p. 35).

PATTERN SPOTTING WITHIN NUMBERS IS MORE IMPORTANT THAN PATTERN AS STRUCTURE

Many patterns exist within data collected for a mathematical investigation. If we look at the Frogs investigation, and the data drawn up in Table 12.1, we can see a number of patterns, some of which are indicated within the assessment schedule. The assessment schedule set out

Table 12.1 *Data collected for Frogs investigation*

Number of counters on each side	Number of moves	Differences
1	3	
2	8	5
3	15	7
4	24	9
5	35	11

earlier indicates that level 5 pupils should have recognized the differences between the numbers of moves as increasing by the odd numbers, and should have used this to extrapolate beyond 4 counters on each side to 5 on each side. The extension of this pattern to 10 on each side and beyond is seen as being worthy of level 6. To go to level 7, the pattern which involves the functional relationship, as opposed to the recursive, is needed. The assessment schedule expresses this pattern in a number of algebraically equivalent ways. These might reflect the ways in which pupils could perceive the pattern of the number of moves; for example, as the product of the number of counters, n, with the number of counters plus 2, $n + 2$, giving $n(n + 2)$, or as the square of the number of counters plus twice the number of counters, $n^2 + 2n$, or again as the square of one more than the number of counters minus 1, $(n + 1)^2 - 1$. However, the assessment schedule does nothing to encourage pupils to look for a pattern which reflects the structure involved in the investigation, since it does not encourage the pupils to look for any form of proof or justification beyond the patterns which are available in the table.

If we tabulate the kinds of moves, as in Table 12.2, instead of the total number of moves, we quickly see that n^2 appears to be the number of hops and $2n$ the number of slides. Thus,

Table 12.2 *Analysis of moves for Frogs investigation*

Number of counters on each side	Number of hops	Number of slides	Total number of moves
1	1	2	3
2	4	4	8
3	9	6	15
4	16	8	24
5	25	10	35

while several expressions are quoted as being equivalent algebraically, one of them reflects the structure behind the investigation, and once this structural pattern has been established, then the result is open to being either proved or justified beyond simple reference to the tables of data.

The devotion to patterns within the numbers rather than patterns which lead to structures can be seen in several other examples. The MEG has published several volumes of exemplar coursework over the years to aid teachers in gauging the standards and expectations of the examination board in terms of coursework. In their volume of 1992, they give an example of the work of a candidate on the problem of how many squares there are on a chessboard (see Figure 12.1). The work is reproduced between pages 33 and 48 inclusive of the volume, with the explanation of the marks awarded on page 32. The work is awarded 29 out of a maximum of 30, including 10 out of 10 for the strand 'reasoning, logic and proof'.

The candidate begins by working through the process indicated previously, beginning with cases involving small numbers, then tabulating the data and next looking for patterns. The particular tool which the candidate calls upon is the use of differences and the knowledge that a constant nth difference implies a relationship which is of degree n. The data which he produces are shown in Table 12.3.

Table 12.3 *Data produced by a pupil in the Chessboard investigation*

Size 'n'	Total number of squares	First difference	Second difference	Third difference
1	1			
2	5	4		
3	14	9	5	
4	30	16	7	2
5	55	25	9	2
6	91	36	11	2
7	140	49	13	2
8	204	64	15	2

The candidate observes the constant third difference and notes that this implies a cubic relationship between the size of the board, n squares by n squares, and the total number of squares. He then postulates a cubic equation in n, with unknown coefficients. These coefficients are found by substituting pairs of values from the table and solving the resulting four simultaneous equations in four unknowns. This is done accurately and successfully, and the work is then extended in the same manner to look at the number of squares on rectangular chessboards. It is clear that the candidate is following a particular prescription for the solution of the initial problem. The need to establish the algebraic relationship, use mathematics of an appropriate level and coordinate a number of variables is paramount in terms of gaining the high marks which were ultimately awarded. Yet these concerns dominate and exclude the pattern of the structure of the problem, denying the very mathematics that such investigations are often said to promote.

While it is given 10 out of 10 for 'reason, logic and proof', as defined by the statement of attainment, 'Handle abstract concepts of proof and definition', and the examiner's comment 'there is no doubt of the candidate's ability to prove correctly by abstract means' (p. 32), it is difficult to see where the abstraction and proof are in the work in question. The formula for the total number of squares is derived correctly, but based upon the assumption that the difference in the third column is constant for all cases not yet considered. Hence, it would be fair to say that a formula which fits the data to hand has been calculated, but it has not been proved that this is the formula which fits all known cases in this particular problem.

It is interesting to note that the patterns in the example of Frogs are also assumed by the assessment schedule to be maintained beyond a limited number of cases. There are many examples where this is not so; see, for instance, 'Patterns which aren't' (Beevers, 1994), and the response by Johnston Anderson (1995), 'Patterns which aren't are!' The point at issue here is that Anderson is able to look for the pattern which reflects the structure of the situation, not any old pattern which may or may not be visible in the data collected.

In terms of the structure of this particular investigation, the first column of differences is the square numbers, and it is clear from the way in which the candidate collects his data that the total number of squares on a chessboard of size n is the sum of the squares of the integers from 1^2 to n^2. Why has the candidate apparently not noticed this? If he had noticed it, there could be grounds for saying that a more mathematical approach would be to establish the structure of the problem through this observation, thereby proving that the result is the sum of the squares of the integers, and looking up the formula in an A level textbook. A candidate with sufficient ability to handle four simultaneous equations in four unknowns might well have sufficient ability to examine the structural patterns if prompted to do so, and if it was worthwhile to do so.

The assessment scheme currently in use would appear to encourage not the pursuit of structural pattern, but that of other more obvious or easily available patterns. Thus, in the commentary provided by another candidate in an exemplar piece of coursework (MEG, 1996b), we find at the beginning of the work: 'First of all I am starting simply and adding single numbers to see if there is a pattern' (p. C1). Later in the same work, '*With n consecutive numbers*', we find: 'First of all I am going to look for a pattern' (p. C7). A variety of patterns is indeed noted, including the recognition of the appearance of the triangle numbers: 'If I fill these results in on my table the pattern is now clear, the gap between the numbers you add on increases by 1 every time. This sequence is called the triangular numbers' (p. C8). However, there is no sign that any of the patterns are to be related by the candidate to the internal structure of the investigation.

The competitions of the YBMA, referred to above, also echo this particular area of concern. A part of one of the investigations set was isomorphic to the 'handshake problem' (see Figure 12.1). All the entrants produced the table of values which corresponded to the number of handshakes generated by specific numbers of people, and noted that these were the triangle numbers and that the formula for the nth triangle number was $\frac{1}{2} n(n + 1)$. Some also noted that the nth triangle number was the sum of the first n integers. But what nobody explained was how this related to the structure of the situation and hence how the formula, taken for $n - 1$ as opposed to n, must always be true.

It might be pertinent to ask what messages pupils are receiving about the nature of mathematics, and proof in particular, if there is no apparent emphasis upon the structure of the situation posed, while the pursuit of number patterns and formulae derived from them is so highly rewarded and reinforced by both the assessment and the teaching? Certainly, the placing of proof at the highest level of the assessment structure and the concomitant association of it with mathematics of the same standard allows the taught process to push on and ignore proof at lower levels, encouraging the search for any patterns in the data which might lead to a generalization and basic extensions within the original context of the problem.

THE SEARCH FOR PATTERNS AMONG NUMBERS WITHOUT CONSIDERATION OF THE OVERALL STRUCTURE MIGHT BE COUNTER-PRODUCTIVE TO ENCOURAGING MATHEMATICAL PROBLEM-SOLVING

Among the assessed exemplar scripts in the Blue Box is that of Paul, Script F. Paul has gained full marks for his attempt at Skeleton Tower, yet he has not followed the prescribed route. Instead, he has observed the overall structure of the tower, its pattern in space, as being composed of four equal right-angled triangles, the total number of blocks in each triangle being achieved by using the formula for the triangle numbers, together with a central column. From this starting point, Paul is in a position from which the whole of the question can be answered with ease, and a proof, based upon the formula for triangle numbers, given. Despite an algebraic error in the final part, Paul is justifiably awarded full marks for his very perceptive piece of work.

Paul was clearly a very able pupil, and it would be dangerous for us to move on from his success without seeking patterns within numbers to saying that it is better not to look for number patterns. After all, what should be sought are the patterns which reflect the structure, so some form of search for pattern is inevitable. Yet there is evidence from other sources that pattern spotting without the search for structure does not aid the process of generalization, and may even hinder it. In Chapter 8, the work of adults tackling questions involving pattern spotting and generalization in a formal examination supports the contention that encouraging the extension of the patterns found by using the strategy of asking for the fiftieth term hinders the development of the generalization. The work of Orton and Orton (1996) referred to in Chapters 7 and 8 also lends support to this view.

The piece of coursework on the number of squares on a chessboard, referred to above, has been the focus of discussion at two seminars given by the author, one to the School of Mathematics at the University of Leeds and the other to the Mathematics Department of the University of California at Los Angeles. At both seminars, the mathematicians, while admitting that the approach through pattern in number might give some insight into the problem, were adamant that the overall structure was what was important, and were disappointed that the candidate had not paid attention to the square numbers so clearly present in the work.

CONCLUSION

It is perhaps inevitable that a mathematical process will become content if routinized, and in doing so will be reduced to the lowest common denominator. There is perhaps no harm in this *per se*, and there may even be some good in it. Hewitt (1992) complains of what he observes in classrooms: the collecting of data and the search for pattern among them without a purpose linked to the source of the data. On the other hand, Andrews (1993) defends the process, pointing out that many pupils can gain success in using this process and that it is often necessary before the inner structure can be perceived. The difficulty is that the assessment structures do not encourage anything other than that of which Hewitt complains.

Burton (1984b) portrays mathematical problem-solving as a helix which winds around a core which is the problem, or in this case the investigation. Each coil of the helix is represented by the process:

Getting a sense of pattern,   Articulating that pattern symbolically,   Manipulating

This is of course very much in keeping with the cyclical process described by Burton (1984a) and Mason *et al*. (1985a). What the current assessment structures have done is to snip one coil of this helix and stretch it out vertically, thus making one coil of the problem-solving process its own hierarchy in the assessment structure:

Getting a sense of pattern
Articulating that pattern symbolically
Manipulating

When married to the need to use as high a mathematical content as possible, the problem-solving process becomes corrupted, causing the focus to be upon pattern spotting and generalization in symbols at the expense of pattern in structure and proof.

The difficulty which has to be faced is that of combining progression in problem-solving with progression in content. If it is recognized that problem-solving is a cyclical process and not a linear one, then the notion of a hierarchy in the problem-solving process must be abandoned, and the full cycle of problem-solving practised and encouraged at all levels of mathematical content. It is hoped that this might encourage the seeking after patterns of structure and the use of situations which are open to such analysis in a fairly direct manner. Building upon this, it might then be possible to construct an assessment structure which anticipated two or more full cycles around the core of the problem, where the investigation begins in some mathematics familiar to the pupil. However, where the investigation begins in relatively new mathematics, the expectation is that there would be only the one cycle around the core. Such cyclical assessment systems are available and have been researched (see, for example, Collis *et al*., 1986).

The evidence would appear to be that the current assessment structures in England and Wales encourage the engagement with patterns but not in a way that respects mathematics as that subject which studies patterns. Hence, the process of investigating degenerates into an algorithm centred upon pattern spotting, of much the same status as the algorithm for long multiplication. This is not the original intention of introducing such activities into the mathematical education of all pupils. It does not show the ability of mathematics to explain, classify and communicate. Rather the opposite, it appears to trivialize the subject, denuding it of its most important element, the power to prove.

Chapter 13

Pattern and Proof

Sue Waring, Anthony Orton and Tom Roper

PROOF IN SCHOOL MATHEMATICS

The place of proof in mathematics teaching and learning has been a difficult, even con-
tentious, issue of debate for many years. In the days before the 'modern mathematics' movement of the 1960s, it was geometry, Euclidean geometry to be precise, which provided the
main opportunity for introducing the idea of proof and logical argument in secondary school
mathematics all around the world. The kind of proof introduced through Euclidean geometry
was, and of course still is, deductive. Other kinds of mathematical proofs would then have
been introduced to those who continued with the study of mathematics in the sixth form
(ages sixteen to eighteen) and beyond. Even then, there were widespread doubts among
school teachers about whether any more than a very small proportion of grammar school
pupils would ever be capable of truly comprehending the nature of Euclidean proof by the
time they sat for public examinations at the age of fifteen or sixteen years (see, for example,
Mathematical Association, 1938, 1959). Indeed, the history of geometry teaching in Britain,
from the latter part of the nineteenth century, has been of frequent attempts to free geometry
more and more from what were sometimes described as the shackles of Euclid.

In many countries around the world, Euclidean geometry still forms the main systematic
study of geometry, and therefore deductive proof is still taught in that context. In Britain,
however, the effect of 'modern mathematics' on geometry teaching has become firmly established, and work with transformations now forms the major component of the geometry curriculum. For most pupils, transformation geometry does not lead to proof. It was realized in
the 1960s that transformation geometry would not be likely to provide the same opportunity
for the study of proof as Euclidean geometry had done for many years (see Willson, 1977, for
an excellent discussion of issues concerning the relative merits of alternative approaches to
geometry and proof). There were two contrasting reactions to this. One was that this was a
good thing, because proof is so difficult for children anyway, so a reduction in the emphasis
on proof was to be welcomed. The other reaction was that it would therefore be necessary to
find other opportunities to introduce ideas concerning proof, perhaps within the algebra content. Of course, the amount of algebra currently taught to the majority of British pupils is now
much less than it was, and consequently the opportunities for introducing proof within that
particular context are much reduced. Thus the problem still remains. An education in mathematics demands that proof is included in the curriculum. This is the firm view held by those

who act as the 'guardians' of the subject, the university mathematicians. To what extent can the approach to algebra through pattern provide opportunities for learning something of the nature of proof in mathematics?

Earlier chapters of this book have raised the issue of proof within the context of the study of pattern. If it is required to find a formula, or general term, when analysing a number pattern such as the triangle numbers,

1,   3,   6,   10,   15,   21,   28,   ... ,

for which in this case the formula is

$T_n = \frac{1}{2} n (n + 1)$,

then a proof of this conclusion or deduction is the essential final step in the analysis. Much debate has taken place in recent years about the unsatisfactory nature of the study of pattern in mathematics, which goes little further than pattern spotting (Hewitt, 1992; Gardiner, 1995), an issue which has been discussed in Chapter 12. A great many pupils, particularly those in the secondary school, can look at a sequence like the triangle numbers, spot the pattern and continue listing terms, but a very much smaller number are capable of building on this approach to find an algebraic expression for the general term, and of those who can reach this stage, hardly ever are they required to prove their result. One of the issues here is whether spotting and continuing patterns is the right approach anyway (see also Chapters 7 and 12, for example). Many questions remain unanswered. Do pupils have the capability to create a proof or justification for generalizations from number patterns? Can the study of patterns be used in a deliberate way to introduce pupils to proof in mathematics? If so, what are appropriate ways to try to move pupils on from work with patterns to the idea of proof? Are pupils who have systematically and extensively studied number patterns and generalizations better at proof than pupils who have not?

Whether pupils can adequately prove their generalizations depends partly on what is accepted as a proof. What might be considered an acceptable proof for twelve-year-olds might not be considered acceptable for mathematics undergraduates. Professional mathematicians do seem to have very firm views about what constitutes an acceptable proof, even at the school level (see, for example, Martin and Harel, 1989; Slomson, 1996). Twelve-year-olds might be quite delighted and even excited by the visual justification of the formula for the triangle numbers, represented by Figure 13.1, but be completely incapable of under-

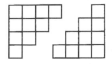

Figure 13.1 *Visual justification of triangle numbers formula*

standing anything more abstract, algebraic, formal or 'rigorous', to use a word frequently invoked by mathematicians when talking about the quality and acceptability of a proof. How do we reconcile the demands of mathematicians and the capabilities of pupils? One of the major difficulties for teachers of mathematics today, operating within statutory curriculum guidelines which do not specify in detail how the concept of mathematical proof is to be developed throughout the years of schooling, is how to foster the developing understanding of proof within their pupils. One thing is certain, however, and that is that the study of patterns does provide certain opportunities. Given the acknowledged importance of proof in mathematics, and the comparative lack of opportunity to study proof within geometry, it is perhaps very important that we explore the opportunities presented by the study of pattern. One experimental study of this kind is described here.

DESIGN OF THE EXPERIMENT

Three groups of Year 10 (aged fourteen to fifteen years) pupils in a selective grammar school took part in an experiment to investigate the benefits of a curriculum enhanced by an emphasis on both proof and pattern (Waring, 1997). The three groups were parallel sets in the sense that all the pupils were from within the tenth to twenty-fifth percentiles of the ability range, and that statistical analysis detected no significant differences between the groups. Naturally, all the pupils had studied the same curriculum prior to entering Year 10. One of the three groups was termed 'experimental' because its curriculum was enhanced, and the other two groups constituted control groups taught according to the standard scheme of work operated in the school. None of the pupils knew that they were taking part in an experiment, and the same written tests were set for pupils in all three groups at the end of the year. Some pupils were also interviewed on completion of the teaching programme, using their responses to the written test and two new tasks. The teaching programme for the experimental group included special worksheets designed to guide pupils through investigations leading to patterns which necessitated analysis, and other aspects of the standard curriculum which offered the opportunity of a pattern-based approach. This experimental group (E) was taught by the researcher, who was also their normal mathematics teacher; one of the control groups (C1) was taught by a teacher who did not use investigative approaches and basically followed the textbook; and the other control group (C2) was taught by a teacher who did use investigative approaches but was in no way directly and intentionally involved in the enhanced course used with group E. Naturally, there were constraints on what could be done with the groups, including the experimental group, because of the demands of the National Curriculum. Piloting of the tasks was carried out using a group of very able Year 8 pupils (aged twelve to thirteen years), and a group of Year 11 pupils (aged fifteen to sixteen years) of similar ability to group E.

The aims of the teaching programme for the pupils in the experimental group included the intentions of first raising levels of awareness of the need for proof, then learning something of what might be considered acceptable as a proof and finally perhaps even creating proofs of their own. Teaching strategies included exposition, informal class discussion, small group work, written work based on structured questions, written work based on open questions, investigations based on diagrams and investigations which involved practical activity. Variety in mathematical content was achieved through, for example, investigations based on number patterns which could be explained by use of algebra and/or diagrams, diagrams which could be explained by use of algebra, spatial problems which led to number patterns and problems which led to solutions which could only be explained in words. The teaching programme also included some elements of geometry in which proofs were based on pattern, but those tasks are not discussed here. In this year-long teaching programme, with pattern and proof activities woven into the normal curriculum at appropriate moments and in a variety of ways, it will be understood that a very large number of tasks and activities was incorporated. Thus, it is possible to provide only a few examples of the tasks here, because of constraints on space.

EXAMPLES FROM THE TEACHING PROGRAMME

Given the importance of the *triangle numbers* in mathematics, the evidence of the difficulties experienced by learners of all ages in finding the general term and providing a proof, and the many references to activities relating to this number sequence throughout this book, it is appropriate to report here on the reactions of group E pupils to the classroom worksheet on the topic. The worksheet is shown here as Task 1.

Task 1

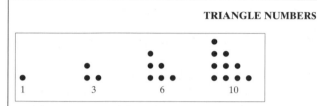

TRIANGLE NUMBERS

Position (n)	Value (T)
1	1
2	3
3	:
4	:
:	:

The first four triangle numbers are shown in the diagram.
Use the following questions to guide your investigation and write a report on triangle numbers.
1. By drawing similar diagrams find the next three triangle numbers and continue the table of results.
2. Write down the next three triangle numbers after the last one you have drawn.
3. Explain how you could obtain the 20th triangle number.
4. Find the most efficient way of doing this.
5. Test it on some of the triangle numbers you have found.
6. Try to write your method as a formula for finding the nth triangle number (T).
7. Test it for $n = 2, 3$, and 4.
8. Explain how and why **your formula** works for the 12th triangle number.
9. Will it always work? How can you be sure?
10. Find the 100th triangle number.

After a period of individual investigation, suggestions for a formula were volunteered, such as '$n + (n + 1)$' from one pupil. Subsequent class discussion led to the tabulation of the first ten terms of the sequence alongside the term number (n). This was followed by the suggestion from one pupil that each of the triangle numbers was formed by 'adding the next integer to the last triangle number', and this was supported by drawing arrows on to the table of results. The pupil who had offered '$n + (n + 1)$' then claimed this was the same method, and it eventually emerged that she had tried to offer 'nth number + $(n - 1)$th triangle number', but had been unable to put this into words which incorporated the necessary precision. When asked for alternatives, the next suggestion was that the fourth triangle number could be formed by adding a row of four dots to the array of dots for the third number. The lesson concluded with a discussion of how to form successive triangle numbers in this way, and eventually to an appreciation of the numbers as the sums of consecutive integers. Pupils were then set the homework task of continuing with the task and producing their own individual written reports.

The reports generally commenced by establishing that triangle numbers were formed by summing consecutive integers, and not surprisingly many pupils extended their list in this way, to twenty terms perhaps, or even to one hundred terms. Two pupils quoted a 'formula', one being '$T = n + t$', for which it was clear that t was intended to represent the previous triangle number, and the other being '$T = n + < n$', obtained by 'adding the next integer to the total so far'. Another pupil suggested that an improvement to finding the twentieth triangle number was to start from the tenth and then add the remaining integers. His report continued by considering odd and even integers separately and establishing that the twentieth triangle number could be calculated as 20×10.5. He then generalized this result as 'the multiplier is half the number plus a half', giving the nth triangle number (T_n) as '$n \times (\frac{1}{2}n + \frac{1}{2})$'. Another pupil began by explaining that when n was odd it was a factor of T_n, and when n was even ($n + 1$) was a factor of T_n, and then continued, 'but I need a formula for this', and wrote '$\frac{1}{2} n(n + 1)$'. He concluded by explaining that the product $n(n + 1)$ is halved because the triangle is half a 'square'. Two other reports included good descriptions of finding T_n as $\frac{1}{2} n(n + 1)$ by reference to the table of results. In all the other reports, the formula $T_n = \frac{1}{2} n(n + 1)$ appeared without explanation, but was used correctly to test other values, and to find T_{100}. About one-third of the pupils attempted to justify this formula later, but many were confused, either about the role of the '1', or about how to relate what they were doing to square numbers, or about whether the product $\frac{1}{2} n(n + 1)$ represented the nth or ($n + 1$)th triangle number.

Four pupils were able to produce proofs. Two used a diagram such as that in Figure 13.1, representing two triangular arrays for T_4 which together formed a 4×5 rectangle, and then explained that in general terms T_n was half of a similar $n \times (n + 1)$ array. The third pupil justified the result for a particular case, T_{12}, drawing a 12×12 square and explaining that half of this would only include half the dots on the diagonal, so it was necessary to add half of twelve to the result. The fourth proof did not refer to a diagram, but explained that the integers in each sum could be paired from each end, giving $\frac{1}{2}n$ pairs each with a total of ($n + 1$). However, the pupil failed to take account of odd numbers. Most pupils did not attempt a proof, and several thought that demonstrating validity for particular examples was sufficient proof, in one case because 'the formula always works because it works for the numbers tested so far'. The aims of the next and final lesson on triangle numbers included the intention to consider, discuss and emphasize the distinction between demonstration and proof, which was clearly a central objective of the entire project.

The next investigation discussed here, entitled 'Growing patterns', was included as an example of a pattern which can clearly be explained in more than one way and also to illustrate pupils' intuitive thinking in the context of visual pattern. The worksheet is shown here as Task 2.

The results for the first five of the pattern of triangles were first recorded on the chalkboard, and by considering successive differences it was established that at each stage the number of triangles added was a multiple of three. Several pupils suggested that this was because triangles have three sides; thus, it became clear that by introducing a ($T - 1$) column in the table, we could then divide these numbers by three. The origin of these numbers as the sums of consecutive integers was discussed, but no one commented on the fact that the outcome was in fact the triangle numbers. The next step was for pupils to produce a written report on the second pattern, involving squares. About half of the reports used the same approach as had been devised in connection with the previous triangular patterns. One pupil produced an exemplary report with the formula '$s = 4$(triangle number stage $- 1$ stage) $+ 1$', accompanied by a diagram, shown here as Figure 13.2, which very clearly indicated the significance of the triangle numbers in his thinking. His report concluded with the statement that the formula could be used in any growing pattern of regular shapes, as the expanding pattern would be the same and the number of unit shapes would be 'number of sides of unit $\times$ (triangle number stage $- 1$ stage) $+ 1$'.

Eight other pupils produced the formula '$s = n^2 + (n - 1)^2$', but were unable to explain it fully. Three pupils confused checking and proof, and three others gave incorrect or confused

Task 2

GROWING PATTERNS

1. Start with a single equilateral triangle drawn on isometric graph paper. At each stage add new equilateral triangles all round the outside.
   Copy and complete the table on the right.

Stage number (n)	Number of 'unit' triangles (T)
1	1
2	4
3	--
4	--
5	--
6	--
10	--
20	--
n	--

Show how you found your formula for n and explain why it will always 'work'.

2. Start with a new single square drawn on squared paper. At each stage add new squares all round the outside.
   Copy and complete the table on the right.

Stage number (n)	Number of 'unit' squares (S)
1	1
2	5
3	--
4	--
5	--
6	--
10	--
20	--
n	--

Show how you found your formula for n and explain why it will always 'work'.

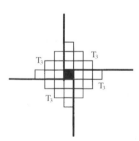

Figure 13.2 *First GROWING PATTERNS illustration*

explanations. However, although this was a difficult pattern to explain, it did provide an opportunity for pupils to produce ideas for discussion by the whole class during the next lesson. Two diagrams were prepared to prompt this discussion, first, the diagram in Figure 13.2, showing clearly the presence of the triangle numbers, and second, the diagrams in Figure 13.3, which show the sums of squares orientated differently. The formula '$S = n^2 + (n - 1)^2$' was then written on the board, and pupils were invited to suggest why this should work. No one was able to explain this adequately, and it emerged that most of those who had obtained it had done so from some other member of the class. However, when their attention was drawn to the second diagram of Figure 13.3, with alternate rows of squares shaded differently, the origins of the formula were much clearer. Pupils also appreciated the opportunity to

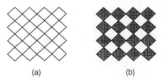

(a)   (b)

Figure 13.3 *Second GROWING PATTERNS illustration*

consider how there could be two formulae, and eventually the algebraic equivalence of 4 (triangle number stage − 1 stage) + 1, translated into $4 \times \frac{1}{2}n(n-1)+1$, and $n^2 + (n-1)^2$ was agreed.

Two other tasks are now discussed more briefly. Written reports on the widely used 'Regions in a circle' investigation (see Task 3) showed that about one-third of the pupils used the idea of doubling the previous value to complete the table for $d = 6$ and $d = 7$, and did not

Task 3

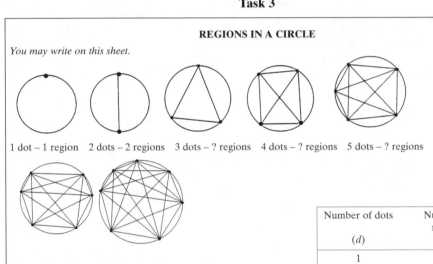

REGIONS IN A CIRCLE

You may write on this sheet.

1 dot – 1 region   2 dots – 2 regions   3 dots – ? regions   4 dots – ? regions   5 dots – ? regions

6 dots – ? regions   7 dots – ? regions

Spend about 20 minutes on questions 1 and 2.
1. Complete the table opposite only up to $d = 5$.
2. a) Can you suggest a suitable formula connecting d and r?
    b) Does it 'work' for $d = 6$ and $d = 7$?

Number of dots (d)	Number of regions (r)
1	1
2	2
3	--
4	--
5	--
6	--
7	--

Spend about 15 minutes on question 3. (Continue overleaf if necessary.)
3. Explain your formula if you found one and/or describe your thinking about the problem.

appear to have checked their results by counting. One pupil did count, but then crossed out his answers obtained this way, clearly having more faith in a formula than in his counting. The best reports were from two girls. One explained, 'I thought I had found a pattern (doubling). It worked for up to $d = 5$, but then it failed'. Another wrote, 'For 1 to 5 the formula is $2r$, that is, the number of regions for the number before times two, but it doesn't work for 6 and 7'. During subsequent class discussion it became clear to all that the suggested formula did not work for $d > 5$. Thus, the importance of justifying formulae was emphasized, and seemed to be appreciated. The main objective of including this task was because it does make this particular point very clearly. Finally, it was explained that it was reasonable to suppose that a formula did exist, but that it was very complicated. Naturally, some pupils wanted to know what it was.

Task 4

| L-SHAPES |

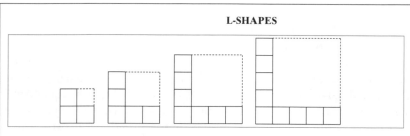

For the above patterns of L-shapes, made from matches:
1. Copy and complete the following table down to $n = 6$.

Side of large square (n)	Number of small squares (s)	Perimeter of L-shape (P)	Number of matches (m)
2	3	8	10
3			
4			
5			
6			
10			
100			

2. Describe any patterns you see.
3. Find formulae for the following in terms of n:
    a) the number of small squares (s);
    b) the perimeter (number of matches around the outside) of the L-shape (P);
    c) the number of matches used (m).
4. Prove that your formulae are correct by explaining how each one is connected to the diagrams.
    (Remember – checking is not the same as proving.)
5. Use your formulae to calculate the values of s, P and m for $n = 10$ and $n = 100$ and put your answers in the table.

The investigation entitled 'L-shapes' (Task 4) enabled pupils to demonstrate their ability to analyse patterns in more than one way. One pupil, in explaining the perimeter formula, $P = 4n$, said she saw lines of matches translated, match by match, to complete a square of side n with perimeter $4n$ (see Figure 13.4). Another pupil explained that he saw the end matches

Figure 13.4 *First L-SHAPES illustration*

added on to the inside lines so that they were of length n, making 4 lines of this length in all (see Figure 13.5). In explaining $s = 2n - 1$, the formula for the number of squares, several pupils explained that n was the bottom row (or side) and $n - 1$ was the other row; or that if the side was to be laid alongside the bottom row there would be a double row with one

Figure 13.5 *Second L-SHAPES illustration*

square missing (it is not clear how to represent this diagrammatically). The formula $m = 6n - 2$ was sometimes derived by substituting in $m = P + s - 1$, which some pupils had obtained. An alternative was to consider the arrangement of the squares as two connected lines of squares, each iteration consisting of two squares and requiring an additional six matches. The emphasis during this discussion was on the fact that there were several equally valid ways of explaining the formulae. All the reports included correctly completed tables and correct formulae, all but one attempted to explain the formulae and about two-thirds of the reports included partially correct explanations. Only three pupils gave explanations for $m = 6n - 2$ which suggested they had a really good understanding, but nearly half were able to explain their justification for the formula. One pupil, for example, derived $m = 3s + 1$ and explained that each new square needed three matches, and one match was needed to start the pattern. Another explained clearly that there were $4n$ matches around the outside, but less clearly that there were $2n - 1 - 1$ matches inside the pattern, and then combined these to give $6n - 2$. All the pupils but one appreciated the need for proof in this investigation, and most were able to make an acceptable attempt at explaining the first two formulae.

The above four tasks, dealt with in varying degrees of detail here, are intended to provide an indication of how pupils were encouraged to find a formula and then explain it, through a mixture of class discussion, group discussion and individual exploration supported by a written report. In fact, it was possible to prove most of the formulae derived from the tasks, and in many cases to highlight the distinction between proof and demonstration. Pupils were receptive, on the whole, to the notion of proving and, even for the more unusual or difficult proofs, were interested and willing when it came to class discussion. The level of difficulty of the patterns was greater than had been anticipated, however. In particular, the pupils found the investigations involving triangle numbers very difficult at first but, for most, their difficulties were eventually resolved through class or group discussion. The question which then remained was: what was the effect of this teaching programme on the pupils' abilities in deriving formulae and providing proofs on their own, as measured by their performance on written tests?

THE WRITTEN TESTS

The post-test in connection with the experiment naturally included a number of tasks of the pattern → formula → proof type, similar to the ones described in the previous section, together with pattern and proof questions which were based within the context of geometry. In scoring pupils' responses, it was possible to separate out their scores for pattern and their scores for proof, as had been planned. At the same time, the pupils completed a test of 'basic' mathematics, representing the rest of their curriculum and taught by more traditional methods. Thus three scores are available for the pupils in all three groups, and the mean percentage scores for the groups are shown in Table 13.1. The groups, being normal secondary school classes, were clearly comparatively small for significance testing purposes. Nevertheless, the basic scores suggest the comparability of the three groups, which was referred to earlier and established by other means, and the pattern and proof scores indicate differences between the groups. For completeness, similarities and differences were investigated using t-tests, and the levels of significance are shown in Table 13.2, with levels of significance of greater than 5 per cent regarded as not significant (NS). The results suggest that the work on pattern and proof throughout the year had made a difference in the experimental group. The results concerning pattern are particularly interesting, remembering that group C1 pupils were not taught pattern at all, but that the curriculum for group C2 pupils had included some work involving pattern.

Table 13.1 *Mean percentage test scores*

	Basic	Pattern	Proof
E ($n = 25$)	82	70	39
C1 ($n = 22$)	75	59	18
C2 ($n = 24$)	81	66	19

Table 13.2 *Levels of significance of differences between group means*

	Basic	Pattern	Proof
E/C1	NS	0.025	0.0005
E/C2	NS	NS	0.0005
C1/C2	NS	NS	NS

Six weeks later, the pupils in all three groups sat a common end-of-year examination, which, in the nature of such examinations, had to represent the work completed throughout the year by all three groups. Thus, two pattern and proof questions were included on one of the two examinations. The mean scores obtained by the pupils in the three teaching groups for 'basic', 'Pattern 1', and 'Pattern 2' are shown in Table 13.3. The 'basic' measure was taken from scores obtained on the rest of the paper on which the two pattern questions were situated, and substantially concerned work completed before entry to Year 10. Here, performances on pattern and proof are not separated.

Table 13.3 *Mean percentage scores on end of year examination*

	Basic	Pattern 1	Pattern 2
E ($n = 24$)	67	86	61
C1 ($n = 22$)	66	63	52
C2 ($n = 24$)	60	62	59

The results from this end-of-year examination basically corroborate the findings of the post-test for the experiment. The two questions are shown here as Pattern 1 and Pattern 2, which is how they were labelled above. Pattern 1 is clearly of a very familiar type to the pupils in group E, whereas Pattern 2 would have been a novelty to all pupils. Detailed scrutiny of where pupils were successful and unsuccessful on these two questions clearly indicates that, on the one hand, pupils in group E were very likely to be able to recognize and to some extent analyse patterns of a type similar to those they had met before, but, on the other hand, they were no more able than group C1 and C2 pupils to recognize and analyse patterns which were unlike those met previously and which did not have an obvious visual structure. In other words, transfer was limited. It must be remembered, however, that these overall test results should be taken as more indicative than conclusive.

PATTERN 1

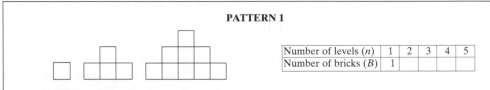

Number of levels (n)	1	2	3	4	5
Number of bricks (B)	1				

John is building a set of 'double staircases' with some bricks.
The diagram shows the view of the stairs he has built for levels 1, 2 and 3.
i)   Draw the view for the stairs with 4 levels.
ii) Copy and complete the table.
iii) How many bricks are needed to build a staircase with 12 levels?
iv) Write down a formula for the number of bricks (B) needed for n levels.
v)   By considering an alternative arrangement of the bricks explain why this formula works.

PATTERN 2

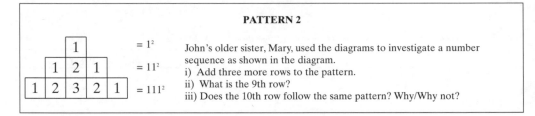

John's older sister, Mary, used the diagrams to investigate a number sequence as shown in the diagram.
i)   Add three more rows to the pattern.
ii) What is the 9th row?
iii) Does the 10th row follow the same pattern? Why/Why not?

PERFORMANCE ON PATTERN AND PROOF ELEMENTS OF THE POST-TEST

The post-test questions which were not based on geometry are shown here as Tasks 5, 6, 7 and 8. The mean percentage scores on the elements of these tasks which were concerned with pattern are shown in Table 13.4. It is clear that all groups of pupils found the pattern elements

Table 13.4 *Mean percentage scores on pattern questions*

Task	5	6	7	8
E	100	95	30	52
C1	95	80	9	34
C2	91	78	38	52

of Task 5 very easy. In Task 6 there was a significant difference ($p < 0.025$) between group E and each of the two control groups. It seems that the experiences with pattern in group C2 had not enhanced their performance on this question, which was surprising considering the nature of the question. It was clear from the responses of a number of pupils in group C2 on this task that they were so intent on using differencing that they lost track of where this method was leading. This same method was widely used in Task 7(c), where, for example, one pupil wrote, 'If you find the differences of the differences, the differences of these seem to be 6', but was unable to continue. The results of this task were interesting, in that group C2 performed better than group E, though the results are not statistically significant, and that group C1 performed very badly and produced a mean score which was significantly different from

Task 5

In the diagram showing the calendar for the month of May a group of four numbers in a square has been highlighted. Adding diagonally opposite numbers in this square gives:

$15 + 23 = 38$

$16 + 22 = 38$

a) Repeat for other squares and describe what you notice about these totals.

b) Explain why this happens.

MAY						
Sun	Mon	Tues	Wed	Thur	Fri	Sat
	1	2	3	4	5	6
7	8	9	10	11	12	13
14	15	16	17	18	19	20
21	22	23	24	25	26	27
28	29	30	31			

Task 6

a) Complete the following table to show the number of rails needed to build each fence.

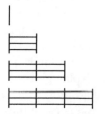

Number of posts	Number of rails
1	0
2	3
3	
4	
5	
6	
20	

b) Describe any patterns you see.

c) Explain how to get the number in the second column from the corresponding number in the first.

d) Write down a formula for the number of rails (r) needed for a fence with p posts.

e) Explain why this formula always works.

Task 7

$\{9, 10, 11, 12, 13\}$ is a set of five consecutive integers.

a) How many multiples of i) 2, ii) 3, iii) 4, iv) 5 are there?

b) What is the maximum number of multiples of i) 2, ii) 3, iii) 4, iv) 5 in any set of five consecutive integers?

c) $2 \times 3 \times 4 = 24$ is a product (multiplication) of three consecutive integers.

　　i) Work out the product of three other consecutive integers.

　　ii) Repeat until you see a pattern.

　　iii) What appears to be true every time?

　　iv) Explain why this will always happen when three consecutive integers are multiplied.

Task 8

a) Find $2^2 - 1^2, 3^2 - 2^2, 4^2 - 3^2$.

b) Continue up to $9^2 - 8^2$ and describe any patterns.

c) If n is the smaller of two consecutive numbers write down an expression for the larger.

d) Explain, using algebra and/or diagrams, why the above result will always happen for the difference between any two consecutive square numbers.

the other two. In Task 8, the means for groups E and C2 were identical, and the mean for group C1 was significantly different from the other two, again suggesting there had been benefits for group C2 in their work with pattern throughout the year. Clearly, however, there are few convincing conclusions that can be drawn from this evidence.

Table 13.5 *Mean percentage scores on proof questions*

Task	5	6	7	8
E	84	64	8	16
C1	61	28	5	5
C2	65	17	2	2

The mean percentage scores on the elements of these tasks which were concerned with proof are shown in Table 13.5. From this, we see that the proof for Task 5 was successfully completed by around 60 per cent of the pupils in the control groups, and by 84 per cent of the experimental group, but that there were few startling successes beyond that. Group E scored 64 per cent on Task 6, but it is questionable whether much more can be claimed at all. Given the original hope that a programme of study on pattern and proof in this age and ability range would lead to increased performance on proof as well as pattern, the results can only be described as somewhat disappointing.

Most of the correct proofs on Task 5 were written informally. For example, 'The totals for the diagonals will always be the same because the top two numbers and the bottom two numbers have a difference of 1. The smaller number on top goes with the larger number on the bottom, and vice versa'. Just one pupil in group E included the algebraic explanation $x + y = (x + 1) + (y - 1)$. For Task 6, two examples of correct explanations from group E were: 'For every post you add three rails but you don't have three rails where there is no post at the end and so you take away three rails' (for $r = 3p - 3$), and 'Get the number of posts minus 1, then times the number by 3 because that is how many rails fit a post; the reason one is minused [*sic*] is because that is the first post which doesn't form any rails' (for $r = 3(p - 1)$). There were only three correct proofs for Task 6 from group C1, and only four from group C2, but there were a number of partially correct answers from these two groups. There were no complete proofs of Task 7 from any group, and only eight pupils (four in group E, two in group C1 and two in group C2) achieved partial explanations. All but one of these realized that a set of three consecutive numbers would contain at least one even number, making the product inevitably even. Algebraic representation was not used by any pupil. For Task 8, only two pupils from Group E were rewarded for drawing diagrams which showed they understood the structure of the pattern. Seven other pupils (four in group E, two in group C1 and one in group C2) gave partial answers, one (from a group E pupil) being: '$(n + 1)^2 - n^2 = A$; $A =$ answer; $2n + 1 = A$; This will always work because the two ^{2} always cancel each other out or the $2n$ is doing the same as squaring would do; the +1 is for the larger number'.

Clearly, the limited success of this experiment indicates that the search for intervention strategies which will enhance the performance of pupils in the area of pattern and proof must continue.

INTERVIEWS WITH PUPILS

Eight pupils from group E were interviewed in order to pursue the idea of proof in a one-to-one environment in which the spoken word could be used to question and explain. All but one of the pupils had found Task 5 easy, but one important point did arise, namely the difficulty of explaining in writing, expressed by one pupil as 'It was hard to explain, but only in that it took a lot of explanation. It's easier to talk.' Six of the pupils had completed Task 6 successfully, perhaps not surprisingly considering it was of a type very widely used in the contemporary approach to algebra. Task 7, however, was more unusual, and generated much more discussion. Six of the pupils had made little progress in the written test, and still required very considerable steering to appreciate the idea that multiples of 6 must feature in 7(c). Typical comments were 'I spent a long time on this; I didn't really understand the way it read', and 'I wasn't really sure what I was doing'. It seems that these pupils were not able to cope with the language of the question. Again, it was in no way a 'standard' pattern task. Some of the pupils had not realized there was a connection between the parts of the question. The other two pupils had made good progress in the written test, but in one case only by spending so long on the question that no other questions were attempted. Nevertheless, both of them were very easily steered to a full understanding of the structure and all the ramifications of the task.

In Task 8, six of the pupils had correct numerical results in the test, and had noticed either that the differences were odd numbers or that they increased by 2, but only two pupils had recognized that it was the sum of the integers. None had drawn a diagram in the test, but five opted to use one in the interview, appreciated its structure for a particular case and were readily moved on to an understanding of the general case. One pupil had not been able to begin to prove anything in the test, but had no difficulty in following a proof based on a diagram. Three pupils opted for an algebraic approach, but all of them at some stage seemed to lose the sense of what they were trying to do, a very common phenomenon in algebra. Eventually, they established that the difference was $2n + 1$, and was therefore an odd number. For one pupil, the discussion became so laboured that the problem was left unfinished. Two pupils had an incomplete appreciation of the situation after some discussion based on an algebraic approach, but the subsequent introduction of a diagram clarified the situation. One said, 'Just looking at the diagram it's easier to see. You can see it both ways, but it's easier looking at it with a diagram.' All the pupils interviewed appreciated the nature of proof, and in most cases either eventually constructed a proof or understood the creation of a proof. Thus, lack of appreciation of proof was not a major cause of the inability of some pupils to construct proofs.

Two new tasks were also used in the interview, and the additional information gained from these supported the conclusions which had emerged from the written test and from the interview discussions based on the written test. In short, with a new question similar to Task 6, these group E pupils confirmed that they could identify and analyse a pattern based on counting numbers and supported by a diagram, sometimes making use of trial and improvement if the structure was not immediately recognized. The second new task was much more unusual, and was more problematical for the pupils.

SOME GENERAL CONCLUSIONS

In evaluating the successes and failures of the teaching programme, it is fair to claim first that, although successes were limited, the group E pupils did have more success than pupils from the control groups. The awareness of the need for proof had certainly been raised in the group E pupils, and this was particularly clear in the interviews. Pupils in group E appeared to be more prepared to look for proofs than they were when the programme started, and than other pupils in the control groups. In fact, group E pupils were likely to want to try to provide a proof and, even if they could not complete one on their own, they were receptive to the teacher then 'piloting' them to a conclusive proof. There was certainly enough evidence that it was quite appropriate to attempt to use pattern as a motivator for the study of proof. Where pupils made progress in their ability to provide a satisfactory proof, however, it was not clear to what extent a pupil's thinking was based on innate ability, on prior knowledge and understanding or on what had been learned from the programme.

Just as with younger children, in experimental studies reported earlier in this book, these Year 10 pupils were inclined to rely too much on differencing, which sometimes inhibited progress towards finding a generalization because it needed to be derived from the mathematical structure of the task. Thus, progress towards finding a proof could be prevented because the focus of analysing the task was wrongly directed, and was not directed towards the underlying structure. It should be recorded, however, that on some occasions pupils were able to relate their sequence to a known sequence like the square numbers, and were able to proceed to a generalization on that basis.

The issue of the place of diagrams arose on many occasions. There were some examples of pupils who lost their way completely when they attempted to use an entirely algebraic approach, and there were many examples of pupils who not only benefited from the availability of a diagram, but also commented on how helpful they found it. This raises other questions, like whether pupils should always be encouraged to refer to a diagram and attempt to analyse the structure of the pattern from that, and whether a diagram would be likely to help all pupils equally (see Krutetskii, 1976). The case for the support of diagrams under all circumstances is a strong one on the basis of our evidence.

Finally, it was clear that transfer was limited. Pupils were more likely to succeed with analysing new patterns if they were of a type similar to ones encountered previously, and conversely were not likely to succeed with patterns arising from completely new contexts. The extent to which transfer of learning is likely to take place has been the subject of debate throughout the twentieth century (see, for example, Cormier and Hagman, 1987). What our evidence suggests is that, even within the fairly limited area of mathematics under consideration here, little transfer of competence in analysing patterns and providing proofs took place within the time scale available.

Chapter 14

Pattern in the Classroom

William Gibbs

This chapter describes a variety of ideas for use in the classroom. In the first three sections some practical ways of creating patterns with simple resources are described. The fourth section looks at the integration of numerical and shape patterns, exemplified by ideas related to work on squared paper, and the fifth describes some pattern activities derived from a variety of cultures.

PRACTICAL PATTERNS WITH PAPER

One of the problems of doing pattern work with shapes in the classroom is having enough shapes for the pupils to work with. This is especially true when one is creating tessellations in a large class and many congruent shapes are needed. One practical solution to this problem is for children to make the shapes themselves, and an easy way to do this is to use A-size paper, or metric paper as it is sometimes called, as the starting point. A-size paper, such as A4, is now the most common paper size in regular use, and it has two mathematical properties that make it ideal for use in the mathematics classroom. First, all A-size rectangles can be folded or overlapped to form a whole range of standard mathematical shapes (Gibbs and Meenan, 1994). Second, because the sides of A-size rectangles are in the ratio 1 to $\sqrt{2}$, when it is folded in half it creates a new rectangle of half the area, but similar (i.e. in proportion) to the original. The process of folding can be repeated to create rectangles of a suitable size for use in the classroom.

Figure 14.1 shows how A-size paper can be folded using two simple folds to create a kite. In a practical activity with a class, it is helpful to use A6 paper of two different colours. The pupils, each having made a kite, then combine them to create patterns. Often the first shape to emerge is the octagon made from eight kites, but further trial leads to the tessellation shown in Figure 14.2. Having kites of two different colours greatly helps the pupils to see the regularity of the tessellation.

Nesting Patterns

One of the other properties of many of the shapes made from different sizes of A-size paper is that they nest inside each other. If, for example, a set of A-size rectangles is cut down to

A-size paper

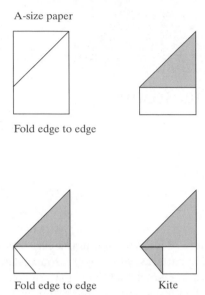

Fold edge to edge

Fold edge to edge   Kite

Figure 14.1 *Creating a kite*

Figure 14.2 *Kite tessellation*

Figure 14.3 *Nesting pattern*

create a set of squares, then these will nest inside each other, and if many individual nesting squares are then combined they can be used to create the pattern in Figure 14.3. Other visually exciting displays can be created from nesting kites or triangles (Gibbs, 1990a) as shown in Figure 14.4 (see colour plates).

Overlapping Patterns

One of the simplest shapes that can be created from A-size paper is the octagon, as shown in Figure 14.5. The papers can be glued in place one by one and once again, if each pupil in the class has produced an octagon, these can be arranged on the floor or pinned to a display

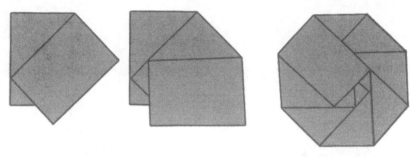

Figure 14.5 *Octagon made from A-size paper*

board to create a mixed tessellation of octagons and squares. The missing squares can them-selves easily be folded and added.

A more dramatic way of displaying the octagon made in this way is to place it on a win-dow. Then other patterns will emerge, hidden at first when the paper octagon is on the table but revealed as the sunlight shines through and gives different tones to the areas of different thickness (Figure 14.6; see colour plates). The results are particularly striking if fairly thin red, yellow or orange papers are used. The shapes can be held in place against the window by cov-ering them with a sheet of non-adhesive book-covering film. Static electricity will hold the display in place.

Other regular polygons can be created using exactly the same method of overlap but with rectangles of different dimensions (Gibbs, 1995). For example, a regular hexagon can be cre-ated using rectangles which are 13 cm by 15 cm. Dimensions for creating other polygons are given in Table 14.1. The general rule for finding the ratio is 1 : 1/sin s where s is 360 divided by the number of sides.

Table 14.1 *Creating polygons from rectangles*

Number of sides	Ratio of sides of rectangles	Convenient measurement (cm)
5	1 : 1.05	10 by 10.5
6	1 : 1.15	13 by 15
8	1 : 1.41	A-size paper
9	1 : 1.55	9 by 14
10	1 : 1.70	10 by 17
12	1 : 2	10 by 20

Another simple method of overlap that can be used by pupils to create regular polygons is shown in Figure 14.7 (colour plate). Using this method, hollow ring polygons are created. Once again, these can be used to investigate which polygons tessellate and what patterns emerge when those that tessellate are combined in a window display. The dimensions of the rectangles to be used for each polygon are exactly the same as those used in Table 14.1. Figure 14.8 (colour plate) shows a pattern made by tessellating hexagons created in this way.

One shape that we commonly wish to investigate is the equilateral triangle, and there are several ways of creating it through folding. However, perhaps one of the simplest is to start with a rectangle with sides in the ratio $\sqrt{3} : 2$ or (9 cm by 10.4 cm) and to fold it as shown in Figure 14.9. We can investigate not only the simple tessellation this triangle creates but also the patterns created when it is tessellated on the window (Figure 14.10: colour plate).

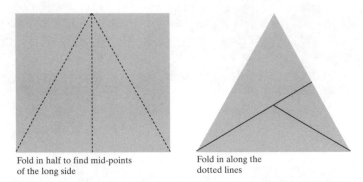

Fold in half to find mid-points
of the long side

Fold in along the
dotted lines

Figure 14.9 *Creating an equilateral triangle*

Creating Tessellations with Circles

A wide range of tessellations can also be created from paper circles (Gibbs, 1990b). The simplest method is by overlapping them as shown in Figure 14.11. More complex and challenging tessellations can be created by folding the circles as shown in Figure 14.12 (colour plate) where the circles are folded so that an edge touches the centre. If circles of three different colours are folded in this way and overlapped, they create the hexagon shown in Figure 14.13 (colour plate), which when combined with other similar hexagons creates a striking tessellation.

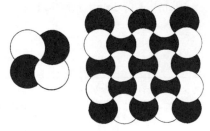

Figure 14.11 *Tessellation created by overlapping circles*

A second method of creating a wide range of patterns from paper circles is to fold them to create an equilateral triangle by folding the circumference to the centre three times. If the flaps are then coloured and interleaved (Figure 14.14: colour plate), the resulting triangles can be combined in a variety of patterns.

USING CARD TO CREATE TESSELLATIONS

A very simple and practical way for pupils to create their own tessellation in the classroom is for each to cut out his or her own irregular cardboard triangle. A small block of wood or fold of card can then be glued or pinned at the centre of the triangle to form a handle. The card triangle can then be placed on a sheet of paper and held firm as its outline is drawn. Then the triangle is rotated so that side touches side, and then drawn around again (Figure 14.15: colour plate). The handle on the shape allows it to be held easily and, more importantly, prevents the shape being turned over. The two common problems in this activity are when pupils turn shapes over, which is prevented by the handle, and when the shape pupils have created has equal sides. To help to overcome this second problem, each side of the triangle can be numbered and pupils encouraged to match each side with itself after turning.

This activity is easily extended to quadrilaterals and, having discovered that their own quadrilaterals tessellate, pupils can also investigate concave quadrilaterals. Having large card triangles and quadrilaterals already prepared and with handles fixed in the centre allows all the activities described above to be done by the teacher on the chalkboard.

Creating original tessellations

From the work of Escher we are now all familiar with the allure of strangely shaped tessellations. Pupils can create their own original tessellations if each is provided with a square or rectangle of card. From one side, a shape of any design is cut out, and then this is fixed with tape to the opposite side of the shape (Figure 14.16: colour plate). The same procedure is then followed on another side of the shape, the cut-out piece once again being joined to the opposite side. The tessellation based on this shape can be created by drawing around the cardboard shape, translating it so that edge meets edge.

Other variations on this technique can be investigated (Figure 14.17: colour plate); for example, by cutting part from the top and part from the bottom or by sticking on the cut-out piece so that it overlaps the edge, or by sticking the cut-out piece on an adjacent side.

USING SQUARED PAPER

A simple way for pupils to create tessellations and tilings is to use squared paper as a base for designing shapes. The grid gives a framework for creating accurate congruent shapes rapidly. This may not be quite so satisfying as actually physically fitting shapes together, but it provides a substitute when shapes are not available, as well as more abstract practice in the rotation and drawing of congruent shapes. It also provides a record of what has been done. Figure 14.18 shows examples of tessellations which have been started on squared paper and can be continued.

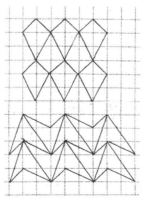

Figure 14.18 *Tessellations on squared paper*

One major drawback with squared paper is that it cannot be used to draw equilateral triangles, regular hexagons or octagons. Isometric dot paper can be used for this, but if we then

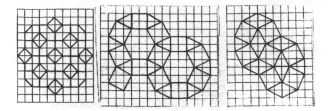

Figure 14.19 *Mixed tessellations on squared paper*

wish to investigate mixed regular tessellations on squared paper it is necessary to resort to topological equivalents (Figure 14.19).

Original tessellations can be created on squared paper by using the same method that created original tessellating patterns with card. Figure 14.20 shows how a square has been modified to create a new shape which tessellates.

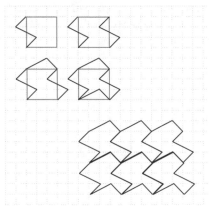

Figure 14.20 *Designing an original tessellating shape on a square grid*

LINKING PATTERN IN SHAPE AND PATTERN IN NUMBER

In this section, some activities are described which illustrate how patterns of number can emerge from the investigation of shapes. The examples chosen are all based on investigations of patterns that can be drawn by pupils on squared paper. The examples have also been chosen to illustrate how the level of complexity of the generalization involved can be organized in a step-by-step progression.

Developing generalizations

One of the problems that pupils face when discovering the generalization that describes the number pattern they have found is that these relationships are often complex. In particular, many patterns lead to the triangle numbers, but this relationship involves both a quadratic expression and the use of fractions (see earlier chapters for evidence of pupils' difficulties with triangle numbers). The examples which follow demonstrate investigations that develop by stages from simple linear to more complex quadratic relations, and in particular in stage 4 how quadratic relationships can be introduced through investigations which involve the multiplication of related numbers.

Stage 1: Linear relations of the form x ± c

Example: Right angles

Draw any closed shape on squared paper by following the lines of the paper. Mark in the right angles outside the shape and the right angles inside. Now investigate other shapes (Figure 14.21) and look for a connection between the number of right angles outside and the number inside.

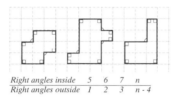

Right angles inside	5	6	7	n
Right angles outside	1	2	3	n - 4

Figure 14.21 *Right angles inside and outside*

Stage 2: Linear relationships of the form *ax*

Example: Crosses in squares

Draw squares of any size on squared paper and inside draw a cross-like shape (Figure 14.22). Find the perimeter of the cross and investigate if there is a relationship between the width of the squares and the perimeter of the crosses.

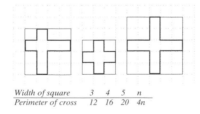

Width of square	3	4	5	n
Perimeter of cross	12	16	20	4n

Figure 14.22 *Crosses in squares*

Stage 3: Linear relationships of the form *ax ± c*

Example: How many squares?

Investigate the number of squares in each of the rectangles (including the hidden squares) and find if there is a connection between the width of the rectangle and the total number of squares (see Figure 14.23).

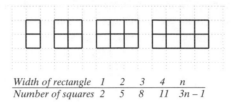

Width of rectangle	1	2	3	4	n
Number of squares	2	5	8	11	3n – 1

Figure 14.23 *How many squares?*

Stage 4: Quadratic relationships of the form $n(n \pm c)$

This is a particularly important and difficult stage, so three examples are given.

Example A: Herring bone patterns

Shown in Figure 14.24 are the first three patterns in a sequence of herring bone designs. Investigate the relationship between the width of the pattern and the total number of line segments in the design.

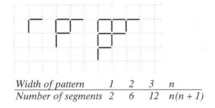

Width of pattern	1	2	3	n
Number of segments	2	6	12	n(n + 1)

Figure 14.24 *Herring bone patterns*

Example B: Spirals in squares

Draw squares of any size and fit a spiral inside. Investigate the length of the spiral and the width of the square (see Figure 14.25).

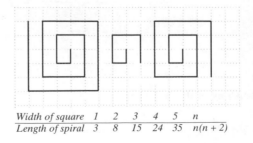

Width of square	1	2	3	4	5	n
Length of spiral	3	8	15	24	35	n(n + 2)

Figure 14.25 *Spirals in squares*

Example C: Longest Journey

Draw squares of even width and find the longest route from corner to corner, assuming the path never meets or intersects with itself (Figure 14.26, right). Look for a connection between the length of the longest route and width. It is also interesting to investigate the length of journeys in squares with odd dimensions (left). The relationship is more complicated, namely $n(n + 1) + 2$.

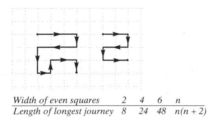

Width of even squares	2	4	6	n
Length of longest journey	8	24	48	$n(n + 2)$

Figure 14.26 *Longest journey in an 'odd' square and an 'even' square*

Stage 5: Quadratic relationships of the form $n(an \pm b)$

Example: U-bend

Draw U-bends of different lengths and fill them with numbers written in order (Figure 14.27). Investigate the length of the tube and the sum of all numbers written inside.

1	2		1	2	3		1	2	3	4
4	3		6	5	4		8	7	6	5

Length of tube	2	3	4	n
Sum of numbers	10	21	36	$n(2n + 1)$

Figure 14.27 *Numbers in U-bends*

Stage 6: Quadratic relationships of the form $n(n + 1)/2$

Example: Hidden rectangles

Investigate the relationship between the number of rectangles that can be found in a row of squares and the length of the row (see Figure 14.28).

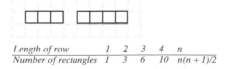

Length of row	1	2	3	4	n
Number of rectangles	1	3	6	10	$n(n + 1)/2$

Figure 14.28 *Hidden rectangles*

Many parallel or similar investigations can be carried out on patterns drawn on isometric paper, but once again the relationships that emerge are often complex quadratic ones. Finding and making a collection of patterns that lead to simple quadratic relationships remains a challenge for all interested in this area of mathematics.

Finally in this section, here is an activity, Fibonacci chains, that delightfully links number and pattern in a different way. The starting point is a numerical sequence, and the representation of this sequence on a grid helps to reveal both the pattern and further sequences.

Fibonacci chains

Start with any pair of numbers and create the next number in the sequence. Record answers in modulo-10 form. For example, starting with 1, 2 leads to the following chain:

1 2 3 5 8 3 1 4 5 9 4 3 7 0 7 7 4 1 5 6 1 7 8 5 ...

This chain returns to its starting point after 50 numbers. If each pair, $(1, 2)$, $(2, 3)$, $(3, 5)$ and so on, is coloured as a coordinate pair on a 10 by 10 grid, then the pattern in Figure 14.29 is revealed. This now helps in finding the missing chains that will complete the pattern – for example, the chain starting 2, 4 – and each of these chains has its own pattern when coloured in on the grid (see Figure 14.30).

Figure 14.29 *Fibonacci chain (1, 2, 3 . . .) on square grid*

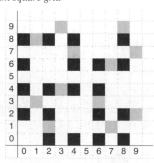

Figure 14.30 *Fibonacci chains (2, 4, 6 . . .) and (1, 3, 4 . . .)*

PATTERNS IN TRADITIONAL ACTIVITIES

In all cultures, the designs people create to decorate their homes, their person or their artefacts provide evidence of a universal drive towards the creation of pattern. Be it in the woven baskets of Bhutan, the cotton embroideries of Bangladesh or the wool blankets of Wales (Figure 14.31: see colour plates), the designs show repetition and regularity, symmetry and structure. To some degree, this is due to the very nature of the material. The natural result of interweaving two strips of leaf is to form a square grid, and any repeated variation of colours woven in the two directions will by the nature of the structure of the weave lead to patterns and, as in Figure 14.32, in some cases to tessellations (Gibbs, 1990c).

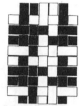 

Figure 14.32 *Star check, a common woven pattern*

In this section, selected designs from around the world are used to exemplify the richness of mathematical ideas that can come from the investigation of their geometrical and numerical patterns.

Bead work

The patterns created in the bead work of Southern Africa are rich, colourful and with added significance for those who know how to interpret the messages conveyed by form and colour. Mathematically they are based on two different structures, either on a regular Cartesian or on an isometric design, as in Figure 14.33 (colour plate). Both designs derive from the particular technique used to string the beads together. Investigating and recording the number of beads used in each part of these patterns provides a rich source for the discovery of numerical relationships. Every bead pattern can lead to some form of generalization. For example, the numbers of beads of each colour in the patterns in Figure 14.34 are given by $4n - 3$ and $8n - 4$.

Figure 14.34 *Patterns in bead work*

Dramis

The wayside shrines and the eaves of houses in Bhutan are often decorated with 'drami' or good luck symbols (Figure 14.35). These are continuous single line designs, an idea that is also found in Celtic knots in Europe, Rangavali doorstep patterns in India and the

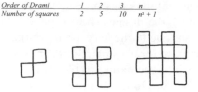

Order of Drami	1	2	3	n
Number of squares	2	5	10	$n^2 + 1$

Figure 14.35 *Drami designs*

sand drawings of Central Africa. One simple way to create Drami patterns of any level of complexity is to start with intersecting lines. Figure 14.36 shows how the third-level Drami can be constructed by first drawing three lines 'vertically' and 'horizontally'. The corners of

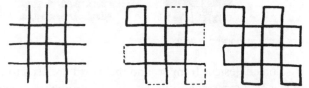

Figure 14.36 *Creating Drami*

alternate pairs of ends are joined to complete the Drami. An extension of this investigation is to create Dramis so that the numbers of vertical lines and horizontal lines we start with are not equal (Figure 14.37).

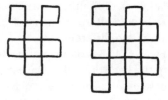

Figure 14.37 *Extension to Drami investigation*

Cross-stitch patterns

Cross-stitch sewing is a popular form of embroidery work in many parts of the world. The example shown here (Figure 14.38) comes from Bangladesh, where organizations like the Bangladesh Rural Advancement Committee (BRAC) are encouraging young and adolescent

Figure 14.38 *Cross-stitch design*

school leavers to sew patterns and sell the products to provide themselves with a little income. The designs produced are essentially mathematical, because the patterns are built up on a square grid drawn on cotton, and so are full of geometric and numerical potential. For example, the numbers of crosses in growing patterns shown in Figure 14.39 are given by $4n + 1$, $2n^2 + 2$ and $2n^2 + 2n + 4$.

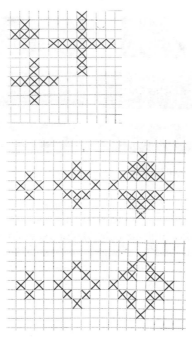

Figure 14.39 *Growing cross-stitch patterns*

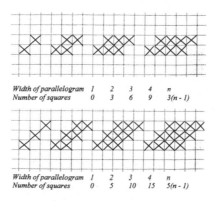

Width of parallelogram	1	2	3	4	n
Number of squares	0	3	6	9	3(n - 1)

Width of parallelogram	1	2	3	4	n
Number of squares	0	5	10	15	5(n - 1)

Figure 14.40 *Squares in cross-stitch parallelograms*

The investigation of cross-stitch patterns can be extended by looking for the number of small squares that emerge from a pattern. For example, Figure 14.40 shows a set of growing parallelograms and the number of small squares that are created by each. The patterns are derived from sets of parallelograms of constant height and increasing width.

String games

All around the world, children create patterns from a simple loop of string. In many places there are stories and games that go with the patterns as they are transformed and passed from child to child. The string patterns shown in Figure 14.41 come from some made by children in

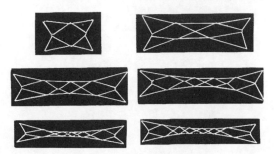

Figure 14.41 *String patterns: 'gates' from Swaziland*

Swaziland, but they are also found in many other parts of the world. Not only does the string provide a cheap and simple way to create mathematical shapes, it also creates patterns that can be investigated (Gibbs and Sihlabela, 1996). For example, in the Swazi patterns there is a relationship between the number of triangles and quadrilaterals in each pattern, and also between the number of polygons and the number of vertices.

Bibliography

Anderson, J. (1995) Patterns which aren't are! *Mathematics in School*, **24**(2), 20–2.

Anderson, J.A., Silverstein, J.W., Ritz, S.A. and Jones, R.S. (1977) Distinctive features, categorical perception, and probability learning: some applications of a neural model. *Psychological Review*, **84**(5), 413–45.

Andrews, P. (1993) Train spotters have feelings too. *Mathematics Teaching*, **142**, 20–2.

Antonouris, G. and Sparrow, L. (1989) Primary mathematics in a multicultural society. *Mathematics Teaching*, **127**, 40–3.

Ashcraft, M.H. (1982) The development of mental arithmetic: a chronometric approach. *Developmental Review*, **2**, 213–36.

Askew, M. and Wiliam, D. (1995) *Recent Research in Mathematics Education 5–16*. London: HMSO.

Assessment of Performance Unit (1980) *Mathematical Development: Primary Survey Report Number 1*. London: HMSO.

Assessment of Performance Unit (undated) *Mathematical Development: a Review of Monitoring in Mathematics 1978 to 1982*. Slough: NFER.

Athey, C. (1990) *Extending Thought in Young Children*. London: Paul Chapman.

Aubrey, C. (1993) An investigation of the mathematical knowledge and competencies which young children bring into school. *British Educational Research Journal*, **19**(1), 27–41.

Backhouse, J., Haggarty, L., Pirie, S. and Stratton, J. (1992) *Improving the Learning of Mathematics*. London: Cassell.

Barnes, P.R. (1989) *Problem Solving Exercises*. Leeds: Leeds Education Authority.

Baroody, A.J. (1985) Mastery of basic number combinations: internalization of relationships or facts? *Journal for Research in Mathematics Education*, **16**(2), 83–98.

Baroody, A.J. and Ginsburg, H.P. (1986) The relationship between initial meaningful and mechanical knowledge in arithmetic. In J. Hiebert (ed.), *Conceptual and Procedural Knowledge: the Case of Mathematics*. Hillsdale, NJ: Lawrence Erlbaum.

Beevers, B. (1994) Patterns which aren't. *Mathematics in School*, **23**(5), 10–12.

Bell, A. (1989) Teaching for the test. *Times Educational Supplement*, 27 October.

Bidwell, J. (1985) Using reflections to find symmetric and asymmetric patterns. *Arithmetic Teacher*, **34**(7), 10–15.

Biggs, E. and Shaw, K. (1985) *Maths Alive!* London: Cassell.

Blane, D. (1992) Curriculum planning, assessment and student learning in mathematics: a top down approach. In G. Leder (ed.), *Assessment and Learning of Mathematics*. Victoria: Australian Council for Educational Research.

Brighouse, A., Godber, D. and Patilla, P. (1981) *Peak Mathematics Book 3*. London: Nelson.

Brownell, W.A. (1945) When is arithmetic meaningful? *Journal of Educational Research*, **38**(3), 481–98.

Bruner, J.S. (1966) *Toward a Theory of Instruction*. Cambridge, MA: Harvard University Press.

Bruner, J.S. and Potter, M.C. (1964) Interference in visual recognition. *Science*, **144**, 424–5.

Bryant, P. (ed.) (1974) *Perception and Understanding in Young Children: an Experimental Approach*. London: Methuen.

Burke, C.S. (1989) Referential thinking: the structures and processes of graphic representation. Unpublished PhD thesis, University of Leeds.

Burton, L. (1984a) *Thinking Things Through: Problem Solving in Mathematics*. Oxford: Basil Blackwell.

Burton, L. (1984b) Mathematical thinking: the struggle for meaning. *Journal for Research in Mathematics Education*, **15**(1), 35–49.

Caine, P.A. (1970) *Number, Shapes and Patterns*. London: Chatto & Windus.

Campbell, J.D. (1987) The role of associative inference in learning and retrieving arithmetic facts. In J. A. Sloboda and D. Rogers (eds), *Cognitive Processes in Mathematics*. Oxford: Oxford University Press.

Campbell, J.I.D. (1991) Conditions of error priming in error fact retrieval. *Memory and Cognition*, **19**(2), 197–209.

Carpenter, T.P. and Moser, J.M. (1983) The acquisition of addition and subtraction concepts. In R. Lesh and M. Landau (eds), *Acquisition of Mathematical Concepts and Processes*. New York: Academic Press.

Chipman, S.F. and Mendelson, M.J. (1979) Influence of six types of visual structure on complexity judgements in children and adults. *Journal of Experimental Psychology: Human Perception and Performance*, **5**(2), 365–78.

Clarke, S. and Atkinson, S. (1996) *Tracking Significant Achievement in Primary Mathematics*. London: Hodder & Stoughton.

Clements, K. (1982) Visual imagery and school mathematics. *For the Learning of Mathematics*, **2**(2), 2–9.

Clemson, D. and Clemson, W. (1994) *Mathematics in the Early Years*. London: Routledge.

Cockcroft, W. H. (1982) *Mathematics Counts*. London: HMSO.

Collis, K., Romberg, T.A. and Jurdak, M.E. (1986) A technique for assessing mathematical problem solving ability. *Journal for Research in Mathematics Education*, **17**(3), 206–21.

Cooper, L.A. (1990) Mental representation of 3-dimensional objects in visual problem-solving and recognition. *Journal of Experimental Psychology: Learning, Memory and Cognition*, **16**, 1097–106.

Corballis, M.C. and Beale, I.L. (1983) *The Ambivalent Mind: the Neuropsychology of Left and Right*. Chicago: Nelson-Hall.

Cormier, S.M. and Hagman, J.D. (eds) (1987) *Transfer of Learning: Contemporary Research and Applications*. San Diego, CA: Academic Press.

Cox, C. and Mouw, J.T. (1992) Disruption of the representativeness heuristic: can we be perturbed into using correct probabilistic reasoning? *Educational Studies in Mathematics*, **23**, 163–78.

Dantzig, T. (1954) *Number, the Language of Science*. New York: Macmillan.

Delaney, K. and Dichmont, J. (1979) Do-it-yourself Islamic patterns. *Mathematics Teaching*, **86**, xvii–xix.

Department for Education/Welsh Office (1995) *Mathematics in the National Curriculum*. London: HMSO.

Department of Education and Science (1983) *9–13 Middle Schools: an Illustrative Survey*. London: HMSO.

Department of Education and Science/Welsh Office (1988) *Mathematics for Ages 5 to 16*. London: HMSO.

Department of Education and Science/Welsh Office (1991) *Mathematics in the National Curriculum (1991)*. London: HMSO.

Deregowski, J.B. (1980) *Illusions, Patterns and Pictures: a Cross-cultural Perspective*. London: Academic Press.

Dickson, L. Brown, M. and Gibson, O. (eds) (1984) *Children Learning Mathematics*. London: Cassell.

Dienes, Z.P. (1963) *An Experimental Study of Mathematics Learning.* London: Hutchinson.
Donahoe, J.W. and Wessels, M.G. (1980) *Learning, Language and Memory.* New York: Harper & Row.

Eagle, M. R. (1995) *Exploring Mathematics through History.* Cambridge: Cambridge University Press.
English, L.D. and Halford, G.S. (1995) *Mathematics Education: Models and Processes.* Mahwah, NJ: Erlbaum.
Eysenck, M. (1984) *Handbook of Cognitive Psychology.* London: Lawrence Erlbaum.

Feldman, J.A. and Ballard, D.H. (1982) Connectionist models and their properties. *Cognitive Science,* **6,** 205–54.
Feller, W. (1968) *An Introduction to Probability Theory and Its Applications, Volume 1.* New York: Wiley.
Fischbein, E. (1975) *The Intuitive Sources of Probabilistic Thinking in Children.* Dordrecht: Reidel.
Fischbein, E. (1987) *Intuition in Science and Mathematics.* Dordrecht: Reidel.
Flavell, J.H., Miller, P.H. and Miller, S.A. (1993) *Cognitive Development,* 3rd edn. Englewood Cliffs, NJ: Prentice Hall.
Frith, U. (1970) Studies in pattern detection in normal and autistic children's reproduction and production of colour sequences. *Journal of Experimental Child Psychology,* **10,** 120–35.
Frobisher, L. (1994) Problems, investigations and an investigative approach. In A. Orton and G. Wain (eds), *Issues in Teaching Mathematics.* London: Cassell.
Frobisher, L.J. and Nelson, N. (1992) Young children's knowledge of odd and even numbers. *Acta Didactica,* **1,** 83–90.

Gardiner, A. (1995) The proof of the pudding is in the ... . *Mathematics in School,* **24**(3), 10–11.
Ghent, I. (1956) Perception of overlapping and embedded figures by children of different ages. *American Journal of Psychology,* **69,** 575–86.
Gibbs, W. (1990a) Paper patterns 1 – with metric paper. *Mathematics in School,* **19**(2), 24–7.
Gibbs, W. (1990b) Paper patterns 3 – with circles. *Mathematics in School,* **19**(4), 2–8.
Gibbs, W. (1990c) Paper patterns 4 – paper weaving. *Mathematics in School,* **19**(5), 16–19.
Gibbs, W. (1995) Window patterns. *Mathematics in School,* **24**(1), 18–25.
Gibbs, W. and Meenan, E. (1994) *Paper Magic, Folding Polygons.* London: Educational Television Company.
Gibbs, W. and Orton, J. (1994) Language and mathematics. In A. Orton and G. Wain (eds), *Issues in Teaching Mathematics.* London: Cassell.
Gibbs, W. and Sihlabela, M. (1996) String figures. *Mathematics in School,* **25**(3), 24–7.
Ginsburg, H. (1977) *Children's Arithmetic: the Learning Process.* New York: Van Nostrand.
Gipps, C. (1994) *Beyond Testing.* London: Falmer Press.
Glenn, J.A. and Sturgess, D.A. (1977) *Towards Mathematics.* Huddersfield: Schofield & Sims.
Gray, E.M. (1991) An analysis of diverging approaches to simple arithmetic: preference and its consequences. *Educational Studies in Mathematics,* **22,** 551–74.
Gray, E.M. (1994) Spectrums of performance in two digit addition and subtraction. In J.P. da Ponte and J.F. Matos (eds), *Proceedings of the Eighteenth International Conference for the Psychology of Mathematics Education, Volume 3.* Lisbon: University of Lisbon, pp. 25–32.
Gray, E.M. and Tall, D.O. (1994) Duality, ambiguity and flexibility: a 'proceptual' view of simple arithmetic. *Journal for Research in Mathematics Education,* **26**(2), 116–40.
Green, D.R. (1982) *Probability Concepts in School Pupils Aged 11–16.* Reading, MA: Addison-Wesley.
Green, D.R. (1991a) *Mathematical Education Report ME9001: Analysis of Probability Concepts Test of 1986.* Loughborough: Loughborough University of Technology.
Green, D.R. (1991b) *Mathematical Education Report ME9002: Analysis of Probability Concepts Test of 1990.* Loughborough: Loughborough University of Technology.
Green, D.R. (1991c) *Mathematical Education Report ME9003: Longitudinal Study of Probability Concepts 1986–90.* Loughborough: Loughborough University of Technology.

Greeno, J.G. and Simon, H.A. (1974) Processes for sequence production. *Psychological Review*, **81**(3), 187–98.

Groen, G.J. and Parkman, J.M. (1972) A chronometric analysis of simple addition. *Psychological Review*, **79**, 329–43.

Grünbaum, B. and Shephard, G. (1986) *Tilings and Patterns: an Introduction*. San Francisco: Freeman.

Gura, P. (1992) *Exploring Learning: Young Children and Block Play*. London: Paul Chapman.

Hadamard, J. (1954) *The Psychology of Invention in the Mathematical Field*. New York: Dover.

Hale, D. (1981) Teaching algebra. In A. Floyd (ed.), *Developing Mathematical Thinking*. London: Addison-Wesley for Oxford University Press.

Hargreaves, M. (1998) Factors influencing the interpretation and generalization of number patterns in children aged 7 to 12. Unpublished PhD thesis, University of Leeds.

Hart, K.M. (ed.) (1981) *Children's Understanding of Mathematics 11–16*. London: John Murray.

Heim, A.W. (1970) *AH4 Group Test of General Intelligence*. Windsor: NFER.

Her Majesty's Inspectorate (1979) *Aspects of Secondary Education in England*. London: HMSO.

Her Majesty's Inspectorate (1989a) *Aspects of Primary Education: the Education of Children under Five*. London: HMSO.

Her Majesty's Inspectorate (1989b) *Aspects of Primary Education: the Teaching and Learning of Mathematics*. London: HMSO.

Hewitt, D. (1992) Trainspotters' paradise. *Mathematics Teaching*, **140**, 6–8.

Jones, L. (1993) Algebra in the primary school. *Education 3–13*, **21**(2), 27–31.

Kahneman, D. and Tversky, A. (1972) Subjective probability: a judgement of representativeness. *Cognitive Psychology*, **3**, 430–54.

Kahneman, D. and Tversky, A. (1973) On the psychology of prediction. *Psychological Review*, **80**(4), 237–51.

Kahneman, D., Slovic, P. and Tversky, A. (eds) (1982*) Judgement under Uncertainty: Heuristics and Biases*. Cambridge: Cambridge University Press.

Kerslake, D. (1979) Visual mathematics. *Mathematics in School*, **8**(2), 34–5.

Kerslake, D., Burton, L., Harvey, R., Street, L. and Walsh, A. (1990) *HBJ Mathematics Y1, Teachers' Resource Book*. London: Harcourt Brace Jovanovich.

Kolinsky, R., Morais, J., Content, A. and Cary, L. (1987) Finding parts within figures: a developmental study. *Perception*,**16**, 339–407.

Kosslyn, S.M. (1981) The medium and the message in mental imagery: a theory. *Psychological Review*, **88**, 46–66.

Krutetskii, V. A. (1976) *The Psychology of Mathematical Abilities in Schoolchildren*. Chicago: University of Chicago Press.

Küchemann, D. (1980) Children's difficulties with single reflections and rotations. *Mathematics in School*, **9**(2), 12–13.

Lee, L. and Wheeler, D. (1987) *Algebraic Thinking in High School Students: Their Conceptions of Generalization and Justification*. Montreal: Concordia University.

Lemaire, P., Barrett, S.E., Fayol, M. and Abdi, H. (1994) Automatic activation of addition and multi-plication facts in elementary school children. *Journal of Experimental Child Psychology*, **57**, 224–58.

Liebeck, P. (1984) *How Children Learn Mathematics*. Harmondsworth: Penguin.

Martin, W.G. and Harel, G. (1989) Proof frames of preservice elementary teachers. *Journal for Research in Mathematics Education*, **20**(1), 41–51.

Mason, J. with Burton, L. and Stacey, K. (1982, 1985a) *Thinking Mathematically*. Wokingham: Addison-Wesley.

Mason, J., Graham, A., Pimm, D. and Gowar, N. (1985b) *Routes to/Roots of Algebra*. Milton Keynes: Open University Press.

Mathematical Association (1938) *A Second Report on the Teaching of Geometry in Schools*. London: G. Bell & Sons.

Mathematical Association (1959) *Mathematics in Secondary Modern Schools*. London: G. Bell & Sons.

Matthews, G. and Matthews, J. (1990) *Early Mathematical Experiences*, 3rd edn. Harlow: Longman.

Midland Examining Group (1992) *Training and Support Materials: Mathematics 1661*. Cambridge: MEG.

Midland Examining Group (1996a) *Mathematics Syllabus A – Syllabus Code 1662*. Cambridge: MEG.

Midland Examining Group (1996b) *Mathematics Syllabus A – Syllabus Code 1662: MEG-marked Tasks Specimen Materials*. Cambridge: MEG.

Montague, M. and Bos, C.S. (1990) Cognitive and metacognitive characteristics of eighth grade students' mathematical problem solving. *Learning and Individual Differences*, **2**, 371–88.

Mottershead, L. (1978) *Sources of Mathematical Discovery*. Oxford: Basil Blackwell.

Mottershead, L. (1985) *Investigations in Mathematics*. Oxford: Basil Blackwell.

Nasser, L., Sant'Anna, N. and Sant'Anna, A.P. (1996) Students' assessment of an alternative approach to geometry. In L. Puig and A. Gutiérrez (eds), *Proceedings of the Twentieth International Conference for the Psychology of Mathematics Education, Volume 4*. Valencia: Universitat de València, pp. 59–66.

National Council of Teachers of Mathematics (1989) *Curriculum and Evaluation Standards for School Mathematics*. Reston, VA: NCTM.

National Curriculum Council (1992) *Using and Applying Mathematics Book B: INSET Handbook for Key Stages 1–4*. York: NCC.

National Curriculum Council (1993) *Mathematics Programmes of Study: INSET for Key Stages 1 and 2*. London: HMSO.

Northern Examinations and Assessment Board (1996) *Syllabus for 1998 – Mathematics Syllabus B, 1132*. Manchester: NEAB.

Orton, A. (1992) *Learning Mathematics: Issues, Theory and Classroom Practice*, 2nd edn. London: Cassell.

Orton, A. (1993) Pattern in mathematics. In G. Wain (ed.), *British Congress on Mathematical Education 1993 Research Papers*. Leeds: The University of Leeds.

Orton, A. (1994a) Half-squares, tessellations and quilting. *Mathematics in School*, **23**(1), 25–8.

Orton, A. (1994b) Tessellations in the curriculum. *Mathematics in School*, **23**(3), 12–15.

Orton, A. and Frobisher, L. (1996) *Insights into Teaching Mathematics*. London: Cassell.

Orton, J. (1993) What is pattern? *Mathematics in School*, **22**(1), 8–10.

Orton, J. (1997) Matchsticks, pattern and generalization. *Education 3–13*, **25**(1), 61–5.

Orton, J. and Orton, A. (1996) Making sense of children's patterning. In L. Puig and A. Gutiérrez (eds), *Proceedings of the Twentieth International Conference for the Psychology of Mathematics Education, Volume 4*. Valencia: Universitat de València, pp. 83–90.

Owen, A. (1995) In search of the unknown: a review of primary algebra. In J. Anghileri (ed.), *Children's Mathematical Thinking in the Primary Years*. London: Cassell.

Palmer, S.E. (1977) Hierarchical structure in perceptual representation. *Cognitive Psychology*, **9**, 441–74.

Paraskevopoulos, I. (1968) Symmetry, recall and preference in relation to chronological age. *Journal of Experimental Child Psychology*, **6**, 254–64.

Paulos, J.A. (1988) *Innumeracy: Mathematical Illiteracy and Its Consequences*. London: Penguin.

Pegg, J. (1992) Research directions in school algebra. In A. Baturo and T. Cooper (eds), *New Directions in Algebra Education*. Red Hill, Australia: Queensland University of Technology.

Pegg, J. and Redden, E. (1990) Procedures for, and experiences in, introducing algebra in New South Wales. *Mathematics Teacher*, **83**(5), 386–91.

Phillips, J.R. (1969) *The Origins of Intellect: Piaget's Theory*. San Francisco: W.H. Freeman.

Piaget, J. and Inhelder, B. (1975) *The Origin of the Idea of Chance in Children*. London: Routledge and Kegan Paul.

Piaget, J., Inhelder, B. and Szeminska, A. (1960) *The Child's Conception of Geometry*. London: Routledge and Kegan Paul.

Picton, J. and Mack, J. (1989) *African Textiles*. London: British Museums Publications.

Pierrault-Le Bonniec, G. (1982) From rhythm to reversibility. In G.E. Forman (ed.), *Action and Thought: from Sensorimotor Schemes to Symbolic Operations*. London: Academic Press.

Plunkett, S.P.O. (1979) Diagrams. *Mathematical Education for Teaching*, **3**(4), 3–15.

Polya, G. (1990) *How to Solve It: a New Aspect of Mathematical Method*. London: Penguin.

Presmeg, N. (1986) Visualization in high school mathematics. *For the Learning of Mathematics*, **6**(3), 42–6.

Presmeg, N. (1995) Preference for visual methods: an international study. In L. Meira and D. Carraher (eds), *Proceedings of the Nineteenth International Conference for the Psychology of Mathematics Education, Volume 3*. Recife, Brazil: Universidade Federal de Pernambuco, pp. 58–65.

Rawson, B. (1993) Searching for pattern. *Education 3–13*, **21**(3), 26–33.

Reed, S.K. (1973) *Psychological Processes in Pattern Recognition*. New York: Academic Press.

Resnick, L.B. and Ford, W.W. (1984) *The Psychology of Mathematics for Instruction*. Hillsdale, NJ: Lawrence Erlbaum.

Resnick, L.B., Cauzinille-Marmèche, E. and Mathieu, J. (1987) Understanding algebra. In J.A. Sloboda and D. Rogers (eds), *Cognitive Processes in Mathematics*. Oxford: Clarendon Press.

Richards, R. and Jones, L. (1990) *An Early Start to Mathematics*. London: Simon and Schuster.

Roper, T. (1985) Students' understanding of selected mechanics concepts. In A. Orton (ed.), *Studies in Mechanics Learning*. Leeds: University of Leeds.

Roper, T. and MacNamara, A. (1994) Can students distinguish between random and invented data? In G. Wain (ed.), *British Congress on Mathematical Education 1993 Research Papers*. Leeds: University of Leeds.

Roth, I. and Frisby, J.P. (eds) (1986) *Perception and Representation: a Cognitive Approach*. Milton Keynes: Open University Press.

Rustigian, A. (1976) The ontogeny of pattern recognition: significance of colour and form in linear pattern recognition among young children. Unpublished PhD thesis, University of Connecticut.

Sawyer, W.W. (1955) *Prelude to Mathematics*. Harmondsworth: Penguin.

Schoenfeld, A.H. and Arcavi, A. (1988) On the meaning of variable. *Mathematics Teacher*, **81**, 420–7.

School Curriculum and Assessment Authority (1995) *Consistency in Teacher Assessment: Exemplification of Standards, Key Stage 3, Levels 4 to 8*. London: SCAA.

School Curriculum and Assessment Authority (1996) *Nursery Education: Desirable Outcomes for Children's Learning on Entering Compulsory Education*. London: DfEE.

School Examinations and Assessment Council (1992) *School Assessment Folder (Part Three). Materials to Support the Assessment of Ma1: Using and Applying Mathematics*. London: SEAC.

School Examinations and Assessment Council (1993) *Pupils' Work Assessed, Mathematics: Three Pupils' Folders*. London: SEAC.

Schools Council (1971) *Mathematical Pattern*. London: Chatto & Windus.

Shaughnessy, J.M. (1977) Misconceptions of probability: an experiment with a small group, activity-based, model building approach to introductory probability at college level. *Educational Studies in Mathematics*, **8**, 295–316.

Shell Centre for Mathematical Education (1984) *Problems with Patterns and Numbers: an O-level Module*. Manchester: Joint Matriculation Board.

Siegler, R.S. and Robinson, M. (1982) The development of numerical understandings. In H.W. Reese and L.P. Lipsett (eds), *Advances in Child Development and Behavior, Volume 16*. New York: Academic Press.

Simon, H.A. (1972) Complexity and the representation of patterned sequences of symbols. *Psychological Review*, **79**(5), 369–82.

Slomson, A. (1996) Mathematical proof and its role in the classroom. *Mathematics Teaching*, **155**, 10–13.

Smith, D.E. (1958) *History of Mathematics,* 2 vols. New York: Dover.

Solano, A. and Presmeg, N.C. (1995) Visualization as a relation of images. In L. Meira and D. Carraher (eds), *Proceedings of the Nineteenth International Conference for the Psychology of Mathematics Education, Volume 3*. Recife, Brazil: Universidade Federal de Pernambuco, pp. 66–78.

Stacey, K. (1989) Finding and using patterns in linear generalizing problems. *Educational Studies in Mathematics*, **20**, 147–64.

Stephens, M. and Money, R. (1993) New developments in senior secondary mathematics. In M. Niss (ed.), *Cases of Assessment in Mathematics Education*. Dordrecht: Kluwer.

Sternberg, L. (1974) An analysis of achievement characteristics of high and low performers in pre-school, kindergarten and first-grade classes on pattern recognition tasks. Unpublished PhD thesis, University of Connecticut.

Storr, A. (1992) *Music and the Mind*. London: QPD.

Straker, A. (1993) *Talking Points in Mathematics*. Cambridge: Cambridge University Press.

Sutherland, R. (1990) The changing role of algebra in school mathematics: the potential of computer-based environments. In P. Dowling and R. Noss (eds), *Mathematics versus the National Curriculum*. London: Falmer Press.

Svenson, O. (1976) Analysis of time required by children for simple additions. *Acta Psychologica*, **39**, 289–302.

Tall, D. (1992) The transition from arithmetic to algebra: number patterns or proceptual programming? In A. Baturo and T. Cooper (eds), *New Directions in Algebra Education*. Red Hill, Australia: Queensland University of Technology.

Thorndike, E.L. (1922) *The Psychology of Arithmetic*. New York: Macmillan.

Threlfall, J., Frobisher, L. and MacNamara, A. (1995) Inferrring the use of recall in simple addition. *British Journal of Educational Psychology*, **65**, 425–39.

Tversky, A. and Kahneman, D. (1971) Belief in the law of small numbers. *Psychological Bulletin*, **26**(2), 105–10.

Tversky, A. and Kahneman, D. (1973) Availability: a heuristic for judging frequency and probability. *Cognitive Psychology*, **5**, 207–32.

Tversky, A. and Kahneman, D. (1974) Judgement under uncertainty: heuristics and biases. *Science*, **185**, 1124–31.

University of London Examinations and Assessment Council (1992) *Specimen Coursework Activities: Mathematics (1384), Options A, B and C*. London: ULEAC.

Ursini, S. (1991) First steps in generalization processes in algebra. In F. Furinghetti (ed.), *Proceedings of the Fifteenth International Conference for the Psychology of Mathematics Education, Volume 3*. Assisi, Italy: Università di Genova, pp. 316–23.

Van Hiele, P.M. (1986) *Structure and Insight*. London: Academic Press.

Van Lehn, K. (1990) *Mind Bugs*. London: MIT Press.

Vernon, M.D. (1970) *Perception through Experience*. London: Methuen.

Vitz, P.C. and Todd, T.C. (1967) A model of learning for simple repeating binary pattern. *Journal of Experimental Psychology*, **75**(1), 108–17.

Vitz, P.C. and Todd, T.C. (1969) A coded element model of the perceptual processing of sequented stimuli. *Psychological Review*, **76**(5), 433–49.

Vitz, P.C. and Todd, T.C. (1971) A model of the perception of simple geometric figures. *Psychological Review*, **78**(3), 207–28.

Waring, S. (1997) Learning and teaching proof and pattern in mathematics in the age range fourteen to sixteen years. Unpublished EdD thesis, University of Leeds.

Warren, E. (1992) Beyond manipulating symbols. In A. Baturo and T. Cooper (eds), *New Directions in Algebra Education*. Red Hill, Australia: Queensland University of Technology.

Watson, F.R. (1981) The role of diagrams in mathematical education. In *Proceedings of the Fifth International Conference for the Psychology of Mathematics Education, Volume 2*. Grenoble, France: Equipe de Recherche Pédagogique, pp. 271–77.

Wells, D. (1988) *Hidden Connections: Double Meanings*. Cambridge: Cambridge University Press.

Wilder, R.L. (1978) *Evolution of Mathematical Concepts*. Milton Keynes: Open University Press.

Wilding, J.M. (ed.)(1982) *Perception from Sense to Object*. London: Hutchinson.

Willerding, M. (1967) *Mathematical Concepts, a Historical Approach*. Boston: Prindle, Weber and Schmidt.

Williams, E. and Shuard, H. (1982) *Primary Mathematics Today*, 3rd edn. Harlow: Longman Group Limited.

Willson, W. W. (1977) *The Mathematics Curriculum: Geometry*. Glasgow: Blackie & Son, for the Schools Council.

Wolf, A. (1989) Testing investigations. In P. Dowling and R. Noss (eds), *Mathematics versus the National Curriculum*. London: Falmer Press.

Wood, D. (1988) *How Children Think and Learn*. Oxford: Blackwell.

Zbrodoff, N.J. (1995) Why is 9 + 7 harder than 2 + 3? Strength and interference as explanations of the problem size effect. *Memory and Cognition*, **23**(6), 689–700.

Index